T0205553

Deriving Priorities from Incomplete Fuzzy Reciprocal Preference Relations

Yejun Xu

Deriving Priorities from Incomplete Fuzzy Reciprocal Preference Relations

Theories and Methodologies

 Springer

Yejun Xu
College of Management and Economy
Tianjin University
Tianjin, China

ISBN 978-981-99-3171-2   ISBN 978-981-99-3169-9   (eBook)
https://doi.org/10.1007/978-981-99-3169-9

This Springer imprint is published by the registered company Springer Nature Singapore Pte Ltd.
The registered company address is: 152 Beach Road, #21-01/04 Gateway East, Singapore 189721,
Singapore

Preface

Pairwise comparison, initiated by Thurstone (1927), is an effective tool to express decision makers' (DMs) preferences. Multiplicative preference relation (or called multiplicative reciprocal preference relation), first proposed by Saaty (1980), is the most widely used pairwise comparison in the multi-criteria decision-making process. With the increasing complexity and uncertainty of practical problems, it is difficult for DMs to give their accurate judgments for objects due to their limited cognitions and incomplete information. In such a case, a fuzzy set, proposed by Zadeh (1965), is also an effective tool to express the specific degree of an element belonging to a set. Orlovsky (1978) incorporated fuzzy set into pairwise comparison and proposed fuzzy preference relation. Tanino (1984) further assumed the fuzzy preference relation satisfying the additive reciprocal condition and actually proposed the fuzzy reciprocal preference relation (although he only called fuzzy preference orderings).

Since the multiplicative reciprocal preference relation and fuzzy reciprocal preference relation have been proposed, it is assumed that the DMs can provide all the $n(n-1)/2$ pairwise comparisons. However, in the real situation, a DM may develop a preference relation with incomplete information due to various reasons. Harker (1987a, 1987b) first proposed incomplete AHP pairwise comparisons. Xu (2004) extended it to fuzzy reciprocal preference relation. Since then, various methods have been proposed to deal with incomplete fuzzy reciprocal preference relation.

When the pairwise comparisons are given, one of the important tasks is to derive priority weights from the preference relations. At present, various estimating methods for deriving weights from multiplicative preference relations under a common framework of effectiveness, distance minimization and correctness in error-free cases, are proposed (Choo & Wedley, 2004). Some of the methods are also extended to explore the weights from the complete fuzzy reciprocal preference relations. However, as far as we know, there is no literature to systematically review and present the methods to derive the priority weights from the incomplete fuzzy reciprocal preference relations. Thus, in the book, we will give various priority methods for incomplete fuzzy reciprocal preference relations. To this end, this book is arranged as follows:

Chapter 1 is the introduction, which introduces the basic concepts about the fuzzy reciprocal preference relations and two consistencies of fuzzy reciprocal preference relations. We also give the relationship between the fuzzy reciprocal elements and the priority weights for additive consistency and multiplicative consistency, respectively.

Chapter 2 presents the normalizing rank aggregation-based method for priority weights from incomplete fuzzy reciprocal preference relations.

Chapter 3 presents the eigenvector method for priority from an incomplete fuzzy reciprocal preference relation. Furthermore, some algorithms are shown to repair the inconsistency of the fuzzy reciprocal preference relation.

Chapter 4 proposes the logarithmic least square method for deriving priorities from group incomplete fuzzy reciprocal preference relations.

Chapter 5 explores the chi-square method for priority derivation from group incomplete fuzzy reciprocal preference relations.

Chapter 6 describes the least deviation method for priority from group incomplete fuzzy reciprocal preference relations.

Chapter 7 introduces the method to derive priorities from fuzzy best-worst method matrix in view of incomplete fuzzy reciprocal preference relations.

Chapter 8 presents the weighted least square method for priority of an incomplete fuzzy reciprocal preference relation.

Chapter 9 proposes the priority weights from incomplete hesitant fuzzy reciprocal preference relations in group decision-making.

We believe that the various priority weights for incomplete fuzzy reciprocal preference relations, proposed in this book, can provide a better understanding of the weight elicitation method for pairwise comparisons, not only for the incomplete fuzzy reciprocal preference relations, but also for the complete fuzzy reciprocal preference relations, and also for multiplicative reciprocal preference relations.

I want to express special thanks to Professor Francisco Herrera, Professor Enrique Herrera-Viedma, Professor Ravi Patnayakuni, Professor Kevin W. Li, and Professor Qingli Da. I also want to express my sincere thanks to the colleagues and students in my group, Professor Huimin Wang, Miss Lei Chen, and Miss Xiaotong Zhu, who have done much work in this field. This book is supported by grants (nos. 71101043, 71471056, 71871085, 72271179) from the National Natural Science Foundation of China.

Tianjin, China   Yejun Xu
March 2023

References

Choo, E. U., & Wedley, W. C. (2004). A common framework for deriving preference values from pairwise comparison matrices. *Computers and Operations Research, 31*, 893–908.

Harker, P. T. (1987a). Alternative modes of questions in the analytic hierarchy process. *Mathematical Modeling, 9*(3–5), 353–360.

Harker, P. T. (1987b). Incomplete pairwise comparisons in the analytic hierarchy process. *Mathematical Modeling, 9*(11), 837–848.

Orlovsky, S. A. (1978). Decision-making with a fuzzy preference relation. *Fuzzy Sets and Systems, 1*(3), 155–167.

Saaty, T. L. (1980). *The analytic hierarchy process*. McGraw-Hill Company.

Tanino, T. (1984). Fuzzy preference orderings in group decision making. *Fuzzy Sets and Systems, 12*(2), 117–131.

Thurstone, L. L. (1927). A law of comparative judgment. *Psychological Review, 34*, 273–286.

Xu, Z. S. (2004). Goal programming models for obtaining the priority vector of incomplete fuzzy preference relation. *International Journal of Approximate Reasoning, 36*(3), 261–270.

Zadeh, L. A. (1965). Fuzzy sets. *Information and Control, 8*, 338–353.

The original version of this book has been revised: typographical errors in the Chapters 3, 4, 5, 6, 7, and 9 have been corrected. The correction to this book can be found at https://doi.org/10.1007/978-981-99-3169-9_10

Contents

1 **Introduction** 1
  1.1   Fuzzy Reciprocal Preference Relations 1
  1.2   Incomplete Fuzzy Reciprocal Preference Relations 4
  1.3   The Relationships Between the Elements of Fuzzy Reciprocal
       Preference Relations and the Weights 8
       1.3.1   The Relationships Between the Elements of Fuzzy
           Reciprocal Preference Relations and the Weights
           for Additive Consistency 8
       1.3.2   The Relationships Between the Elements of Fuzzy
           Reciprocal Preference Relations and the Weights
           for Multiplicative Consistency 18
  1.4   Summary 18
  References 18

2 **Normalizing Rank Aggregation-Based Method** 23
  2.1   Normalizing Rank Aggregation Method 1 23
       2.1.1   An Approach to Constructing a Complete Fuzzy
           Reciprocal Preference Relation from an Incomplete
           Fuzzy Reciprocal Preference Relation When $\beta = n/2$ 23
       2.1.2   An Illustrative Example 25
       2.1.3   An Algorithm for Decision-Making with Incomplete
           Fuzzy Reciprocal Preference Relation 27
  2.2   Normalizing Rank Method 2 28
       2.2.1   An Approach to Constructing a Complete Fuzzy
           Reciprocal Preference Relation from an Incomplete Fuzzy
           Reciprocal Preference Relation When $\beta = (n - 1)/2$ 28
       2.2.2   An Illustrative Example 30
       2.2.3   An Algorithm for the Decision-Making with an
           Incomplete Fuzzy Reciprocal Preference Relation 32

2.2.4 Performance Comparisons   32
2.3 Normalizing Rank Aggregation Method for Group
Decision-Making with Incomplete Fuzzy Reciprocal Preference
Relations   36
 2.3.1 An Algorithm for Group Decision-Making with
  Incomplete Fuzzy Reciprocal Preference Relations   36
 2.3.2 Performance Comparisons   38
 2.3.3 Illustrative Examples   39
2.4 Goal Programming Method   45
2.5 Least Deviation Method   48
2.6 Quadratic Programming Method   51
2.7 Summary   55
References   55

3 Eigenvector Method   57
3.1 EM for Priority from an Incomplete Fuzzy Reciprocal
Preference Relation   57
3.2 Algorithms for Repairing the Inconsistency of the Incomplete
Fuzzy Reciprocal Preference Relation   63
3.3 Illustrative Example   65
3.4 Summary   71
References   71

4 Logarithmic Least Squares Method   73
4.1 Logarithmic Least Squares Method for Priority from Incomplete
Fuzzy Reciprocal Preference Relations   73
4.2 An Algorithm for Repairing the Inconsistency of an Incomplete
Fuzzy Reciprocal Preference Relation   78
4.3 Numerical Examples   79
4.4 Summary   84
References   84

5 A Chi-Square Method   87
5.1 Chi-Square Method for Priority from Group Incomplete Fuzzy
Reciprocal Preference Relations   87
5.2 A Method for Repairing Inconsistency of Incomplete Fuzzy
Reciprocal Preference Relations   93
5.3 Illustrative Examples   94
5.4 Summary   106
References   106

6 A Least Deviation Method   107
6.1 Least Deviation Method for Priority from Group Incomplete
Fuzzy Reciprocal Preference Relations   107
6.2 A Method for Repairing Inconsistency of an Incomplete
Fuzzy Reciprocal Preference Relation   114

6.3 Illustrative Examples.................................... 114
6.4 Statistical Comparative Study........................... 122
6.5 Complexity of Computation of Different Algorithms.......... 123
6.6 Summary.. 124
References.. 124

7 Priorities from Fuzzy Best-Worst Method Matrix.............. 125
7.1 FBWM and Its Structure............................... 125
7.2 Methods for Priorities from FBWM Matrix................. 129
    7.2.1 Methods for Priorities from an FBWM Matrix......... 129
    7.2.2 Priority Methods from FBWM Matrices in Group
          Decision-Making................................. 135
7.3 Monte Carlo Simulations and Discussions.................. 138
7.4 Illustrative Examples and Comparative Analyses............. 141
    7.4.1 Comparative Analyses............................ 144
7.5 Summary.. 147
References.. 147

8 Weighted Least Square Method........................... 149
8.1 WLSM for Priority from an Incomplete Fuzzy Reciprocal
    Preference Relation.................................... 149
8.2 The Improvement of ICWLSM............................ 151
8.3 Illustrative Examples.................................. 152
8.4 Summary.. 156
References.. 156

**9 Priorities from Incomplete Hesitant Fuzzy Reciprocal Preference
  Relations**.. 157
9.1 Preliminaries... 157
    9.1.1 HFS.. 157
    9.1.2 Hesitant Fuzzy Preference Relation................. 158
    9.1.3 Incomplete Hesitant Fuzzy Reciprocal Preference
          Relation.. 158
9.2 The Models to Derive Priority Weights from Incomplete
    Hesitant Fuzzy Reciprocal Preference Relations............. 160
9.3 Illustrative Cases of Study............................. 167
    9.3.1 Case of Study with Four Decision Alternatives
          and an Incomplete Hesitant Fuzzy Reciprocal Preference
          Relation.. 167
    9.3.2 GDM Problem with Three Alternatives and Three
          Experts.. 170
9.4 Summary.. 174
References.. 174

**Correction to: Deriving Priorities from Incomplete Fuzzy Reciprocal
Preference Relations**... C1

Chapter 1
Introduction

The basic concepts related with fuzzy reciprocal preference relations are introduced in this chapter. Two main consistencies, i.e., additive consistency and multiplicative consistency of fuzzy reciprocal preference relations, are reviewed. The relationships between the elements of fuzzy reciprocal preference relations and the weights for additive consistency and multiplicative consistency are presented.

1.1 Fuzzy Reciprocal Preference Relations

Denote $N = \{1, 2, \ldots, n\}$, $M = \{1, 2, \ldots, m\}$. Let $X = \{x_1, x_2, \ldots, x_n\}$ ($n \geq 2$) be a finite set of alternatives, where x_i denotes the ith alternative. In the multiple attribute decision-making problems, the DM needs to rank the alternatives $x_1, x_2, \ldots, x_n$ from the best to the worst according to the preference information. A brief description of the multiplicative reciprocal preference relation and fuzzy reciprocal preference relation is given below.

The multiplicative reciprocal preference relation is a positive preference relation $A \subset X \times X$, $A = (a_{ij})_{n \times n}$, where a_{ij} denotes the relative weight of alternative x_i with respect to x_j. The measurement of a_{ij} is described using a ratio scale and in particular, as shown by Saaty (1980), $a_{ij} \in \{1/9, 1/8, \ldots, 1, 2, \ldots, 9\}$: $a_{ij} = 1$ denotes the indifference between x_i and x_j, $a_{ij} = 9$ (or $a_{ji} = 1/9$) denotes that x_i is unanimously preferred to x_j, and $a_{ij} \in \{2, 3, \ldots, 8\}$ denotes the intermediate evaluations. It is multiplicative reciprocal, i.e., $a_{ij}a_{ji} = 1$, $\forall i, j \in N$ and in particular, $a_{ij} = 1$, $\forall i, j \in N$. Thus, we have the following definitions (Saaty, 1980):

Definition 1.1 (Saaty, 1980) Let $A = (a_{ij})_{n \times n}$ be a multiplicative reciprocal preference relation; then A is called a consistent multiplicative reciprocal preference relation if $a_{ij} = a_{ik}a_{kj}$, for all i, j, k.

Y. Xu, *Deriving Priorities from Incomplete Fuzzy Reciprocal Preference Relations*, https://doi.org/10.1007/978-981-99-3169-9_1

It has been found that a consistent multiplicative reciprocal preference relation can be precisely characterized by a priority vector $w = (w_1, w_2, \ldots, w_n)^T$, which satisfies $\sum_{i=1}^{n} w_i = 1, 0 \leq w_i \leq 1, i \in N$. That is,

$$a_{ij} = \frac{w_i}{w_j} \tag{1.1}$$

The fuzzy preference relation R is described as follows: $R \subset X \times X, R = (r_{ij})_{n \times n}$, with membership function $u_R: X \times X \longrightarrow [0, 1]$, where $u_R(x_i, x_j) = r_{ij}$ denotes the preference degree of the alternative x_i over x_j, $r_{ij} = 0.5$ denotes indifference between x_i and x_j, $r_{ij} = 1$ denotes that x_i is unanimously preferred to x_j, and $0.5 < r_{ij} < 1$ (or $0 < r_{ji} < 0.5$) denotes that x_i is preferred to x_j.

Definition 1.2 (Tanino, 1984) Let $R = (r_{ij})_{n \times n}$ be a preference relation; then R is called a fuzzy reciprocal preference relation if

$$r_{ij} + r_{ji} = 1, r_{ii} = 0.5, r_{ij} \in [0, 1], \forall i, j \in N \tag{1.2}$$

Remark 1.1 Generally, the multiplicative reciprocal preference relation is only called multiplicative preference relation, or AHP pairwise comparison matrix, and the reciprocal condition ($a_{ij}a_{ji} = 1$) is always assumed. Fuzzy means the values in the interval [0, 1], and reciprocal may be additive reciprocal ($r_{ij} + r_{ji} = 1$) or multiplicative reciprocal ($a_{ij}a_{ji} = 1$). Fuzzy preference relation may not be reciprocal (Fodor and Roubens, 1994; Orlovsky, 1978). Thus, we call fuzzy reciprocal preference relation when R satisfies Eq. (1.2). In the references, it is also called fuzzy preference relation (Tanino, 1984; Herrera-Viedma et al., 2004), reciprocal preference relation (Xu and Chen, 2008; Li et al., 2019; De Baets et al., 2006), and additive preference relation (Li et al., 2019).

Definition 1.3 (Tanino, 1984) Let $R = (r_{ij})_{n \times n}$ be a fuzzy reciprocal preference relation; then R is called an additive transitive fuzzy reciprocal preference relation, if the following additive transitivity is satisfied:

$$\left(r_{ij} - 0.5\right) + \left(r_{jk} - 0.5\right) = \left(r_{ik} - 0.5\right), \forall i, j, k \in N \tag{1.3}$$

or equivalently:

$$r_{ij} = r_{ik} - r_{jk} + 0.5, \forall i, j, k \in N \tag{1.4}$$

We also call the additive transitive perfectly consistent.

From Definition 1.1, we can get the following results easily:

Theorem 1.1 *Let $R = (r_{ij})_{n \times n}$ be a fuzzy reciprocal preference relation; then the sum of all the elements of R is $n^2/2$, that is,*

$$\sum_{i=1}^{n}\sum_{j=1}^{n}r_{ij}=n^2/2 \tag{1.5}$$

and the sum of all the elements of R except the diagonal elements is n(n − 1)/2, that is,

$$\sum_{\substack{i=1 \\ }}^{n}\sum_{\substack{j=1 \\ j\neq i}}^{n}r_{ij}=\sum_{\substack{i=1 \\ }}^{n}\sum_{\substack{j=1 \\ j\neq i}}^{n}r_{ij}-\sum_{i=1}^{n}r_{ii}=\frac{n^2}{2}-\frac{n}{2}=\frac{n(n-1)}{2} \tag{1.6}$$

Definition 1.4 (Tanino, 1984) Let $R = (r_{ij})_{n\times n}$ be a fuzzy reciprocal preference relation; then R has multiplicative transitivity property if

$$\frac{r_{ij}}{r_{ji}}\frac{r_{jk}}{r_{kj}}=\frac{r_{ik}}{r_{ki}},\forall i,j,k \in N \tag{1.7}$$

or

$$\left(\frac{1}{r_{ij}}-1\right)\left(\frac{1}{r_{jk}}-1\right)=\frac{1}{r_{ik}}-1,\forall i,j,k \in N \tag{1.8}$$

Chiclana et al. (2001) established a relationship between multiplicative reciprocal preference relation and fuzzy reciprocal preference relation as follows:

Theorem 1.2 (Chiclana et al., 2001) *Suppose that we have a set of alternatives* $X = \{x_1, x_2, \ldots, x_n\}$, *and associated with it a multiplicative reciprocal preference relation* $A = (a_{ij})_{n\times n}$. *Then the corresponding fuzzy reciprocal preference relation* $R = (r_{ij})_{n\times n}$, *associated with A, is given below:*

$$r_{ij}=\frac{1}{2}\left(1+\log_{9}a_{ij}\right) \tag{1.9}$$

According to Eq. (1.9), we have the following:

1. If $a_{ij} = 1/9$, then $r_{ij} = 0$, which indicates that x_j is absolutely preferred to x_i.
2. If $a_{ij} = 1$, then $r_{ij} = 0.5$, which indicates indifference between x_i and x_j.
3. If $a_{ij} = 9$, then $r_{ij} = 1$, which indicates that x_i is absolutely preferred to x_j.
4. If $a_{ij} > 1$, then $r_{ij} > 0.5$, which indicates that x_i is preferred to x_j.

Theorem 1.3 (Xu and Da, 2005) $A = (a_{ij})_{n\times n}$ *is a consistent multiplicative reciprocal preference relation, if and only if the corresponding reciprocal preference relation* $R = (r_{ij})_{n\times n}$ *derived by (1.9) is an additive transitive reciprocal preference relation.*

1.2   Incomplete Fuzzy Reciprocal Preference Relations

Since the multiplicative reciprocal preference relation and fuzzy reciprocal preference relation were proposed, they are assumed that the DMs can provide all the
$n(n - 1)/2$ pairwise comparisons. However, in the real situation, a DM may develop
a preference relation with incomplete information. Because of (1) time pressure, lack
of knowledge, and DM's limited expertise with problem domain (Chiclana et al.,
2008; Liu et al., 2012; Xu et al., 2009, 2011, 2013; Xu, 2004, 2005) and (2) when the
number of alternatives, n, is large, it may be practically impossible, or at least
unacceptable from the point of view of the DM, to perform all the $n(n - 1)/2$
required comparisons to complete the pairwise comparison matrices (Fedrizzi and
Giove, 2007); (3) it can be convenient/necessary to skip some direct critical comparison between alternatives, even if the total number of alternatives is small
(Fedrizzi and Giove, 2007); and (4) an expert would not be able to efficiently express
any kind of preference degree among two or more of the available options. This may
be due to an expert not possessing a precise or sufficient level of knowledge of part
of the problem, or because that the expert is unable to discriminate the degree to
which some options are better than others (Alonso et al., 2008; Herrera-Viedma
et al., 2007a, 2007b). Harker (1987a, 1987b) first proposed incomplete AHP
pairwise comparisons. Xu (2004) extended it to fuzzy reciprocal preference relation.
Alonso et al. (2004) also gave the definition of incomplete fuzzy reciprocal preference relation as follows:

Definition 1.5 (Alonso et al., 2004) A membership function $f: X \rightarrow Y$ is called partial
if at least one element in the set X is not mapped to an element in the set Y. If every
element from the set X is mapped to an element in Y, then we have a total function.

Definition 1.6 (Alonso et al., 2004) A fuzzy reciprocal preference relation C on a
set of alternatives X with a partial membership function is an incomplete fuzzy
reciprocal preference relation.

   Xu (2004) also defined the concept of an incomplete fuzzy reciprocal preference
relation; it regards that some of the elements in R are not given by the DM, and others
can be provided by the DM.

   For any $i, j \in N$, let c_{ij} be the ijth entry of an incomplete fuzzy reciprocal
preference relation $C = (c_{ij})_{n \times n}$,

$$\delta_{ij} = \begin{cases} 1 & c_{ij} \neq - \\ 0 & c_{ij} = - \end{cases} \tag{1.10}$$

and $c_{ij} = -$ indicates a missing element c_{ij}. According to Definition 1.6, $\delta_{ij} = 1$ if and
only if there exists $c_{ij} = u_C(x_i, x_j)$, and $\delta_{ij} = 0$ denotes that the preference value
$c_{ij} = u_C(x_i, x_j)$ is not furnished or missing.

Definition 1.7 Let $C = (c_{ij})_{n \times n}$ be an incomplete fuzzy reciprocal preference relation; then C is called an additively consistent incomplete fuzzy reciprocal preference relation, if all the known elements satisfy

$$c_{ij_1} + c_{j_1 j_2} + \ldots + c_{j_{t-1} j_t} + c_{j,i} = \frac{t+1}{2}, \forall j_o, o = 1, 2, \ldots, t, c_{ij} \neq - \quad (1.11)$$

Definition 1.8 (Xu and Wang, 2013) Let $C = (c_{ij})_{n \times n}$ be an incomplete fuzzy reciprocal preference relation; then C is called a multiplicative consistent incomplete fuzzy reciprocal preference relation, if all the known elements satisfy the multiplicative transitivity:

$$c_{i_1 i_2} \cdot c_{i_2 i_3} \cdot \ldots \cdot c_{i_k i_j} = c_{i_2 i_1} \cdot c_{i_3 i_2} \cdot \ldots \cdot c_{i_j i_k}, c_{ij} \neq - , \forall i, j \in N \quad (1.12)$$

Remark 1.2 Xu et al. (2014b) showed that Eqs. (1.4) and (1.11) are equivalent for the complete additively consistent fuzzy reciprocal preference relation. Xu (2004) only extended Eqs. (1.4) and (1.7) to incomplete additively consistent and multiplicative consistent fuzzy reciprocal preference relation, respectively. However, Xu and Wang (2013) proved that the multiplicative consistency Eq. (1.7) for incomplete fuzzy reciprocal preference relation is not proper and gave the revised Definition 1.8. For the same reason, we should say that the simple extension of additive consistency Eq. (1.4) for incomplete fuzzy reciprocal preference relation is also wrong. Thus, we give the revised additive consistency for incomplete fuzzy reciprocal preference relation in Definition 1.7.

Definition 1.9 The elements c_{ij}, c_{kl} of C are called adjacent, if $(i, j) \bigcap (k, l) \neq \emptyset$. For the unknown element, c_{ij}, c_{ij} can be determined indirectly, if there exist a series of known elements c_{ij_1}, $c_{j_1 j_2}$, ..., $c_{j_{t-1} j}$.

Definition 1.10 (Xu, 2004) Let $C = (c_{ij})_{n \times n}$ be an incomplete fuzzy reciprocal preference relation; if the missing elements of C can be determined by the known elements, then C is called an acceptable incomplete fuzzy reciprocal preference relation; otherwise, C is not an acceptable incomplete fuzzy reciprocal preference relation.

Theorem 1.4 (Jiang and Fan, 2008) *Let $C = (c_{ij})_{n \times n}$ be an incomplete fuzzy reciprocal preference relation. Then C can be completed by the known elements if there exists at least one known non-diagonal element in each row or column of C. This implies that an incomplete fuzzy reciprocal preference relation C which can be completed has at least $(n-1)$ non-diagonal judgments.*

Let $C = (c_{ij})_{n \times n}$ be an incomplete fuzzy reciprocal preference relation and $w = (w_1, w_2, \ldots, w_n)^T$ be its priority weight vector; its fuzzy consistency index and fuzzy consistency ratio are denoted by FCI and FCR for short, and their formulas are presented as follows (Xu et al., 2013):

$$\begin{cases} \text{FCI} = \dfrac{1}{n(n-1)} \displaystyle\sum_{1 \le i < j \le n} \sigma_{ij}\delta_{ij}\left(\dfrac{c_{ij}\,w_j}{c_{ji}\,w_i} + \dfrac{c_{ji}\,w_i}{c_{ij}\,w_j} - 2\right) \\[4mm] \text{FCR} = \dfrac{\text{FCI}}{\text{RI}} \end{cases} \qquad (1.13)$$

where δ_{ij} is defined in Eq. (1.10), and σ_{ij} is defined as

$$\sigma_{ij} = \begin{cases} 0, & \text{if } c_{ij} = 0 \quad \text{or} \quad 1, \\ 1, & \text{otherwise.} \end{cases}, i, j \in N \qquad (1.14)$$

and RI is the mean consistency index of randomly generated multiplicative reciprocal preference matrices as given in Table 1.1.

By adapting the acceptable consistency threshold 0.1 proposed by Saaty (1980), we have the following:

Definition 1.11 (Xu et al., 2013) Let $C = (c_{ij})_{n \times n}$ be an incomplete fuzzy reciprocal preference relation; if FCR < 0.1, then C is of acceptable consistency; otherwise, C's consistency level is unacceptable.

Remark 1.3 In Eq. (1.13), we still think that the number of elements in the fuzzy reciprocal preference relation is $n(n-1)$ except the diagonal elements, because when $c_{ij} = -$, we use the value $\frac{w_i}{w_i + w_j}$ to instead the unknown element c_{ij}, and then $\frac{c_{ij}}{c_{ji}}\frac{w_j}{w_i} + \frac{c_{ji}}{c_{ij}}\frac{w_i}{w_j} - 2 \equiv 0$, which denotes that the unknown elements are always consistent. Thus, it does not need to compute when $c_{ij} = -$, and then there is no impact on the fuzzy consistency index (FCI). That is, we look it as complete fuzzy reciprocal preference relation.

As the preference relation is incomplete, there exist some elements unknown, and there are some important problems for incomplete preference relations: (1) estimating the missing values (Herrera-Viedma et al., 2007a, 2007b; Alonso et al., 2008, 2009; Chiclana et al., 2008, 2009; Atiq-ur-Rehman et al., 2015; Xu et al., 2014b, 2014c; Zhang et al., 2014; Fedrizzi and Giove, 2013; Liang et al., 2017; Cabrerizo et al., 2020; Ureña et al., 2015; Hu and Tsai, 2006; Szádoczki et al., 2022); (2) consistency problem (Xu et al., 2014a; Kułakowski and Talaga, 2020; Ágoston and Csató, 2022; Zhang et al., 2022; Bozóki et al., 2011; Wedley, 1993; Forman, 1990); and (3) deriving priorities from incomplete preference relations (Csató and Rónyai, 2016; Carmone Jr et al., 1997; Shen, 1992; Xu et al., 2015a, 2015b, 2016, 2009, 2011; Xu and Da, 2008, 2009; Xu, 2004, 2005). In this book, we concentrate on the last issue. Thus, in the following, we give the relationship between the elements of fuzzy reciprocal preference relations and the weights for additive consistency and multiplicative consistency, respectively.

Table 1.1 The mean consistency index of randomly generated matrix (Saaty, 1980)

n	1	2	3	4	5	6	7	8	9	10	11	12	13	14	15
RI	0	0	0.52	0.89	1.12	1.26	1.36	1.41	1.46	1.49	1.52	1.54	1.56	1.58	1.59

1.3   The Relationships Between the Elements of Fuzzy Reciprocal Preference Relations and the Weights

1.3.1   The Relationships Between the Elements of Fuzzy Reciprocal Preference Relations and the Weights for Additive Consistency

As we stated above, suppose that we have a set of alternatives, $X = \{x_1, x_2, \ldots, x_n\}$, and the expert gives his/her fuzzy reciprocal preference relation and construct the judgment matrix R:

$$R = \begin{bmatrix} r_{11} & r_{12} & \cdots & r_{1n} \\ r_{21} & r_{22} & \cdots & r_{2n} \\ \cdots & \cdots & \cdots & \cdots \\ r_{n1} & r_{n2} & \cdots & r_{nn} \end{bmatrix}$$

Let $w_1, w_2, \ldots, w_n$ be the corresponding ranking vector of each alternative $x_1, x_2, \ldots,$ x_n, where $\sum_{i=1}^{n} w_i = 1$, $w_i \geq 0$. Based on the description of the fuzzy reciprocal preference relation given in Sect. 1.1, r_{ij} denotes the pairwise preference degree of alternative x_i over x_j. Since it is well known that the preference information between alternative x_i and x_j can also be reflected in their ranking values w_i and w_j, there exists an explicit function relation of r_{ij} and the ranking values w_i and w_j. From the description of the fuzzy reciprocal preference relations, r_{ij} denotes the preference degree of the alternative x_i over x_j; the greater r_{ij}, the stronger the preference of alternative x_i over x_j; $r_{ij} = 0.5$ denotes the indifference between x_i and x_j. Thus, $w_i - w_j$ is also the preference degree of x_i over x_j, and the greater $w_i - w_j$, the stronger the preference of alternative x_i over x_j. So, there exists some relationship between r_{ij} and $w_i - w_j$. We use function f to denote the relationship, which is $r_{ij} = f(w_i - w_j)$ (Zhang, 2000).

In the following, we infer the properties of f:

1. From the above analysis, we know that the greater r_{ij}, the stronger the preference degree of x_i over x_j. Similarly, the greater $w_i - w_j$, the stronger the preference degree of x_i over x_j. So, the function $f(x)$ should be the increasing function on $[-1, 1]$ (since $-1 \leq w_i - w_j \leq 1$).
2. f is a continuous function.
3. From Weierstrass theorem, for function $f(x) \in [-1, 1]$ and $\forall \varepsilon > 0$, there always exists a polynomial $h(x)$, that is, $\|f(x) - h(x)\| \leq \varepsilon$ on $[-1, 1]$; assume that

$$f(x) = a_0 + a_1 x + a_2 x^2 + \ldots + a_n x^n \tag{1.15}$$

4. From the properties of function f, we can deduce the specific form:

(a) For $r_{ij} = 1 - r_{ji}$, we have $f(x) = f(w_i - w_j) = 1 - f(w_j - w_i)$, writing $x = w_i - w_j$, so $f(x) = 1 - f(-x)$; then we have

$$f(x) + f(-x) = 1 \qquad (1.16)$$

Using $f(x) = a_0 + a_1 x + a_2 x^2 + \ldots + a_n x^n$ instead into the above equation, we have

$$2a_0 + 2a_2 x^2 + 2a_4 x^4 + \ldots + a_{2k} x^{2k} = 1 \qquad (1.17)$$

that is

$$(2a_0 - 1) + 2a_2 x^2 + 2a_4 x^4 + \ldots + a_{2k} x^{2k} = 0 \qquad (1.18)$$

For all $x \in [-1, 1]$, Eq. (1.18) should exist (where $n = 2k$ or $n = 2k + 1$). Because there exist $2k$ solutions for $2k$ polynomial at most, for all $x \in [-1, 1]$, if Eq. (1.18) holds, there must be

$$2a_0 - 1 = 2a_2 = 2a_4 = \ldots = 2a_{2k} = 0 \qquad (1.19)$$

Then, $a_0 = 1/2$, $a_2 = a_4 = \ldots = a_{2k} = 0$. Thus, function f can be expressed as follows:

$$f(x) = 0.5 + a_1 x + a_3 x^3 + \ldots + a_{2k-1} x^{2k-1} \qquad (1.20)$$

Writing $g(x) = a_1 x + a_3 x^3 + \ldots + a_{2k-1} x^{2k-1}$, the expression of f becomes

$$f(x) = 0.5 + g(x) \qquad (1.21)$$

(b) For $r_{ij} = r_{ik} - r_{jk} + 0.5$, we have

$$f(w_i - w_j) = f(w_i - w_k) - f(w_j - w_k) + 0.5 \qquad (1.22)$$

Writing $x = w_i - w_k$, $y = w_j - w_k$, we have

$$f(x - y) = f(x) - f(y) + 0.5 \qquad (1.23)$$

and $f(x) = 0.5 + g(x)$, and also along with Eq. (1.23), we have

$$g(x - y) + 0.5 = g(x) + 0.5 - (g(y) + 0.5) + 0.5 \qquad (1.24)$$

that is

$$g(x-y)=g(x)-g(y) \tag{1.25}$$

and

$$g(x)=a_1x+a_3x^3+\ldots+a_{2k-1}x^{2k-1} \tag{1.26}$$

$$g(y)=a_1y+a_3y^3+\ldots+a_{2k-1}y^{2k-1} \tag{1.27}$$

$$g(x-y)=a_1(x-y)+a_3(x-y)^3+\ldots+a_{2k-1}(x-y)^{2k-1} \tag{1.28}$$

So, if $g(x-y)=g(x)-g(y)$, for all x, $y \in [-1, 1]$, there must be

$$a_3=a_5=\ldots=a_{2k-1}=0 \tag{1.29}$$

In fact, because $g(x-y)=g(x)-g(y)$, for all x, $y \in [-1, 1]$, especially, if $y=cx$ (c is an arbitrary constant), then

$$g(x-y)=a_1(1-c)x+a_3(1-c)^3x^3+\ldots+a_{2k-1}(1-c)^{2k-1}x^{2k-1} \tag{1.30}$$

$$g(x)-g(y)=a_1(1-c)x+a_3(1-c^3)x^3+\ldots+a_{2k-1}(1-c^{2k-1})x^{2k-1} \tag{1.31}$$

So $a_1(1-c)x+a_3(1-c)^3x^3+\ldots+a_{2k-1}(1-c)^{2k-1}x^{2k-1}=a_1^{2k-1}x+a_3(1-c^3)x^3+\ldots+a_{2k-1}(1-c^{2k-1})x^{2k-1}$, for all $x \in [-1, 1]$. Because there exist $2k-1$ solutions for $2k-1$ polynomial at most, then

$$a_1(1-c)=a_1(1-c), a_3=a_3(1-c^3), \ldots, a_{2k-1}=a_{2k-1}(1-c^{2k-1})$$

Because c is an arbitrary constant, we can again get

$$a_3=a_5=\ldots=a_{2k-1}=0$$

and

$$g(x)=a_1x$$

Thus,

$$f(x)=0.5+a_1x.$$

(c) For $r_{ij}=f(w_i-w_j)$ and $f(x)=0.5+a_1x$, we have

$$r_{ij}=0.5+a_1(w_i-w_j) \tag{1.32}$$

As stated above, we have the following results:

Theorem 1.5 *Let $R = (r_{ij})_{n \times n}$ be a fuzzy reciprocal preference relation and $w = (w_1, w_2, \ldots, w_n)^T$ be the corresponding weighting vector, where $0 \le w_i \le 1$, $i \in N$, $\sum_{i=1}^{n} w_i = 1$; then there exists a positive number β, and such a relation can be expressed as follows:*

$$r_{ij} = 0.5 + \beta(w_i - w_j) \tag{1.33}$$

Furthermore,

$$w_i = \frac{1}{2n\beta}\left(2\sum_{k=1}^{n} r_{ik} - n\right) + \frac{1}{n} \tag{1.34}$$

where $\beta \ge \max\{\frac{n}{2} - \sum_{k=1}^{n} r_{ik}\}$. Furthermore, if $\sum_{k=1}^{n} r_{ik} \ge \sum_{k=1}^{n} r_{jk}$, then $w_i \ge w_j$. Specially, (i) if $\beta = \frac{n-1}{2}$, $w_i = \frac{2\sum_{k=1}^{n} r_{ik} - 1}{n(n-1)}$, and (ii) if $\beta = \frac{n}{2}$, $w_i = \frac{2\sum_{k=1}^{n} r_{ik}}{n^2}$.

Proof Equation (1.33) has been proved. Summing on both sides of Eq. (1.33) with respect to j, we have

$$\sum_{j=1}^{n} r_{ij} = \sum_{j=1}^{n} (0.5 + \beta(w_i - w_j))$$

$$= \frac{n}{2} + \beta\sum_{j=1}^{n} w_i - \beta\sum_{j=1}^{n} w_j$$

$$= \frac{n}{2} + n\beta w_i - \beta$$

that is

$$w_i = \frac{1}{2n\beta}\left(2\sum_{k=1}^{n} r_{ik} - n\right) + \frac{1}{n}$$

which is Eq. (1.34).

For an additive fuzzy reciprocal preference relation, by Eq. (1.5), we have

$$\sum_{i=1}^{n}\sum_{k=1}^{n} r_{ik} = \frac{n^2}{2} \ge n \times \min\left\{\sum_{k=1}^{n} r_{ik}\right\}$$

i.e.,

$$\frac{n}{2} \geq \min\left\{\sum_{k=1}^{n} r_{ik}\right\}$$

Thus,

$$\max\left\{\frac{n}{2} - \sum_{k=1}^{n} r_{ik}\right\} \geq 0$$

Then, for the parameter β, we have

$$\beta \geq \max\left\{\frac{n}{2} - \sum_{k=1}^{n} r_{ik}\right\} \geq 0$$

And it can be verified that

$$
\begin{aligned}
w_i &= \frac{1}{2n\beta}\left(2\sum_{k=1}^{n} r_{ik} - n\right) + \frac{1}{n} \\
&= \frac{\left(2\sum_{k=1}^{n} r_{ik} - n\right) + 2\beta}{2n\beta} \\
&= \frac{2\left[\beta - \left(\frac{n}{2} - \sum_{k=1}^{n} r_{ik}\right)\right]}{2n\beta} \\
&\geq \frac{2\left[\max\left\{\frac{n}{2} - \sum_{k=1}^{n} r_{ik}\right\} - \left(\frac{n}{2} - \sum_{k=1}^{n} r_{ik}\right)\right]}{2n\beta} \\
&\geq 0
\end{aligned}
$$

And with Theorem 1.1,

$$
\begin{aligned}
\sum_{i=1}^{n} w_i &= \sum_{i=1}^{n} \frac{1}{2n\beta}\left(2\sum_{k=1}^{n} r_{ik} - n\right) + 1 \\
&= \left(\frac{2\sum_{i=1}^{n}\sum_{k=1}^{n} r_{ik} - n^2}{2n\beta}\right) + 1 = \left(\frac{2 \times \frac{n^2}{2} - n^2}{2n\beta}\right) + 1 = 1
\end{aligned}
$$

If R is additively consistent, plugging the aforesaid w_i, we have

$$0.5 + \beta(w_i - w_j) = 0.5 + \frac{1}{n}\sum_{k=1}^{n}(r_{ik} - r_{jk}) = 0.5 + \frac{1}{n}\sum_{k=1}^{n}\left(r_{ij} - \frac{1}{2}\right) = r_{ij}$$

Furthermore, since $\beta > 0$, if $\sum_{k=1}^{n} r_{ik} \geq \sum_{k=1}^{n} r_{jk}$, by the definition of w_i in (1.34), one has $w_i \geq w_j$. This shows that the ranking order is preserved regardless of the value of β. Especially, if $\beta = \frac{n-1}{2}$, $w_i = \frac{2\sum_{k=1}^{n} r_{ik} - 1}{n(n-1)}$, and (ii) if $\beta = \frac{n}{2}$, $w_i = \frac{2\sum_{k=1}^{n} r_{ik}}{n^2}$. In both cases, $\beta \geq \max\{\frac{n}{2} - \sum_{k=1}^{n} r_{ik}\}$, and hence $w_i \geq 0$.

Theorem 1.5 is equivalent to the following Theorem 1.6. $\square$

Theorem 1.6 *For a complete fuzzy reciprocal preference relation $R = (r_{ij})_{n \times n}$, if R is additively consistent, there always exists a priority weight vector $w = (w_1, w_2, \ldots, w_n)^T$ such that*

$$w_i \geq 0(i = 1, 2, \ldots, n), \quad \sum_{i=1}^{n} w_i = 1 \tag{1.35}$$

The relationship between w_i and r_{ij} is

$$w_i = \left(\frac{2}{n}\sum_{k=1}^{n} r_{ik} - 1\right)c + \frac{1}{n}, r_{ij} = \frac{w_i - w_j}{2c} + \frac{1}{2} \tag{1.36}$$

where $c \in (0, d]$, and $d = 1/(n - 2\min_{1 \leq i \leq n}\{\sum_{k=1}^{n} r_{ik}\})$. Furthermore, if $\sum_{k=1}^{n} r_{ik} \geq \sum_{k=1}^{n} r_{jk}$, then $w_i \geq w_j$.

Proof By Theorem 1.1, we know that

$$n - 2\min_{1 \leq i \leq n}\left\{\sum_{k=1}^{n} r_{ik}\right\} \geq 0$$

and because $c \in (0, d]$,
   it can be verified that

$$w_i = \left(\frac{2}{n}\sum_{k=1}^{n} r_{ik} - 1\right)c + \frac{1}{n}$$

$$\geq \left(\frac{2}{n}\min_{1 \leq i \leq n}\left\{\sum_{k=1}^{n} r_{ik}\right\} - 1\right)c + \frac{1}{n}$$

$$= -\left(n - 2 \min_{1 \le i \le n}\left\{\sum_{k=1}^{n} r_{ik}\right\}\right)\frac{c}{n} + \frac{1}{n}$$

$$\ge -\left(n - 2 \min_{1 \le i \le n}\left\{\sum_{k=1}^{n} r_{ik}\right\}\right)\frac{d}{n} + \frac{1}{n}$$

$$= -\frac{1}{n} + \frac{1}{n} = 0$$

And with Theorem 1.1,

$$\sum_{i=1}^{n} w_i = \sum_{i=1}^{n}\left(\frac{2}{n}\sum_{k=1}^{n} r_{ik} - 1\right)c + 1 = \left(\frac{2}{n}\sum_{i=1}^{n}\sum_{k=1}^{n} r_{ik} - n\right)c + 1 = \left(\frac{2}{n} \times \frac{n^2}{2} - n\right)c$$
$$+ 1 = 1$$

On the other hand,

$$\frac{w_i - w_j}{2c} + \frac{1}{2} = \frac{1}{n}\sum_{k=1}^{n}(r_{ik} - r_{jk}) + \frac{1}{2} = \frac{1}{n}\sum_{k=1}^{n}\left(r_{ij} - \frac{1}{2}\right) + \frac{1}{2} = r_{ij}$$

Furthermore, because $c > 0$, if $\sum_{k=1}^{n} r_{ik} \ge \sum_{k=1}^{n} r_{jk}$, then $w_i \ge w_j$. This shows that the ranking order is preserved whatever c is different, which completes the proof of Theorem 1.6. $\qquad\square$

Example 1.1 Example 6 in Liu et al. (2012):
In Liu et al. (2012), we obtain the collective fuzzy preference relation R as

$$R = \begin{bmatrix} 0.5 & 0.473 & 0.573 & 0.536 \\ 0.527 & 0.5 & 0.6 & 0.563 \\ 0.427 & 0.4 & 0.5 & 0.463 \\ 0.464 & 0.437 & 0.537 & 0.5 \end{bmatrix}$$

We have

$$r_1 = \sum_{k=1}^{4} r_{1k} = 0.5 + 0.473 + 0.573 + 0.536 = 2.082,$$

$$r_2 = \sum_{k=1}^{4} r_{2k} = 0.527 + 0.5 + 0.6 + 0.563 = 2.190,$$

$$r_3 = \sum_{k=1}^{4} r_{3k} = 0.427 + 0.4 + 0.5 + 0.463 = 1.790,$$

$$r_4 = \sum_{k=1}^{4} r_{4k} = 0.464 + 0.437 + 0.537 + 0.5 = 1.938.$$

Thus,

$$\min_{1 \leq i \leq n} \sum_{k=1}^{n} r_{ik} = r_3 = 1.790 > \frac{4-1}{2} = 1.5$$

In Liu et al. (2012), we have

$$c = \min\{1, 1/(4 - 2\min\{2.082, 2.190, 1.790, 1.938\})\}$$
$$= \min\{1, 1/(4 - 2 \times 1.790)\} = 1$$

The priority weight vector $w = (w_1, w_2, w_3, w_4)$ is obtained by the equation $w_i = (\frac{2}{n}\sum_{k=1}^{n} r_{ik} - 1)c + \frac{1}{n}$, and then we have

$$w = (w_1, w_2, w_3, w_4) = (0.291, 0.345, 0.145, 0.219)$$

Now, we will use Theorem 1.6 to obtain the priority weight vector. By Eq. (1.36), we have

$$w_1 = \left(\frac{2}{n}\sum_{k=1}^{n} r_{ik} - 1\right)c + \frac{1}{n} = 0.25 + 0.041c,$$
$$w_2 = 0.25 + 0.095c,$$
$$w_3 = 0.25 - 0.105c,$$
$$w_4 = 0.25 - 0.031c,$$

where $d = 1/(n - 2\min_{1 \leq i \leq n}\{\sum_{k=1}^{n} r_{ik}\}) = 1/(4 - 2 \times 1.790) = 2.381$; therefore, $c \in (0, 2.381]$.

From the above constraints, we can get numerous priority weight vectors w. For example, if $c = 1$, we will get $w = (w_1, w_2, w_3, w_4) = (0.291, 0.345, 0.145, 0.219)$, which is the same as our previous work in Liu et al. (2012). If $c = 2.381$, $w = (w_1, w_2, w_3, w_4) = (0.3476, 0.4762, 0, 0.1762)$. If $c = 1/n = 0.25$, we get $w = (w_1, w_2, w_3, w_4) = (0.2602, 0.2737, 0.2238, 0.2422)$. We can also get different weight vectors by

Fig. 1.1 The relationship
between c and w of Example
1.1

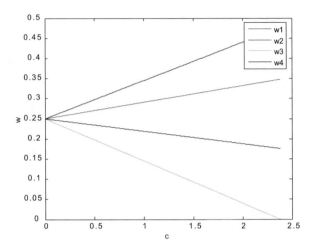

setting different c. And all the weight vectors satisfy the normalization constraint
(i.e., Eq. (1.35)), and all the weight vectors get the same rankings, that is, $x_2 \succ x_1 \succ x_4 \succ x_3$. This can also be seen from Fig. 1.1.

Remark 1.4 From Theorems 1.5 and 1.6, we know that if a fuzzy reciprocal
preference relation R is additively consistent, there are numerous normalization
weight vectors, and the vectors can inversely deduce the same additively consistent
fuzzy reciprocal preference relation R by Eq. (1.33) or (1.36). However, if $\beta = 1/2$,
which is widely used and originally proposed by Tanino (1984), Fedrizzi and
Brunelli (2009) pointed out that there does not exist normalization weight vector
and proposed the unnormalized weight vectors, or alternative normalization weight
vector (Fedrizzi and Brunelli, 2009) (that is, $w_n = 0$). Furthermore, if $\beta = 1/2$, Shen
et al. (2009) also pointed out that the normalized weight vector does not exist. Our
results show that not only can we obtain one normalized weight vector, but also there
exist numerous normalized weight vectors. It only needs not to fix the parameter β to
be 1/2.

As f is a continuous and increasing function, $\beta > 0$. In the following, we will
deduce how to take the value of β corresponding to the fuzzy reciprocal preference
relation R.

Theorem 1.7 *Let $R = (r_{ij})_{n \times n}$ be a fuzzy reciprocal preference relation; we take the
below transformation:*

$$p_{ij} = 0.5 + \alpha \left(\sum_{l=1}^{n} r_{il} - \sum_{l=1}^{n} r_{jl} \right), \forall i, j, l \in N$$

where $\alpha \geq \frac{1}{2(n-1)}$.

(i) *The transformation $P = (p_{ij})_{n \times n}$ will be additive transitive perfectly consistent.*

(ii) *If $\alpha = 1/n$, the preference relation R is additive transitive perfectly consistent if and only if $R = P$.*

Proof

(i) As $p_{ij} = 0.5 + \alpha \left(\sum_{l=1}^{n} r_{il} - \sum_{l=1}^{n} r_{jl} \right)$, then

$$p_{ij} + p_{ji} = 0.5 + \alpha \left(\sum_{l=1}^{n} r_{il} - \sum_{l=1}^{n} r_{jl} \right) + 0.5 + \alpha \left(\sum_{l=1}^{n} r_{jl} - \sum_{l=1}^{n} r_{il} \right) = 1$$

So, $P = (p_{ij})_{n \times n}$ is a fuzzy reciprocal preference relation.
On the other hand,

$$p_{ij} = 0.5 + \alpha \left(\sum_{l=1}^{n} r_{il} - \sum_{l=1}^{n} r_{jl} \right)$$

$$= 0.5 + \alpha \left[\left(\sum_{l=1}^{n} r_{il} - \sum_{l=1}^{n} r_{kl} \right) - \left(\sum_{l=1}^{n} r_{jl} - \sum_{l=1}^{n} r_{kl} \right) \right]$$

$$= 0.5 + \left[0.5 + \alpha \left(\sum_{l=1}^{n} r_{il} - \sum_{l=1}^{n} r_{kl} \right) \right] - \left[0.5 + \alpha \left(\sum_{l=1}^{n} r_{jl} - \sum_{l=1}^{n} r_{kl} \right) \right]$$

$$= 0.5 + p_{ik} - p_{jk}$$

From Definition 1.3, we know that $P = (p_{ij})_{n \times n}$ is additive transitive perfectly consistent.

(ii) If R is additive transitive perfectly consistent, then

$$r_{ij} = r_{ik} - r_{jk} + 0.5$$

For all $\forall i, j, k \in N$, we have

$$p_{ij} = 0.5 + \alpha \left(\sum_{k=1}^{n} r_{ik} - \sum_{k=1}^{n} r_{jk} \right)$$

$$= 0.5 + \alpha \sum_{k=1}^{n} \left(r_{ij} - 0.5 \right)$$

$$= 0.5 + \alpha \left(r_{ij} - 0.5 \right) \times n$$

So, if $\alpha = 1/n$, then $p_{ij} = r_{ij}$, that is, $R = P$. On the other hand, if $R = P$, from (i), we know that $P = (p_{ij})_{n \times n}$ is additive transitive perfectly consistent, so R is also additive transitive perfectly consistent, which completes the proof of Lemma 1.2. $\square$

It is clear from Lemma 1.2 that if $\alpha = 1/n$, then the transformation preference relation $P = (p_{ij})_{n \times n}$ is more closer to the initial preference relation $R = (r_{ij})_{n \times n}$. If $\alpha \neq 1/n$, then the transformation preference relation $P = (p_{ij})_{n \times n}$ is deviation from the initial preference relation $R = (r_{ij})_{n \times n}$, that is to say, if the initial preference relation $R = (r_{ij})_{n \times n}$ is additive transitive perfectly consistent, the transformation preference relation $P = (p_{ij})_{n \times n}$ is also additive transitive perfectly consistent, but they are not equal ($P \neq R$); thus, the transformation changed the initial information and cannot express true options of the DM.

1.3.2   The Relationships Between the Elements of Fuzzy Reciprocal Preference Relations and the Weights for Multiplicative Consistency

Let $w = (w_1, w_2, \ldots, w_n)^T$ be the priority weight vector for the fuzzy reciprocal preference relation $R = (r_{ij})_{n \times n}$, where $\sum_{i=1}^{n} w_i = 1$, $w_i > 0$, $i \in N$. If $R = (r_{ij})_{n \times n}$ is a complete fuzzy reciprocal preference relation with multiplicative transitivity, then it can be expressed as

$$r_{ij} = \frac{w_i}{w_i + w_j}, i, j \in N \tag{1.37}$$

1.4   Summary

In this chapter, we have introduced the basic concept of fuzzy reciprocal preference relation and incomplete fuzzy reciprocal preference relation. The relationship between the elements of fuzzy reciprocal preference relation and the weights for additive and multiplicative consistence is presented; all of these will be used in the following chapters.

References

Ágoston, K. C., & Csató, L. (2022). Inconsistency thresholds for incomplete pairwise comparison matrices. *Omega, 108*, 102576.

Alonso, S., Chiclana, F., Herrera, F., & Herrera-Viedma, E. (2004). A learning procedure to estimate missing values in fuzzy preference relations based on additive consistency. In V. Torra & Y. Narukawa (Eds.), *MDAI, 2004, LNAI 3131* (pp. 227–238). Springer-Verlag.

Alonso, S., Chiclana, F., Herrera, F., Herrera-Viedma, E., Alcala-Fdez, J., & Porcel, C. (2008). A consistency-based procedure to estimate missing pairwise preference values. *International Journal of Intelligence Systems, 23*(2), 155–175.

Alonso, S., Herrera-Viedma, E., Chiclana, F., & Herrera, F. (2009). Individual and social strategies to deal with ignorance situations in multi-person decision making. *International Journal of Information Technology & Decision Making, 8*(2), 313–333.

Atiq-ur-Rehman, Kerre, E. E., & Ashraf, S. (2015). Group decision making by using incomplete fuzzy preference relations based on T-consistency and the order consistency. *International Journal of Intelligence Systems, 30*, 120–143.

Bozóki, S., Fülöp, J., & Koczkodaj, W. W. (2011). An LP-based inconsistency monitoring of pairwise comparison matrices. *Mathematical and Computer Modelling, 54*, 789–793.

Cabrerizo, F. J., Al-Hmouz, R., Morfeq, A., Martínze, M. Á., Pedrycz, W., & Herrera-Viedma, E. (2020). Estimating incomplete information in group decision making: A framework of granular computing. *Applied Soft Computing, 86*, 105930.

Carmone, F. J., Jr., Kara, A., & Zanakis, S. H. (1997). A Monte Carlo investigation of incomplete pairwise comparison matrices in AHP. *European Journal of Operational Research, 102*, 538–553.

Chiclana, F., Herrera-Viedma, E., & Alonso, S. (2009). A note on two methods for estimating missing pairwise preference values. *IEEE Transactions on Systems, Man, and Cybernetics, Part B: Cybernetics, 39*(6), 1628–1633.

Chiclana, F., Herrera-Viedma, E., Alonso, S., & Herrera, F. (2008). A note on the estimation of missing pairwise preference values: A U-consistency based method. *International Journal of Uncertainty Fuzziness, 16*(2), 19–32.

Chiclana, F., Herrera, F., & Herrera-Viedma, E. (2001). Integrating multiplicative preference relations in a multipurpose decision-making model based on fuzzy preference relations. *Fuzzy Sets and Systems, 122*(2), 277–291.

Csató, L., & Rónyai, L. (2016). Incomplete pairwise comparison matrices and weighting methods. *Fundamenta Informaticae, 144*, 309–320.

De Baets, B., De Meyer, H., De Schuymer, B., & Jenei, S. (2006). Cyclic evaluation of transitivity of reciprocal relations. *Social Choice and Welfare, 26*, 217–238.

Fedrizzi, M., & Brunelli, M. (2009). On the normalisation of a priority vector associated with a reciprocal relation. *International Journal of General Systems, 38*(5), 579–586.

Fedrizzi, M., & Giove, S. (2007). Incomplete pairwise comparison and consistency optimization. *European Journal of Operational Research, 183*(1), 303–313.

Fedrizzi, M., & Giove, S. (2013). Optimal sequencing in incomplete pairwise comparisons for large-dimensional problems. *International Journal of General Systems, 42*(4), 366–375.

Fodor, J. C., & Roubens, M. R. (1994). *Fuzzy preference modelling and multicriteria decision support*. Springer Science & Business Media.

Forman, E. H. (1990). Random indices for incomplete pairwise comparison matrices. *European Journal of Operational Research, 48*, 153–155.

Harker, P. T. (1987a). Alternative modes of questions in the analytic hierarchy process. *Mathematical Modeling, 9*(3-5), 353–360.

Harker, P. T. (1987b). Incomplete pairwise comparisons in the analytic hierarchy process. *Mathematical Modeling, 9*(11), 837–848.

Herrera-Viedma, E., Alonso, S., Chiclana, F., & Herrera, F. (2007a). A consensus model for group decision making with incomplete fuzzy preference relations. *IEEE Transactions on Fuzzy Systems, 15*(5), 863–877.

Herrera-Viedma, E., Chiclana, F., Herrera, F., & Alonso, S. (2007b). Group decision-making model with incomplete fuzzy preference relations based on additive consistency. *IEEE Transactions on Systems, Man, and Cybernetics, Part B: Cybernetics, 37*(1), 176–189.

Herrera-Viedma, E., Herrera, F., Chiclana, F., & Luque, M. (2004). Some issues on consistency of fuzzy preference relations. *European Journal of Operational Research, 154*(1), 98–109.

Hu, Y. C., & Tsai, J. F. (2006). Backpropagation multi-layer perceptron for incomplete pairwise comparison matrices in analytic hierarchy process. *Applied Mathematical Modelling, 180*, 53–62.

Jiang, Y. P., & Fan, Z. P. (2008). An approach to group decision making based on incomplete fuzzy preference relations. *International Journal of Uncertainty Fuzziness, 16*(01), 83–94.

Kułakowski, K., & Talaga, D. (2020). Inconsistency indices for incomplete pairwise comparisons matrices. *International Journal of General Systems, 49*(2), 174–200.

Li, C. C., Dong, Y. C., Xu, Y. J., Chiclana, F., Herrera-Viedma, E., & Herrera, F. (2019). An overview on managing additive consistency of reciprocal preference relations for consistency-driven decision making and fusion: Taxonomy and future directions. *Information Fusion, 52*, 143–156.

Liang, Q., Liao, X. W., & Liu, J. P. (2017). A social ties-based approach for group decision-making problems with incomplete additive preference relations. *Knowledge-Based Systems, 119*, 68–86.

Liu, X. W., Pan, Y. W., Xu, Y. J., & Yu, S. (2012). Least square completion and inconsistency repair methods for additively consistent fuzzy preference relations. *Fuzzy Sets and Systems, 198*, 1–19.

Orlovsky, S. A. (1978). Decision-making with a fuzzy preference relation. *Fuzzy Sets and Systems, 1*(3), 155–167.

Saaty, T. L. (1980). *The analytic hierarchy process*. McGraw-Hill.

Shen, P. D., Chyr, W. L., Lee, H. S., & Lin, K. (2009). Correspondence between incomplete fuzzy preference relation and its priority vector. In *Knowledge-based and intelligent information and engineering systems* (pp. 745–751). Springer.

Shen, Y. J. (1992). An incomplete design in the analytic hierarchy process. *Mathematical and Computer Modelling, 16*(5), 121–129.

Szádoczki, Z., Bozóki, S., & Tekile, H. A. (2022). Filling in pattern designs for incomplete pairwise comparison matrices: (Quasi-)regular graphs with minimal diameter. *Omega, 107*, 102557.

Tanino, T. (1984). Fuzzy preference orderings in group decision making. *Fuzzy Sets and Systems, 12*(2), 117–131.

Ureña, R., Chiclana, F., Morente-Molinera, J. A., & Herrera-Viedma, E. (2015). Managing incomplete preference relations in decision making: A review and future trends. *Information Sciences, 302*, 14–32.

Wedley, W. C. (1993). Consistency prediction for incomplete AHP matrices. *Mathematical and Computer Modelling, 17*(4/5), 151–161.

Xu, Y. J., Chen, L., Li, K. W., & Wang, H. M. (2015a). A chi-square method for priority derivation in group decision making with incomplete reciprocal preference relations. *Information Sciences, 306*, 166–179.

Xu, Y. J., Chen, L., Rodríguez, R. M., Herrera, F., & Wang, H. M. (2016). Deriving the priority weights from incomplete hesitant fuzzy preference relations in group decision making. *Knowledge-Based Systems, 99*, 71–78.

Xu, Y. J., Chen, L., & Wang, H. M. (2015b). A least deviation method for priority derivation in group decision making with incomplete reciprocal preference relations. *International Journal of Approximate Reasoning, 66*, 91–102.

Xu, Y. J., & Da, Q. L. (2008). Weighted least-square method and its improvement for priority of incomplete complementary judgement matrix. *Systems Engineering and Electronics, 30*(7), 1273–1276.

Xu, Y. J., & Da, Q. L. (2009). Methods for priority of incomplete complementary judgement matrices. *Systems Engineering and Electronics, 31*(1), 95–99.

Xu, Y. J., Da, Q. L., & Liu, L. H. (2009). Normalizing rank aggregation method for priority of a fuzzy preference relation and its effectiveness. *International Journal of Approximate Reasoning, 50*(8), 1287–1297.

Xu, Y. J., Da, Q. L., & Wang, H. M. (2011). A note on group decision-making procedure based on incomplete reciprocal relations. *Soft Computing, 15*(7), 1289–1300.

Xu, Y. J., Gupta, J. N. D., & Wang, H. M. (2014a). The ordinal consistency of an incomplete reciprocal preference relation. *Fuzzy Sets and Systems, 246*, 62–77.

Xu, Y. J., Li, K. W., & Wang, H. M. (2014b). Incomplete interval fuzzy preference relations and their applications. *Computers and Industrial Engineering, 67*, 93–103.

Xu, Y. J., Ma, F. K.-B. S., Tao, F. F., & Wang, H. M. (2014c). Some methods to deal with unacceptable incomplete 2-tuple fuzzy linguistic preference relations in group decision making. *Knowledge-Based Systems, 56*, 179–190.

Xu, Y. J., Patnayakuni, R., & Wang, H. M. (2013). Logarithmic least squares method to priority for group decision making with incomplete fuzzy preference relations. *Applied Mathematical Modelling, 37*(4), 2139–2152.

Xu, Y. J., & Wang, H. M. (2013). Eigenvector method, consistency test and inconsistency repairing for an incomplete fuzzy preference relation. *Applied Mathematical Modelling, 37*(7), 5171–5183.

Xu, Z. S. (2004). Goal programming models for obtaining the priority vector of incomplete fuzzy preference relation. *International Journal of Approximate Reasoning, 36*(3), 261–270.

Xu, Z. S. (2005). A procedure for decision making based on incomplete fuzzy preference relation. *Fuzzy Optimization and Decision Making, 4*(3), 175–189.

Xu, Z. S., & Chen, J. (2008). Group decision-making procedure based on incomplete reciprocal relations. *Soft Computing, 12*(6), 515–521.

Xu, Z. S., & Da, Q. L. (2005). A least deviation method to obtain a priority vector of a fuzzy preference relation. *European Journal of Operational Research, 164*(1), 206–216.

Zhang, J. J. (2000). Fuzzy analytical hierarchy process. *Fuzzy Systems and Mathematics, 14*, 80–88.

Zhang, J. W., Liu, F., Tu, H. N., & Herrera-Viedma, E. (2022). A decision-making model with sequential incomplete additive pairwise comparisons. *Knowledge-Based Systems, 236*, 107766.

Zhang, Y., Ma, H. X., Li, Q., Liu, B. H., & Liu, J. (2014). Conditions of two methods for estimating missing preference information. *Information Sciences, 279*, 186–198.

Chapter 2
Normalizing Rank Aggregation-Based Method

In Chap. 1, we have introduced the relationship between the elements of fuzzy reciprocal preference relations and the weights for additive consistency, and it is described in Eq. (1.33). In this chapter, we further investigate the parameter β and call it normalizing rank aggregation-based method when $\beta = n/2$ or $\beta = (n-1)/2$. Additionally, we will show that it is more reasonable when $\beta = n/2$ or $\beta = (n-1)/2$ than $\beta = 0.5$, which is extensively used in the existing literatures.

2.1 Normalizing Rank Aggregation Method 1

2.1.1 An Approach to Constructing a Complete Fuzzy Reciprocal Preference Relation from an Incomplete Fuzzy Reciprocal Preference Relation When $\beta = n/2$

In the following, we first give some results when $\beta = n/2$.

Theorem 2.1 (Xu et al., 2009) *If the priority vector of the additive transitive perfectly consistent fuzzy reciprocal preference relation R is derived by normalizing rank aggregation method, then $\beta = \frac{n}{2}$.*

Proof If the priority vector of the additive transitive perfectly consistent fuzzy reciprocal preference relation R is derived by normalizing rank aggregation method, then

$$w_i = \frac{\sum_{k=1}^{n} r_{ik}}{\sum_{i=1}^{n} \sum_{k=1}^{n} r_{ik}} = \frac{\sum_{k=1}^{n} r_{ik}}{\frac{n^2}{2}}, \quad i \in N \tag{2.1}$$

© The Author(s), under exclusive license to Springer Nature Singapore Pte Ltd. 2023
Y. Xu, *Deriving Priorities from Incomplete Fuzzy Reciprocal Preference Relations*,
https://doi.org/10.1007/978-981-99-3169-9_2

$$w_i = \frac{\sum_{k=1}^{n} r_{jk}}{\sum_{i=1}^{n} \sum_{k=1}^{n} r_{jk}} = \frac{\sum_{k=1}^{n} r_{jk}}{\frac{n^2}{2}}, i \in N \tag{2.2}$$

Put (2.1) and (2.2) into (1.33); then,

$$r_{ij} = \beta\left(w_i - w_j\right) + 0.5$$

$$= \beta \frac{\sum_{k=1}^{n} \left(r_{ik} - r_{jk}\right)}{\frac{n^2}{2}} + 0.5$$

Since $r_{ij} = r_{ik} - r_{jk} + 0.5$,

$$r_{ij} = \beta \frac{\sum_{k=1}^{n} \left(r_{ij} - 0.5\right)}{\frac{n^2}{2}} + 0.5 = \beta \frac{n r_{ij} - \frac{n}{2}}{\frac{n^2}{2}} + 0.5 \tag{2.3}$$

So, we can get $\beta = \frac{n}{2}$, which completes the proof.   □

Theorem 2.2 *If $\beta = \frac{n}{2}$, then the priority vector of the additive transitive perfectly consistent fuzzy reciprocal preference relation R derived by Eq. (1.33) is normalizing rank aggregation method, that is,*

$$w_i = \frac{\sum_{j=1}^{n} r_{ij}}{\frac{n^2}{2}} = \frac{\sum_{j=1}^{n} r_{ij}}{\sum_{i=1}^{n} \sum_{j=1}^{n} r_{ij}} \tag{2.4}$$

Proof If $\beta = \frac{n}{2}$, by (1.33), we have

$$w_i = \frac{r_{ij} - 0.5}{\frac{n}{2}} + w_j \tag{2.5}$$

Summing on both sides of Eq. (2.5) with respect to j, then

$$\sum_{j=1}^{n} w_i = \frac{\sum_{j=1}^{n} \left(r_{ij} - 0.5\right)}{\frac{n}{2}} + \sum_{j=1}^{n} w_j \tag{2.6}$$

i.e.,

$$n w_i = \frac{\sum_{j=1}^{n} r_{ij} - 0.5 n}{\frac{n}{2}} + 1$$

Therefore,

$$w_i = \frac{\sum_{j=1}^{n} r_{ij} - 0.5n}{n^2/2} + \frac{1}{n} = \frac{\sum_{j=1}^{n} r_{ij}}{n^2/2} = \frac{\sum_{j=1}^{n} r_{ij}}{\sum_{i=1}^{n} \sum_{j=1}^{n} r_{ij}}$$

which completes the proof.   □

We call the method normalizing rank aggregation method.

For a fuzzy reciprocal preference relation, which all the elements are known, from Theorem 2.1, we have proved that it is more reasonable to take $\beta = \frac{n}{2}$; therefore,

$$c_{ij} = \frac{n}{2}\left(w_i - w_j\right) + 0.5 \tag{2.7}$$

and we extend the conclusion to the unknown elements of the incomplete fuzzy reciprocal preference relation, that is, if $c_{ij} = -$, then we instead $-$ by $\frac{n}{2}\left(w_i - w_j\right) + 0.5$.

Let $C = (c_{ij})_{n \times n}$ be an incomplete fuzzy reciprocal preference relation; we construct an auxiliary fuzzy reciprocal preference relation $\overline{C} = (\overline{c}_{ij})_{n \times n}$, and its element is

$$\overline{c}_{ij} = \begin{cases} c_{ij} & c_{ij} \neq - \\ \frac{n}{2}\left(w_i - w_j\right) + 0.5 & c_{ij} = - \end{cases} \tag{2.8}$$

2.1.2   An Illustrative Example

Example 2.1   For a decision-making problem, there are three decision alternatives. The DM provides his/her preference over these three decision alternatives and gives an incomplete fuzzy reciprocal preference relation as follows:

$$C = \begin{bmatrix} 0.5 & 0.4 & - \\ 0.6 & 0.5 & 0.7 \\ - & 0.3 & 0.5 \end{bmatrix}$$

From the incomplete fuzzy reciprocal preference relation C, we construct the auxiliary fuzzy reciprocal preference relation $\overline{C} = (\overline{c}_{ij})_{n \times n}$ as follows (where $n = 3$):

$$\overline{C} = \begin{bmatrix} 0.5 & 0.4 & \frac{3}{2}(w_1 - w_3) + 0.5 \\ 0.6 & 0.5 & 0.7 \\ \frac{3}{2}(w_3 - w_1) + 0.5 & 0.3 & 0.5 \end{bmatrix}$$

We use normalizing rank aggregation method to obtain the priority vector, that is,

$$w_i = \frac{\sum_{j=1}^{n} c_{ij}}{\sum_{i=1}^{n}\sum_{j=1}^{n} c_{ij}} = \frac{\sum_{j=1}^{n} c_{ij}}{\frac{n^2}{2}}, i \in N$$

We get the following linear equations:

$$\begin{cases} w_1 = \dfrac{0.5 + 0.4 + 1.5(w_1 - w_3) + 0.5}{4.5} \\ w_2 = \dfrac{0.6 + 0.5 + 0.7}{4.5} \\ w_3 = \dfrac{1.5(w_3 - w_1) + 0.5 + 0.3 + 0.5}{4.5} \end{cases}$$

i.e.,

$$\begin{bmatrix} 3 & 0 & 1.5 \\ 0 & 4.5 & 0 \\ 1.5 & 0 & 3 \end{bmatrix} \begin{bmatrix} w_1 \\ w_2 \\ w_3 \end{bmatrix} = \begin{bmatrix} 1.4 \\ 1.8 \\ 1.3 \end{bmatrix}$$

Solving the linear equations, we obtain $w_1 = 1/3$, $w_2 = 2/5$, and $w_3 = 4/15$. And the priority vector is $w = (1/3, 2/5, 4/15)^T$. And we can also get the unknown elements as follows:

$$\overline{c}_{13} = 1.5(w_1 - w_3) + 0.5 = 0.6, \overline{c}_{31} = 1.5(w_3 - w_1) + 0.5 = 0.4$$

and then

$$C = \begin{bmatrix} 0.5 & 0.4 & 0.6 \\ 0.6 & 0.5 & 0.7 \\ 0.4 & 0.3 & 0.5 \end{bmatrix}$$

Obviously, C is an additively consistent fuzzy reciprocal preference relation. If we take $\beta = 1/2$, which was computed by Xu (2004), we have $w = (0.31, 0.14, 0.29)^T$, $c_{13} = 0.5(w_1 - w_3 + 1) = 0.51$, and $c_{31} = 0.5(w_3 - w_1 + 0.5) = 0.49$. Then,

$$C = \begin{bmatrix} 0.5 & 0.4 & 0.51 \\ 0.6 & 0.5 & 0.7 \\ 0.49 & 0.3 & 0.5 \end{bmatrix}$$

Obviously, C is not an additive consistent fuzzy reciprocal preference relation. Again, we can see that it is more reasonable to take $\beta = n/2$ than $\beta = 1/2$.

2.1.3 An Algorithm for Decision-Making with Incomplete Fuzzy Reciprocal Preference Relation

Based on the above example, we develop a procedure for the decision-making with an incomplete fuzzy reciprocal preference relation in the following:

Algorithm 2.1

Let $w = (w_1, w_2, \ldots, w_n)^T$ be the weighting vector of the incomplete fuzzy reciprocal preference relation $C = (c_{ij})_{n \times n}$.

Step 1. Replace the unknown element c_{ij} in C with $\frac{n}{2}(w_i - w_j) + 0.5$, and construct the auxiliary relation $\overline{C} = (\overline{c}_{ij})_{n \times n}$, with $\overline{c}_{ij}$ satisfying Eq. (2.8).

Step 2. Utilize the normalizing rank aggregation method to obtain the weighting vector w. First, calculate the collective preference degree $p_i(w)$ of the alternative x_i over all the other alternatives:

$$p_i(w) = \sum_{j=1}^{n} \overline{c}_{ij}, i \in N \tag{2.9}$$

And establish the following linear system of equations:

$$w_i = \frac{p_i(w)}{\sum_{j=1}^{n} p_j(w)} = \frac{p_i(w)}{n^2/2}, i \in N \tag{2.10}$$

which can be further rewritten as the following form:

$$Aw = b \tag{2.11}$$

where b is a positive vector and A is a real symmetrical matrix, whose ith main diagonal element is $\frac{n^2}{2} - \frac{n}{2} m_i$; here, m_i is the count of the missing elements in the ith line in the matrix C.

Step 3. Solving Eq. (2.11), we can get the priority vector $w = (w_1, w_2, \ldots, w_n)^T$.
Step 4. Rank all the alternatives and select the best one(s) in accordance with the
   values of w_i ($i \in N$).
Step 5. End.

2.2 Normalizing Rank Method 2

2.2.1 An Approach to Constructing a Complete Fuzzy Reciprocal Preference Relation from an Incomplete Fuzzy Reciprocal Preference Relation When $\beta = (n - 1)/2$

Similarly, we give some results when $\beta = (n - 1)/2$.

Theorem 2.3 (Xu et al., 2011) *If the priority vector of the additive transitive perfectly consistent fuzzy reciprocal preference relation R except the diagonal elements is derived by normalizing rank aggregation method, then $\beta = \frac{n-1}{2}$.*

Proof If the priority vector of the additive transitive perfectly consistent fuzzy reciprocal preference relation R except the diagonal elements is derived by normalizing rank aggregation method, then

$$w_i = \frac{\sum_{k=1}^{n} r_{ik} - 0.5}{\sum_{i=1}^{n} \sum_{k=1, k \neq i}^{n} r_{ik}} = \frac{\sum_{k=1}^{n} r_{ik} - 0.5}{\frac{n(n-1)}{2}}, i \in N \tag{2.12}$$

$$w_j = \frac{\sum_{k=1}^{n} r_{jk} - 0.5}{\sum_{i=1}^{n} \sum_{k=1, k \neq j}^{n} r_{ik}} = \frac{\sum_{k=1}^{n} r_{jk} - 0.5}{\frac{n(n-1)}{2}}, i \in N \tag{2.13}$$

Put (2.12) and (2.13) into (1.33); then

$$r_{ij} = \beta(w_i - w_j) + 0.5$$

$$= \beta \frac{\sum_{k=1}^{n}(r_{ik} - r_{jk})}{\frac{n(n-1)}{2}} + 0.5$$

since $r_{ij} = r_{ik} - r_{jk} + 0.5$.
   Then

$$r_{ij} = \beta \frac{\sum_{k=1}^{n}(r_{ij} - 0.5)}{\frac{n(n-1)}{2}} + 0.5 = \beta \frac{nr_{ij} - \frac{n}{2}}{\frac{n(n-1)}{2}} + 0.5 \tag{2.14}$$

So, we can get $\beta = \frac{n-1}{2}$, which completes the proof. □

Theorem 2.4 *If $\beta = \frac{n-1}{2}$, then the priority vector of the additive transitive perfectly consistent fuzzy reciprocal preference relation R except the diagonal elements derived by Eq. (1.33) is normalizing rank aggregation method, that is,*

$$w_i = \frac{\sum_{j=1}^{n} r_{ij} - 0.5}{n(n-1)/2} = \frac{\sum_{j=1, j \neq i}^{n} r_{ij}}{\sum_{i=1}^{n} \sum_{j=1, j \neq i}^{n} r_{ij}} \tag{2.15}$$

Proof If $\beta = \frac{n-1}{2}$, by (1.33), we have

$$w_i = \frac{r_{ij} - 0.5}{\frac{n-1}{2}} + w_j \tag{2.16}$$

Summing on both sides of Eq. (2.16) with respect to j, then

$$\sum_{j=1}^{n} w_i = \frac{\sum_{j=1}^{n} (r_{ij} - 0.5)}{\frac{n-1}{2}} + \sum_{j=1}^{n} w_j \tag{2.17}$$

i.e.,

$$n w_i = \frac{\sum_{j=1}^{n} r_{ij} - 0.5n}{\frac{n-1}{2}} + 1$$

Therefore,

$$w_i = \frac{\sum_{j=1}^{n} r_{ij} - 0.5n}{n(n-1)/2} + \frac{1}{n} = \frac{\sum_{j=1}^{n} r_{ij} - 0.5}{n(n-1)/2} = \frac{\sum_{j=1, j \neq i}^{n} r_{ij}}{\sum_{i=1}^{n} \sum_{j=1, j \neq i}^{n} r_{ij}}$$

which completes the proof.   □

We also call the method normalizing rank aggregation method.

For a fuzzy reciprocal preference relation, which all the elements are known, from Theorem 2.3, we have proved that it is more reasonable to take $\beta = \frac{n-1}{2}$; therefore,

$$c_{ij} = \frac{n-1}{2}(w_i - w_j) + 0.5 \tag{2.18}$$

For an incomplete fuzzy reciprocal preference relation $C = (c_{ij})_{n \times n}$, we can replace the unknown element "$-$" with $\frac{n-1}{2}(w_i - w_j) + \frac{1}{2}$ and then construct an auxiliary fuzzy reciprocal preference relation $\overline{C} = (\overline{c}_{ij})_{n \times n}$ (we also call $\overline{C}$ the fitting relation of C), where

$$\bar{c}_{ij} = \begin{cases} c_{ij}, & c_{ij} \neq - \\ \dfrac{n-1}{2}(w_i - w_j) + \dfrac{1}{2}, & c_{ij} = - \end{cases} \tag{2.19}$$

2.2.2   An Illustrative Example

Example 2.2 For a decision-making problem, there are four decision alternatives x_i $(i = 1, 2, 3, 4)$. The DM provides his/her preference over these four decision alternatives and gives an incomplete fuzzy reciprocal preference relation as follows (the example has been examined by Xu and Chen (2008)):

$$C = \begin{bmatrix} 0.5 & - & 0.4 & 0.8 \\ - & 0.5 & 0.3 & 0.7 \\ 0.6 & 0.7 & 0.5 & - \\ 0.2 & 0.3 & - & 0.5 \end{bmatrix}$$

Let $w = (w_1, w_2, w_3, w_4)^T$ be the weight vector of C; then we construct an auxiliary fuzzy reciprocal preference relation $\bar{C} = (\bar{c}_{ij})_{4\times4}$ (where $n = 4$):

$$\bar{C} = \begin{bmatrix} 0.5 & 1.5(w_1 - w_2) + 0.5 & 0.4 & 0.8 \\ 1.5(w_2 - w_1) + 0.5 & 0.5 & 0.3 & 0.7 \\ 0.6 & 0.7 & 0.5 & 1.5(w_3 - w_4) + 0.5 \\ 0.2 & 0.3 & 1.5(w_4 - w_3) + 0.5 & 0.5 \end{bmatrix}$$

Then, we use the normalizing rank aggregation method to get the weighting vector as follows:

$$w_1 = \frac{\sum_{j=2}^{4} \bar{c}_{1j}}{\sum_{i=1}^{4} \sum_{j=2}^{4} \bar{c}_{1j}} = \frac{1.5(w_1 - w_2) + 0.5 + 0.4 + 0.8}{6},$$

$$w_2 = \frac{\sum_{j=1, j\neq 2}^{4} \bar{c}_{2j}}{\sum_{i=1}^{4} \sum_{j=1, j\neq 2}^{4} \bar{c}_{2j}} = \frac{1.5(w_2 - w_1) + 0.5 + 0.3 + 0.7}{6},$$

$$w_3 = \frac{\sum_{j=1, j\neq 3}^{4} \bar{c}_{3j}}{\sum_{i=1}^{4} \sum_{j=1, j\neq 3}^{4} \bar{c}_{3j}} = \frac{0.6 + 0.7 + 1.5(w_3 - w_4) + 0.5}{6},$$

$$w_4 = \frac{\sum_{j=1, j\neq 4}^{4} \bar{c}_{4j}}{\sum_{i=}^{4} \sum_{j=1, j\neq 4}^{4} \bar{c}_{4j}} = \frac{0.2 + 0.3 + 1.5(w_4 - w_3) + 0.5}{6}.$$

i.e.,

$$
\begin{bmatrix} 4.5 & 1.5 & 0 & 0 \\ 1.5 & 4.5 & 0 & 0 \\ 0 & 0 & 4.5 & 1.5 \\ 0 & 0 & 1.5 & 4.5 \end{bmatrix} \begin{bmatrix} w_1 \\ w_2 \\ w_3 \\ w_4 \end{bmatrix} = \begin{bmatrix} 1.7 \\ 1.5 \\ 1.8 \\ 1 \end{bmatrix}
$$

Solving the linear system of equations, we get $w_1 = 0.3$, $w_2 = 0.233$, $w_3 = 0.3667$, and $w_4 = 0.1$, and the priority vector is $w = (0.3, 0.233, 0.3667, 0.1)^T$. And we can also get the unknown elements as follows:

$$
\bar{c}_{12} = 1.5(w_1 - w_2) + 0.5 = 0.6, \bar{c}_{34} = 1.5(w_3 - w_4) + 0.5 = 0.9.
$$

And thus, we can get a complete reciprocal fitting relation $\bar{C}$:

$$
\bar{C} = \begin{bmatrix} 0.5 & 0.6 & 0.4 & 0.8 \\ 0.4 & 0.5 & 0.3 & 0.7 \\ 0.6 & 0.7 & 0.5 & 0.9 \\ 0.2 & 0.3 & 0.1 & 0.5 \end{bmatrix}
$$

Obviously, we can verify that $\bar{C}$ is an additive transitivity reciprocal preference relation according to Definition 1.3. If we take $\beta = 1/2$, which was computed by Xu and Chen (2008), we have

$$
w = (0.2863, 0.2467, 0.3137, 0.1533)^T, \bar{c}_{12} = \frac{1}{2}(w_1 - w_3 + 1) = 0.5198,
$$

$$
\bar{c}_{34} = 0.5(w_3 - w_1 + 1) = 0.5802.
$$

Then

$$
\bar{C} = \begin{bmatrix} 0.5 & 0.5198 & 0.4 & 0.8 \\ 0.4802 & 0.5 & 0.3 & 0.7 \\ 0.6 & 0.7 & 0.5 & 0.5802 \\ 0.2 & 0.3 & 0.4198 & 0.5 \end{bmatrix}
$$

Obviously, $\bar{C}$ is not an additive consistent reciprocal preference relation. Therefore, we can see that it is more reasonable to take $\beta = (n - 1)/2$ than $\beta = 1/2$.

2.2.3   An Algorithm for the Decision-Making with an Incomplete Fuzzy Reciprocal Preference Relation

Based on the above example, we develop a procedure for the decision-making with an incomplete fuzzy reciprocal preference relation in the following:

Algorithm 2.2

Let $w = (w_1, w_2, \ldots, w_n)^T$ be the weighting vector of the incomplete fuzzy reciprocal preference relation $C = (c_{ij})_{n \times n}$.

Step 1. Replace the unknown element c_{ij} in C with $\frac{n-1}{2}(w_i - w_j) + 0.5$, and construct the auxiliary relation $\overline{C} = (\overline{c}_{ij})_{n \times n}$, with $\overline{c}_{ij}$ satisfying Eq.(2.19).

Step 2. Utilize the normalizing rank aggregation method to obtain the weighting vector w. First, calculate the collective preference degree $p_i(w)$ of the alternative x_i over all the other alternatives:

$$p_i(w) = \sum_{j=1, j \neq i}^{n} \overline{c}_{ij}, i \in N \tag{2.20}$$

And establish the following linear system of equations:

$$w_i = \frac{p_i(w)}{\sum_{j=1}^{n} p_j(w)} = \frac{p_i(w)}{n(n-1)/2}, i \in N \tag{2.21}$$

which can be further rewritten as the following form:

$$Aw = b \tag{2.22}$$

where b is a positive vector and A is a real symmetrical matrix, whose ith main diagonal element is $\frac{n(n-1)}{2} - \frac{n-1}{2} m_i$; here, m_i is the count of the missing elements in the ith line in the matrix C.

Step 3. Solving Eq. (2.22), we can get the priority vector $w = (w_1, w_2, \ldots, w_n)^T$.

Step 4. Rank all the alternatives and select the best one(s) in accordance with the values of w_i ($i \in N$).

Step 5. End.

2.2.4   Performance Comparisons

To further compare the performances of $\beta = (n - 1)/2$ than $\beta = 1/2$ in fitting the fuzzy reciprocal preference relation, we introduce the following definition and criteria:

Definition 2.1 Let $w = (w_1, w_2, \ldots, w_n)^T$ be the weighting vector which is computed by the above Algorithm 2.1; then we call $C^* = (c_{ij}^*)_{n \times n} = (\frac{n-1}{2}(w_i - w_j) + 0.5)_{n \times n}$ the characteristic matrix of $\overline{C}$.

Theorem 2.5 $\overline{C} = (\overline{c}_{ij})_{n \times n}$ *is a complete additively consistent fuzzy reciprocal preference relation if and only if* $\overline{C} = C^*$.

Proof Necessary condition: If $\overline{C} = (\overline{c}_{ij})_{n \times n}$ is an additive consistency reciprocal preference relation, then, for all i, j, k, $\overline{c}_{ij} = \overline{c}_{ik} - \overline{c}_{jk} + 0.5$, and based on Eq. (2.15), we have

$$c_{ij}^* = \frac{n-1}{2}(w_i - w_j) + 0.5$$

$$= \frac{n-1}{2}\left(\frac{\sum_{k=1}^{n}\overline{c}_{ik} - 0.5}{n(n-1)/2} - \frac{\sum_{k=1}^{n}\overline{c}_{jk} - 0.5}{n(n-1)/2}\right) + 0.5$$

$$= \frac{n-1}{2}\left(\frac{\sum_{k=1}^{n}(\overline{c}_{ik} - \overline{c}_{jk})}{n(n-1)/2}\right) + 0.5$$

$$= \frac{\sum_{k=1}^{n}(\overline{c}_{ij} - 0.5)}{n} + 0.5$$

$$= \overline{c}_{ij}$$

Thus, $\overline{C} = C^*$.

Sufficient condition: If $\overline{C} = C^*$, then for all $i, j, k \in N$, we have

$$\overline{c}_{ik} - \overline{c}_{jk} = c_{ik}^* - c_{jk}^*$$

$$= \frac{n-1}{2}(w_i - w_k) + 0.5 - \left(\frac{n-1}{2}(w_j - w_k) + 0.5\right)$$

$$= \frac{n-1}{2}(w_i - w_j)$$

$$= c_{ij}^* - 0.5$$

$$= \overline{c}_{ij} - 0.5$$

i.e., $\overline{c}_{ik} - \overline{c}_{jk} = \overline{c}_{ij} - 0.5$; thus, $\overline{C}$ is an additive consistency reciprocal preference relation, which completes the proof. □

Further, from the above proof process of Theorem 2.5, we can prove that if $\beta = 1/2$ (i.e., $c_{ij}^* = 0.5(w_i - w_j + 1)$), the above Theorem 2.5 will not hold. This means that if $\overline{C} = (\overline{c}_{ij})_{n \times n}$ is an additive consistency reciprocal preference relation and the weighting vector is computed by Algorithm 2.1 or Algorithm 2.2 in which the unknown element $\overline{c}_{ij}$ in $\overline{C}$ is instead by $0.5(w_i - w_j + 1)$, and then the characteristic matrix C^* is computed by $c_{ij}^* = 0.5(w_i - w_j + 1)$, it will be $\overline{C} \neq C^*$. Thus, it is more reasonable to take $\beta = (n-1)/2$ than $\beta = 1/2$.

Definition 2.2 Let $D = (d_{ij})_{n \times n}$ be the difference matrix between $\overline{C}$ and C^*, where $d_{ij} = \overline{c}_{ij} - c_{ij}^*$.

Obviously, $d_{ij} = -d_{ji}$.

From Theorem 2.5, we know that $\overline{C}$ is an additive consistency fuzzy reciprocal preference relation if and only if $D = 0$. Thus, the smaller the value of D, the better. That is,

$$TD = \sum_{i=1}^{n} \sum_{j=1}^{n} |d_{ij}| = \sum_{i=1}^{n} \sum_{j=1}^{n} |\overline{c}_{ij} - c_{ij}^*| \tag{2.23}$$

where $d_{ij} = \overline{c}_{ij} - c_{ij}^*$ is the fitting error for the element $\overline{c}_{ij}$ of the collective auxiliary fuzzy reciprocal preference relation $\overline{C} = (\overline{c}_{ij})_{n \times n}$. It is easy to find that $|d_{ij}| \equiv |d_{ji}|$. Obviously, the smaller the TD, the better the fitting performance of the weighting vector w.

Again, for Example 2.2, as we compute in the above, if we take $\beta = (n-1)/2$, we get

$$w = (0.3, 0.233, 0.3667, 0.1)^T$$

And thus, the characteristic matrix C^* is computed by $c_{ij}^* = 1.5(w_i - w_j + 1)$, and we get

$$C^* = \begin{bmatrix} 0.5 & 0.6 & 0.4 & 0.8 \\ 0.4 & 0.5 & 0.3 & 0.7 \\ 0.6 & 0.7 & 0.5 & 0.9 \\ 0.2 & 0.3 & 0.1 & 0.5 \end{bmatrix}$$

Therefore, $TD = \sum_{i=1}^{n} \sum_{j=1}^{n} |d_{ij}| = \sum_{i=1}^{n} \sum_{j=1}^{n} |\overline{c}_{ij} - c_{ij}^*| = 0$.

If we take $\beta = 1/2$, we have $w = (0.2863, 0.2467, 0.3137, 0.1533)^T$ and

$$\overline{C} = \begin{bmatrix} 0.5 & 0.5198 & 0.4 & 0.8 \\ 0.4802 & 0.5 & 0.3 & 0.7 \\ 0.6 & 0.7 & 0.5 & 0.5802 \\ 0.2 & 0.3 & 0.4198 & 0.5 \end{bmatrix}$$

And thus, the characteristic matrix C^* is computed by $c_{ij}^* = 0.5(w_i - w_j + 1)$, and we get

$$C^* = \begin{bmatrix} 0.5 & 0.5198 & 0.4863 & 0.5665 \\ 0.4802 & 0.5 & 0.4665 & 0.5467 \\ 0.5137 & 0.5335 & 0.5 & 0.5802 \\ 0.4335 & 0.4533 & 0.4198 & 0.5 \end{bmatrix}$$

Therefore,

$$D = \begin{bmatrix} 0 & 0 & -0.0863 & 0.2335 \\ 0 & 0 & -0.1665 & 0.1533 \\ 0.0863 & 0.1655 & 0 & 0 \\ -0.2335 & -0.1533 & 0 & 0 \end{bmatrix}$$

and

$$\text{TD} = \sum_{i=1}^{n}\sum_{j=1}^{n}|d_{ij}| = \sum_{i=1}^{n}\sum_{j=1}^{n}|\bar{c}_{ij} - c_{ij}^*| = 1.2792.$$

As is known, smaller deviation means better performance. Obviously, from the above results, we know that it is more reasonable to take $\beta = (n-1)/2$ than $\beta = 1/2$.

Example 2.3 If the DM provides no preferences over these four decision alternatives, then the incomplete fuzzy reciprocal preference relation C is reduced to the following (this example was examined by Xu and Chen (2008)):

$$C = \begin{bmatrix} 0.5 & - & - & - \\ - & 0.5 & - & - \\ - & - & 0.5 & - \\ - & - & - & 0.5 \end{bmatrix}$$

In this case, if we take $\beta = 1.5$, then we can construct the following auxiliary fuzzy reciprocal preference relation $\bar{C} = (\bar{c}_{ij})_{4\times4}$:

$$\bar{C} = \begin{bmatrix} 0.5 & 1.5(w_1-w_2)+0.5 & 1.5(w_1-w_3)+0.5 & 1.5(w_1-w_4)+0.5 \\ 1.5(w_2-w_1)+0.5 & 0.5 & 1.5(w_2-w_3)+0.5 & 1.5(w_2-w_4)+0.5 \\ 1.5(w_3-w_1)+0.5 & 1.5(w_3-w_2)+0.5 & 0.5 & 1.5(w_3-w_4)+0.5 \\ 1.5(w_4-w_1)+0.5 & 1.5(w_4-w_2)+0.5 & 1.5(w_4-w_3)+0.5 & 0.5 \end{bmatrix}$$

Then, we use the normalizing rank aggregation method to get the weighting vector as follows:

$$w_i = \frac{\sum\limits_{j \neq i} \left(1.5 \left(w_i - w_j\right) + 0.5\right)}{6}$$

i.e.,

$$\begin{bmatrix} 1.5 & 1.5 & 1.5 & 1.5 \\ 1.5 & 1.5 & 1.5 & 1.5 \\ 1.5 & 1.5 & 1.5 & 1.5 \\ 1.5 & 1.5 & 1.5 & 1.5 \end{bmatrix} \begin{bmatrix} w_1 \\ w_2 \\ w_3 \\ w_4 \end{bmatrix} = \begin{bmatrix} 1.5 \\ 1.5 \\ 1.5 \\ 1.5 \end{bmatrix} \qquad (2.24)$$

Obviously, there are infinite solutions for the above equation, i.e., for any $w_i \in [0, 1]$, and $\sum_{i=1}^{4} w_i = 1$, Eq. (2.24) always holds. But if we take $\beta = 0.5$, we will get $w = (0.25, 0.25, 0.25, 0.25)^T$. Xu and Chen (2008) interpreted that, in the situations where no preference information is provided, each alternative should be assigned with the same weight. And with the weighting vector, the auxiliary fuzzy reciprocal preference relation $\overline{C} = (\overline{c}_{ij})_{4 \times 4}$ should be

$$\overline{C} = \begin{bmatrix} 0.5 & 0.5 & 0.5 & 0.5 \\ 0.5 & 0.5 & 0.5 & 0.5 \\ 0.5 & 0.5 & 0.5 & 0.5 \\ 0.5 & 0.5 & 0.5 & 0.5 \end{bmatrix}$$

That is, we can only construct the unique fuzzy reciprocal preference relation. But in our view, C is a complete unknown fuzzy reciprocal preference relation; in this circumstance, we can construct numerous auxiliary fuzzy reciprocal preference relation and only need to satisfy the conditions $w_i \in [0, 1]$ and $\sum_{i=1}^{4} w_i = 1$. Again, this also denotes that it is more reasonable to take $\beta = (n - 1)/2$ than $\beta = 0.5$. In the following, we will further investigate the problem in the group decision-making.

2.3 Normalizing Rank Aggregation Method for Group Decision-Making with Incomplete Fuzzy Reciprocal Preference Relations

2.3.1 An Algorithm for Group Decision-Making with Incomplete Fuzzy Reciprocal Preference Relations

Now, we consider a group decision-making problem. Let $E = \{e_1, e_2, \ldots, e_m\}$ be a set of DMs, and let $\lambda = (\lambda_1, \lambda_2, \ldots, \lambda_m)^T$ be the weighting vector of DMs, with $\sum_{k=1}^{m} \lambda_k = 1, \lambda_k \geq 0$, and $k \in M$. Suppose that these m DMs provide their preferences over a set of n decision alternatives $X = \{x_1, x_2, \ldots, x_n\}$ and give m incomplete fuzzy reciprocal preference relations $C_k = (c_{ij}^{(k)})_{n \times n}$ $(k \in M)$.

Similar to the procedure in Sect. 2.2.1 which is for the decision-making with an incomplete fuzzy reciprocal preference relation, in the following, we develop a procedure for group decision-making with incomplete fuzzy reciprocal preference relations.

Algorithm 2.3

Let $v = (v_1, v_2, \ldots, v_n)^T$ be the collective weighting vector of the incomplete fuzzy reciprocal preference relations $C_k = (c_{ij}^{(k)})_{n \times n}$ $(k \in M)$.

Step 1. Replace the unknown element $c_{ij}^{(k)}$ in $C^{(k)}$ with $\frac{n-1}{2}(v_i - v_j) + 0.5$, and construct the auxiliary relation $\overline{C}_k = (\overline{c}_{ij}^{(k)})_{n \times n}$, where

$$\overline{c}_{ij}^{(k)} = \begin{cases} c_{ij}^{(k)}, & c_{ij}^{(k)} \neq - \\ \dfrac{n-1}{2}(v_i - v_j) + \dfrac{1}{2}, & c_{ij}^{(k)} = - \end{cases} \qquad (2.25)$$

Step 2. Utilize the additive weighted averaging (AWA) operator

$$\overline{c}_{ij} = \text{AWA}_h\left(\overline{c}_{ij}^{(1)}, \overline{c}_{ij}^{(2)}, \ldots, \overline{c}_{ij}^{(m)}\right) = \sum_{k=1}^{m} \lambda_k \overline{c}_{ij}^{(k)}, i, j \in N \qquad (2.26)$$

To aggregate all the auxiliary fuzzy reciprocal preference relations $\overline{C}_k = (\overline{c}_{ij}^{(k)})_{n \times n}$ into a collective auxiliary fuzzy reciprocal preference relation $\overline{C} = (\overline{c}_{ij})_{n \times n}$.

Step 3. Utilize the normalizing rank aggregation method to obtain the weighting vector v. First, calculate the collective preference degree $p_i(v)$ of the alternative x_i over all the other alternatives:

$$p_i(v) = \sum_{j=1, j \neq i}^{n} \overline{c}_{ij}, i \in N \qquad (2.27)$$

And establish the following linear system of equations:

$$v_i = \frac{p_i(v)}{\sum\limits_{j=1}^{n} p_j(v)} = \frac{p_i(v)}{n(n-1)/2}, i \in N \qquad (2.28)$$

which can be further rewritten as the following form:

$$Av = b \tag{2.29}$$

where b is a positive vector and A is a real symmetrical matrix.

Step 4. Solving Eq. (2.29), we can get the priority vector $v = (v_1, v_2, \ldots, v_n)^T$.
Step 5. Rank all the alternatives and select the best one(s) in accordance with the values of v_i ($i \in N$).
Step 6. End.

2.3.2 Performance Comparisons

The above algorithm is similar to Xu and Chen (2008)'s method; the difference of the algorithm between Xu and Chen (2008) and this paper is that in Step 1. In this note, we replace the unknown element $c_{ij}^{(k)}$ in C_k with $\frac{n-1}{2}(v_i - v_j) + 0.5$, while Xu and Chen (2008) utilized $0.5(v_i - v_j + 1)$ to replace the unknown element $c_{ij}^{(k)}$ in C_k and then both to construct the auxiliary fuzzy reciprocal preference relations.

Based on the idea in Sect. 2.3, we introduce the following definition and criteria:

Definition 2.3 Let $v = (v_1, v_2, \ldots, v_n)^T$ be the weighting vector which is computed by the above Algorithm 2.2; then we call $C^* = (c_{ij}^*)_{n \times n} = (\frac{n-1}{2}(v_i - v_j) + 0.5)_{n \times n}$ the collective characteristic matrix of $\overline{C}$.

To further compare the performances of Algorithm 2.2 of this paper with Xu and Chen (2008)'s algorithm for group decision-making with incomplete fuzzy reciprocal preference relations, we introduce the following performance evaluation criteria:

Total deviation of group (TDG) between each auxiliary fuzzy reciprocal preference relation and the collective characteristic matrix:

$$\text{TDG} = \sum_{k=1}^{m} \sum_{i=1}^{n} \sum_{j=1}^{n} \left| d_{ij}^{(k)} \right| = \sum_{k=1}^{m} \sum_{i=1}^{n} \sum_{j=1}^{n} \left| \overline{c}_{ij}^{(k)} - c_{ij}^* \right| \tag{2.30}$$

where $d_{ij}^{(k)} = \overline{c}_{ij}^{(k)} - c_{ij}^*$ is the fitting error for $c_{ij}^{(k)}$ of the fuzzy reciprocal preference relation $\overline{C}_k = (\overline{c}_{ij}^{(k)})_{n \times n}$. It is easy to find that $|d_{ij}^{(k)}| \equiv |d_{ji}^{(k)}|$. Obviously, the smaller the TD and TDG, the better the fitting performance of the weighting vector v.

2.3.3 Illustrative Examples

Example 2.4 Consider a group decision-making problem; there are three DMs e_k $(k = 1, 2, 3)$, and let $\lambda = (0.5, 0.3, 0.2)^T$ be the weighting vector of DMs. The DMs provide three incomplete fuzzy reciprocal preference relations as follows:

$$C_1 = \begin{bmatrix} 0.5 & 0.6 & 0.7 & 0.3 & 0.6 \\ 0.4 & 0.5 & - & - & - \\ 0.3 & - & 0.5 & - & - \\ 0.7 & - & - & 0.5 & - \\ 0.4 & - & - & - & 0.5 \end{bmatrix}, C_2 = \begin{bmatrix} 0.5 & - & - & - & - \\ - & 0.5 & 0.6 & 0.2 & 0.5 \\ - & 0.4 & 0.5 & - & - \\ - & 0.8 & - & 0.5 & - \\ - & 0.5 & - & - & 0.5 \end{bmatrix},$$

$$C_3 = \begin{bmatrix} 0.5 & - & - & - & 0.6 \\ - & 0.5 & - & - & 0.5 \\ - & - & 0.5 & - & 0.4 \\ - & - & - & 0.5 & 0.8 \\ 0.4 & 0.5 & 0.6 & 0.2 & 0.5 \end{bmatrix}$$

Let $v = (v_1, v_2, \ldots, v_5)^T$ be the collective weight vector of the incomplete fuzzy reciprocal preference relations $C_k = (c_{ij}^{(k)})_{5 \times 5}$ $(k = 1, 2, 3)$ (where $\beta = (n - 1)/2 = 2$).

Step 1. Replace each unknown element $c_{ij}^{(k)}$ in C_k with $2(v_i - v_j) + 0.5$, and construct the auxiliary fuzzy reciprocal preference relations:

$$\overline{C}_1 = \begin{bmatrix} 0.5 & 0.6 & 0.7 & 0.3 & 0.6 \\ 0.4 & 0.5 & 2(v_2 - v_3) + 0.5 & 2(v_2 - v_4) + 0.5 & 2(v_2 - v_5) + 0.5 \\ 0.3 & 2(v_3 - v_2) + 0.5 & 0.5 & 2(v_3 - v_4) + 0.5 & 2(v_3 - v_5) + 0.5 \\ 0.7 & 2(v_4 - v_2) + 0.5 & 2(v_4 - v_3) + 0.5 & 0.5 & 2(v_4 - v_5) + 0.5 \\ 0.4 & 2(v_5 - v_2) + 0.5 & 2(v_5 - v_3) + 0.5 & 2(v_5 - v_4) + 0.5 & 0.5 \end{bmatrix}$$

$$\overline{C}_2 = \begin{bmatrix} 0.5 & 2(v_1 - v_2) + 0.5 & 2(v_1 - v_3) + 0.5 & 2(v_1 - v_4) + 0.5 & 2(v_1 - v_5) + 0.5 \\ 2(v_2 - v_1) + 0.5 & 0.5 & 0.6 & 0.2 & 0.5 \\ 2(v_3 - v_1) + 0.5 & 0.4 & 0.5 & 2(v_3 - v_4) + 0.5 & 2(v_3 - v_5) + 0.5 \\ 2(v_4 - v_1) + 0.5 & 0.8 & 2(v_4 - v_3) + 0.5 & 0.5 & 2(v_4 - v_5) + 0.5 \\ 2(v_5 - v_1) + 0.5 & 0.5 & 2(v_5 - v_3) + 0.5 & 2(v_5 - v_4) + 0.5 & 0.5 \end{bmatrix}$$

$$\overline{C}_3 = \begin{bmatrix} 0.5 & 2(v_1-v_2)+0.5 & 2(v_1-v_3)+0.5 & 2(v_1-v_4)+0.5 & 0.6 \\ 2(v_2-v_1)+0.5 & 0.5 & 2(v_2-v_3)+0.5 & 2(v_2-v_4)+0.5 & 0.5 \\ 2(v_3-v_1)+0.5 & 2(v_3-v_2)+0.5 & 0.5 & 2(v_3-v_4)+0.5 & 0.4 \\ 2(v_4-v_1)+0.5 & 2(v_4-v_2)+0.5 & 2(v_4-v_3)+0.5 & 0.5 & 0.8 \\ 0.4 & 0.5 & 0.6 & 0.2 & 0.5 \end{bmatrix}$$

Step 2. Utilize Eq. (2.26) to aggregate all the auxiliary fuzzy reciprocal preference relations $\overline{C}_k = (\overline{c}_{ij}^{(k)})_{5\times5}$ ($k = 1, 2, 3$) into the collective auxiliary fuzzy reciprocal preference relation:

$$\overline{C} = \begin{bmatrix} 0.5 & v_1-v_2+0.55 & v_1-v_3+0.6 \\ v_2-v_1+0.45 & 0.5 & 1.4(v_2-v_3)+0.53 \\ v_3-v_1+0.4 & 1.4(v_3-v_2)+0.47 & 0.5 \\ v_4-v_1+0.6 & 1.4(v_4-v_2)+0.59 & 2(v_4-v_3)+0.5 \\ 0.6(v_5-v_1)+0.43 & v_5-v_2+0.5 & 1.6(v_5-v_3)+0.52 \end{bmatrix}$$

$$\begin{bmatrix} v_1-v_4+0.4 & 0.6(v_1-v_5)+0.57 \\ 1.4(v_2-v_4)+0.41 & v_2-v_5+0.5 \\ 2(v_3-v_4)+0.5 & 1.6(v_3-v_5)+0.48 \\ 0.5 & 1.6(v_4-v_5)+0.56 \\ 1.6(v_5-v_4)+0.44 & 0.5 \end{bmatrix}$$

Step 3. Utilize the normalizing rank aggregation method to obtain the weighting vector v. We can establish the following linear system of equations:

$$\begin{cases} v_1 = \dfrac{v_1-v_2+0.55+v_1-v_3+0.6+v_1-v_4+0.4+0.6(v_1-v_5)+0.57}{10} \\[2mm] v_2 = \dfrac{v_2-v_1+0.45+1.4(v_2-v_3)+0.53+1.4(v_2-v_4)+0.41+v_2-v_5+0.5}{10} \\[2mm] v_3 = \dfrac{v_3-v_1+0.4+1.4(v_3-v_2)+0.47+2(v_3-v_4)+0.5+1.6(v_3-v_5)+0.48}{10} \\[2mm] v_4 = \dfrac{v_4-v_1+0.6+1.4(v_4-v_2)+0.59+2(v_4-v_3)+0.5+1.6(v_4-v_5)+0.56}{10} \\[2mm] v_5 = \dfrac{0.6(v_5-v_1)+0.43+v_5-v_2+0.5+1.6(v_5-v_3)+0.52+1.6(v_5-v_4)+0.44}{10} \end{cases}$$

i.e.,

$$\begin{bmatrix} 6.4 & 1 & 1 & 1 & 0.6 \\ 1 & 5.2 & 1.4 & 1.4 & 1 \\ 1 & 1.4 & 4 & 2 & 1.6 \\ 1 & 1.4 & 2 & 4 & 1.6 \\ 0.6 & 1 & 1.6 & 1.6 & 5.2 \end{bmatrix} \begin{bmatrix} v_1 \\ v_2 \\ v_3 \\ v_4 \\ v_5 \end{bmatrix} = \begin{bmatrix} 2.12 \\ 1.89 \\ 1.85 \\ 2.25 \\ 1.89 \end{bmatrix}$$

Step 4. Solve the above system of equations, and thus we have

$$v = (0.22, 0.17, 0.12, 0.32, 0.17)^T$$

Step 5. Rank all the alternatives x_i ($i = 1, 2, 3, 4, 5$) in accordance with the values of v_i ($i = 1, 2, 3, 4, 5$).

$$x_4 \succ x_1 \succ x_2 \sim x_5 \succ x_3$$

Thus, the best alternative is x_4.

Furthermore, we can get $\overline{C}^{(k)}$ ($k = 1, 2, 3$), collective auxiliary fuzzy reciprocal preference relation $\overline{C}$, and characteristic matrix C^* that are all the same, i.e.,

$$\overline{C}_1 = \overline{C}_2 = \overline{C}_3 = \overline{C} = C^* = \begin{bmatrix} 0.5 & 0.6 & 0.7 & 0.3 & 0.6 \\ 0.4 & 0.5 & 0.6 & 0.2 & 0.5 \\ 0.3 & 0.4 & 0.5 & 0.1 & 0.4 \\ 0.7 & 0.8 & 0.9 & 0.5 & 0.8 \\ 0.4 & 0.5 & 0.6 & 0.2 & 0.5 \end{bmatrix}$$

And TD and TDG are computed by Eqs. (2.23) and (2.30), respectively, and we have

$$TD = 0, TDG = 0.$$

The above results show that all the matrices ($\overline{C}_k$ ($k = 1, 2, 3$), $\overline{C}$ and C^*) are the same, and also, we can verify that they are all the additively consistent fuzzy reciprocal preference relations according to Definition 1.3.

If we take Xu and Chen (2008)'s method (i.e., $\beta = 0.5$) to get the weighting vector, we have the following steps:

Step 1. Replace each unknown element $\bar{c}_{ij}^{(k)}$ in C_k with $0.5(v_i - v_j + 1)$, and construct the auxiliary fuzzy reciprocal preference relations:

$$\bar{C}_1 = \begin{bmatrix} 0.5 & 0.6 & 0.7 & 0.3 & 0.6 \\ 0.4 & 0.5 & 0.5(v_2 - v_3 + 1) & 0.5(v_2 - v_4 + 1) & 0.5(v_2 - v_5 + 1) \\ 0.3 & 0.5(v_3 - v_2 + 1) & 0.5 & 0.5(v_3 - v_4 + 1) & 0.5(v_3 - v_5 + 1) \\ 0.7 & 0.5(v_4 - v_2 + 1) & 0.5(v_4 - v_3 + 1) & 0.5 & 0.5(v_4 - v_5 + 1) \\ 0.4 & 0.5(v_5 - v_2 + 1) & 0.5(v_5 - v_3 + 1) & 0.5(v_5 - v_4 + 1) & 0.5 \end{bmatrix}$$

$$\bar{C}_2 = \begin{bmatrix} 0.5 & 0.5(v_1 - v_2 + 1) & 0.5(v_1 - v_3 + 1) & 0.5(v_1 - v_4 + 1) & 0.5(v_1 - v_5 + 1) \\ 0.5(v_2 - v_1 + 1) & 0.5 & 0.6 & 0.2 & 0.5 \\ 0.5(v_3 - v_1 + 1) & 0.4 & 0.5 & 0.5(v_3 - v_4 + 1) & 0.5(v_3 - v_5 + 1) \\ 0.5(v_4 - v_1 + 1) & 0.8 & 0.5(v_4 - v_3 + 1) & 0.5 & 0.5(v_4 - v_5 + 1) \\ 0.5(v_5 - v_1 + 1) & 0.5 & 0.5(v_5 - v_3 + 1) & 0.5(v_5 - v_4 + 1) & 0.5 \end{bmatrix}$$

$$\bar{C}_3 = \begin{bmatrix} 0.5 & 0.5(v_1 - v_2 + 1) & 0.5(v_1 - v_3 + 1) & 0.5(v_1 - v_4 + 1) & 0.6 \\ 0.5(v_2 - v_1 + 1) & 0.5 & 0.5(v_2 - v_3 + 1) & 0.5(v_2 - v_4 + 1) & 0.5 \\ 0.5(v_3 - v_1 + 1) & 0.5(v_3 - v_2 + 1) & 0.5 & 0.5(v_3 - v_4 + 1) & 0.4 \\ 0.5(v_4 - v_1 + 1) & 0.5(v_4 - v_2 + 1) & 0.5(v_4 - v_3 + 1) & 0.5 & 0.8 \\ 0.4 & 0.5 & 0.6 & 0.2 & 0.5 \end{bmatrix}$$

Step 2. Utilize Eq. (2.26) to aggregate all the auxiliary fuzzy reciprocal preference relations $\bar{C}_k = (\bar{c}_{ij}^{(k)})_{5 \times 5}$ ($k = 1, 2, 3$) into the collective auxiliary fuzzy reciprocal preference relation:

$$\bar{C} = \begin{bmatrix} 0.5 & 0.25(v_1 - v_2) + 0.55 & 0.25(v_1 - v_3) + 0.6 \\ 0.25(v_2 - v_1) + 0.45 & 0.5 & 0.35(v_2 - v_3) + 0.53 \\ 0.25(v_3 - v_1) + 0.4 & 0.35(v_3 - v_2) + 0.47 & 0.5 \\ 0.25(v_4 - v_1) + 0.6 & 0.35(v_4 - v_2) + 0.59 & 0.5(v_4 - v_3) + 0.5 \\ 0.15(v_5 - v_1) + 0.43 & 0.25(v_5 - v_2) + 0.5 & 0.4(v_5 - v_3) + 0.52 \end{bmatrix}$$
$$\begin{matrix} 0.25(v_1 - v_4) + 0.4 & 0.15(v_1 - v_5) + 0.57 \\ 0.35(v_2 - v_4) + 0.41 & 0.25(v_2 - v_5) + 0.5 \\ 0.5(v_3 - v_4) + 0.5 & 0.4(v_3 - v_5) + 0.48 \\ 0.5 & 0.4(v_4 - v_5) + 0.56 \\ 0.4(v_5 - v_4) + 0.44 & 0.5 \end{matrix}$$

Step 3. Utilize the normalizing rank aggregation method to obtain the weighting vector v. We can establish the following linear system of equations:

$$
\begin{cases}
v_1 = \dfrac{0.25(v_1-v_2)+0.55+0.25(v_1-v_3)+0.6+0.25(v_1-v_4)+0.4+0.15(v_1-v_5)+0.57}{10} \\[2mm]
v_2 = \dfrac{0.25(v_2-v_1)+0.45+0.35(v_2-v_3)+0.53+0.35(v_2-v_4)+0.41+0.25(v_2-v_5)+0.5}{10} \\[2mm]
v_3 = \dfrac{0.25(v_3-v_1)+0.4+0.35(v_3-v_2)+0.47+0.5(v_3-v_4)+0.5+0.4(v_3-v_5)+0.48}{10} \\[2mm]
v_4 = \dfrac{0.25(v_4-v_1)+0.6+0.35(v_4-v_2)+0.59+0.5(v_4-v_3)+0.5+0.4(v_4-v_5)+0.56}{10} \\[2mm]
v_5 = \dfrac{0.15(v_5-v_1)+0.43+0.25(v_5-v_2)+0.5+0.4(v_5-v_3)+0.52+0.4(v_5-v_4)+0.44}{10}
\end{cases}
$$

i.e.,

$$
\begin{bmatrix}
9.1 & 0.25 & 0.25 & 0.25 & 0.15 \\
0.25 & 8.8 & 0.35 & 0.35 & 0.25 \\
0.25 & 0.35 & 8.5 & 0.5 & 0.4 \\
0.25 & 0.35 & 0.5 & 8.5 & 0.4 \\
0.15 & 0.25 & 0.4 & 0.4 & 8.8
\end{bmatrix}
\begin{bmatrix} v_1 \\ v_2 \\ v_3 \\ v_4 \\ v_5 \end{bmatrix}
=
\begin{bmatrix} 2.12 \\ 1.89 \\ 1.85 \\ 2.25 \\ 1.89 \end{bmatrix}
$$

Step 4. Solve the above system of equations, and thus we have

$$
v = (0.2134, 0.187, 0.1813, 0.2312, 0.1871)^T
$$

Step 5. Rank all the alternatives x_i ($i = 1, 2, 3, 4, 5$) in accordance with the values of v_i ($i = 1, 2, 3, 4, 5$):

$$
x_4 \succ x_1 \succ x_5 \succ x_2 \succ x_3
$$

Thus, the best alternative is x_4.

Furthermore, by the weighting vector v, we can get $\overline{C}_k$ ($k = 1, 2, 3$), collective auxiliary fuzzy reciprocal preference relation $\overline{C}$, and characteristic matrix C^* (in this case, $c_{ij}^* = 0.5(v_i - v_j) + 0.5$) easily, and we can verify that they are not the same. At the same time, we can further get TD and TDG by Eqs. (2.23) and (2.30), respectively. Table 2.1 shows the performances of the two methods.

From the above results, we see that the ranking order is somewhat different between Xu and Chen (2008)'s method and ours. In our method, the weights of x_2 and x_5 are the same, which means that x_2 and x_5 are of same importance. But in Xu and Chen (2008)'s method, x_5 is preferred to x_2. From the original incomplete fuzzy reciprocal preference relations $R^{(2)}$ and $R^{(3)}$, we see that the two DMs think that x_2

Table 2.1 Performance evaluation for Example 2.4

Criteria	$\beta = 2$	$\beta = 0.5$
TD	0	0.9583
TDG	0	2.7721

and x_5 are of same importance. As is known, smaller deviation means better performances. Obviously, our method has better performance in the two criteria. This shows the advantages of our method. Evidently, Xu and Chen (2008)'s method suffers from rank reversal phenomenon, and their method will distort the DM's information in some time.

Example 2.5 Let us suppose that a company wants to renew its cars. There exist five models of car available, $X = \{x_1, x_2, \ldots, x_5\}$, and three DMs e_k ($k = 1, 2, 3$), and let $\lambda = (0.5, 0.3, 0.2)^T$ be the weighting vector of DMs. The DMs provide three incomplete fuzzy reciprocal preference relations as follows (the example has been examined by Xu and Chen (2008)):

$$C_1 = \begin{bmatrix} 0.5 & 0.6 & 0.7 & 0.3 & 0.6 \\ 0.4 & 0.5 & - & 0.8 & 0.6 \\ 0.3 & - & 0.5 & 0.3 & 0.5 \\ 0.7 & 0.2 & 0.7 & 0.5 & 0.8 \\ 0.4 & 0.4 & 0.5 & 0.2 & 0.5 \end{bmatrix}, C_2 = \begin{bmatrix} 0.5 & 0.7 & 0.4 & - & 0.6 \\ 0.3 & 0.5 & 0.3 & 0.6 & 0.5 \\ 0.6 & 0.7 & 0.5 & 0.4 & - \\ - & 0.4 & 0.6 & 0.5 & 0.6 \\ 0.4 & 0.5 & - & 0.4 & 0.5 \end{bmatrix},$$

$$C_3 = \begin{bmatrix} 0.5 & - & 0.8 & 0.4 & 0.5 \\ - & 0.5 & - & - & - \\ 0.2 & - & 0.5 & 0.3 & 0.6 \\ 0.6 & - & 0.7 & 0.5 & 0.7 \\ 0.5 & - & 0.4 & 0.3 & 0.5 \end{bmatrix}$$

Xu and Chen (2008) got the priority vector as $v = (0.2193, 0.2095, 0.1766, 0.2327,$ $0.1618)^T$. But after our careful computation, the result of Xu and Chen (2008)'s linear systems (see Xu and Chen (2008), Eq. (17)) is $v = (0.2199, 0.2071, 0.1772,$ $0.2335, 0.1623)^T$. By using our method, we get $v = (0.2193, 0.2124, 0.1733, 0.2348,$ $0.1601)^T$. Both the priority vectors lead to the ranking of $x_4 \succ x_1 \succ x_2 \succ x_3 \succ x_5$. The fitting performances of the two methods are assessed in terms of the criteria defined by Eqs. (2.23) and (2.30). The results are shown in Table 2.2, from which it is clear that our method still has smaller deviation, that is, our method still performs better than Xu and Chen (2008)'s method.

In Eq. (2.25) of Algorithm 2.3, and in Definition 2.3, we set $\beta = (n - 1)/2$. Obviously, we can also set $\beta = n/2$; if so, for Example 2.5, we will obtain the corresponding values of TD and TDG, which are listed in the last column of

Table 2.2 Performance evaluation for Example 2.5

Criteria	$\beta = 2$	$\beta = 0.5$	$\beta = 2.5$
TD	1.4515	2.0163	1.4511
TDG	5.1564	6.1471	5.156

Table 2.2. It shows that the values of TD and TDG are almost same; it further shows that it is more reasonable to set $\beta = n/2$ or $\beta = (n-1)/2$ than $\beta = 0.5$.

2.4   Goal Programming Method

In Sects. 2.1 and 2.2, it is shown that $\beta = n/2$ or $\beta = (n-1)/2$ is more reasonable than $\beta = 0.5$, and we call them normalizing rank aggregation method. In the following, we derive the priority weights from other points of view.

Generally, Eq. (2.7) does not hold, and we introduce the deviation function (Xu & Da, 2009):

$$f_{ij} = \left| c_{ij} - \frac{n}{2}(w_i - w_j) - 0.5 \right| \tag{2.31}$$

As C is an incomplete fuzzy reciprocal preference relation, we can use Eq. (2.8) to construct an auxiliary fuzzy reciprocal preference relation $\overline{C} = (\overline{c}_{ij})_{n \times n}$, and construct the following multiple objective programming model:

$$\min \varepsilon_{ij} = \left| \delta_{ij} c_{ij} - \delta_{ij}\left(\frac{n}{2}(w_i - w_j) + 0.5\right) \right|, i, j \in N, i \neq j$$

$$\text{s.t.} \begin{cases} \sum_{i=1}^{n} w_i = 1 \\ w_i \geq 0, i \in N \end{cases} \tag{M-2.1}$$

Solution to the above minimization problem is found by solving the following goal programming model:

$$\min z = \sum_{i=1}^{n} \sum_{\substack{j=1 \\ j \neq i}}^{n} \left(s_{ij} d_{ij}^+ + t_{ij} d_{ij}^- \right)$$

$$\text{s.t.} \begin{cases} \delta_{ij}\left[c_{ij} - \frac{1}{2}(w_i - w_j) - 0.5 \right] - d_{ij}^+ + d_{ij}^- = 0, i, j \in N \\ \sum_{i=1}^{n} w_i = 1 \\ w_i \geq 0, i \in N \\ d_{ij}^+ \geq 0, d_{ij}^- \geq 0, i \neq j, i, j \in N \end{cases} \tag{M-2.2}$$

where d_{ij}^+ is the positive deviation from the target of the goal ε_{ij}, defined as

$$d_{ij}^+ = \delta_{ij}\left(c_{ij} - \frac{n}{2}\left(w_i - w_j\right) - 0.5\right) \vee 0$$

d_{ij}^- is the negative deviation from the target of the goal ε_{ij}, defined as

$$d_{ij}^- = \delta_{ij}\left(\frac{n}{2}\left(w_i - w_j\right) + 0.5 - c_{ij}\right) \vee 0$$

s_{ij} is the weighting factor corresponding to the positive deviation d_{ij}^+, and t_{ij} is the weighting factor corresponding to the negative deviation d_{ij}^-.

Consider that all the goal functions ε_{ij} are fair, and then we can set $s_{ij} = t_{ij} = 1$, $i, j \in N$; then, the model (M-2.2) can be rewritten as

$$\min z = \sum_{i=1}^{n} \sum_{\substack{j=1 \\ j \neq i}}^{n} \left(d_{ij}^+ + d_{ij}^-\right)$$

$$\text{s.t.} \begin{cases} \delta_{ij}\left[c_{ij} - \frac{n}{2}\left(w_i - w_j\right) - 0.5\right] - d_{ij}^+ + d_{ij}^- = 0, i \neq j, i, j \in N \\ \sum_{i=1}^{n} w_i = 1 \\ w_i \geq 0, i \in N \\ d_{ij}^+, d_{ij}^- \geq 0, i \neq j, i, j \in N \end{cases} \quad \text{(M-2.3)}$$

As $c_{ij} = 1 - c_{ji}$, (M-2.3) is equivalent to the following (M-2.4):

$$\min z = \sum_{i=1}^{n} \sum_{j=i+1}^{n} \left(d_{ij}^+ + d_{ij}^-\right)$$

$$\text{s.t.} \begin{cases} \delta_{ij}\left[c_{ij} - \frac{n}{2}\left(w_i - w_j\right) - 0.5\right] - d_{ij}^+ + d_{ij}^- = 0, i < j, i, j \in N \\ \sum_{i=1}^{n} w_i = 1 \\ w_i \geq 0, i \in N \\ d_{ij}^+, d_{ij}^- \geq 0, i < j, i, j \in N \end{cases} \quad \text{(M-2.4)}$$

Similarly, Eq. (2.18) does not hold, and we can establish the following function:

$$f_{ij} = \left|c_{ij} - \frac{n-1}{2}\left(w_i - w_j\right) - 0.5\right| \quad (2.32)$$

Furthermore, we can construct the following goal programming model:

$$\min z = \sum_{i=1}^{n} \sum_{\substack{j=1 \\ j \neq i}}^{n} \left(d_{ij}^+ + d_{ij}^- \right)$$

$$\text{s.t.} \begin{cases} \delta_{ij} \left[c_{ij} - \dfrac{n-1}{2} \left(w_i - w_j \right) - 0.5 \right] - d_{ij}^+ + d_{ij}^- = 0, i \neq j, i, j \in N \\ \sum_{i=1}^{n} w_i = 1 \\ w_i \geq 0, i \in N \\ d_{ij}^+, d_{ij}^- \geq 0, i \neq j, i, j \in N \end{cases} \quad \text{(M-2.5)}$$

It is equivalent to the following model (M-2.6):

$$\min z = \sum_{i=1}^{n} \sum_{j=i+1}^{n} \left(d_{ij}^+ + d_{ij}^- \right)$$

$$\text{s.t.} \begin{cases} \delta_{ij} \left[c_{ij} - \dfrac{n-1}{2} \left(w_i - w_j \right) - 0.5 \right] - d_{ij}^+ + d_{ij}^- = 0, i < j, i, j \in N \\ \sum_{i=1}^{n} w_i = 1 \\ w_i \geq 0, i \in N \\ d_{ij}^+, d_{ij}^- \geq 0, i < j, i, j \in N \end{cases} \quad \text{(M-2.6)}$$

Example 2.6 Example 2.2 continued:
If we use model (M-2.4) to obtain the weight vector in Example 2.2, we can construct the following model:

$$\min z = d_{13}^+ + d_{13}^- + d_{14}^+ + d_{14}^- + d_{23}^+ + d_{23}^- + d_{24}^+ + d_{24}^-$$

$$\text{s.t.} \begin{cases} 0.4 - 2 \times \left(w_1 - w_3 \right) - 0.5 - d_{13}^+ + d_{13}^- = 0 \\ 0.8 - 2 \times \left(w_1 - w_4 \right) - 0.5 - d_{14}^+ + d_{14}^- = 0 \\ 0.3 - 2 \times \left(w_2 - w_3 \right) - 0.5 - d_{23}^+ + d_{23}^- = 0 \\ 0.7 - 2 \times \left(w_2 - w_4 \right) - 0.5 - d_{24}^+ + d_{24}^- = 0 \\ w_1 + w_2 + w_3 + w_4 = 1 \\ w_1, w_2, w_3, w_4, d_{13}^+, d_{13}^-, d_{14}^+, d_{14}^-, d_{23}^+, d_{23}^-, d_{24}^+, d_{24}^- \geq 0 \end{cases}$$

Solving the model, we obtain $w_1 = 0.2875$, $w_2 = 0.2375$, $w_3 = 0.3375$, and $w_4 = 0.1375$. And we can also get the unknown elements as follows:

$$\bar{c}_{12} = 2(w_1 - w_2) + 0.5 = 0.6, \bar{c}_{21} = 2(w_2 - w_1) + 0.5 = 0.4,$$
$$\bar{c}_{34} = 2(w_3 - w_4) + 0.5 = 0.9, \bar{c}_{42} = 2(w_4 - w_3) + 0.5 = 0.1.$$

And thus, we can get a complete fuzzy reciprocal fitting relation $\bar{C}$:

$$\bar{C} = \begin{bmatrix} 0.5 & 0.6 & 0.4 & 0.8 \\ 0.4 & 0.5 & 0.3 & 0.7 \\ 0.6 & 0.7 & 0.5 & 0.9 \\ 0.2 & 0.3 & 0.1 & 0.5 \end{bmatrix}$$

If we set $\beta = (n - 1)/2$, use (M-2.6) to construct the following model:

$$\min z = d_{13}^+ + d_{13}^- + d_{14}^+ + d_{14}^- + d_{23}^+ + d_{23}^- + d_{24}^+ + d_{24}^-$$

$$\text{s.t.} \begin{cases} 0.4 - 1.5 \times (w_1 - w_3) - 0.5 - d_{13}^+ + d_{13}^- = 0 \\ 0.8 - 1.5 \times (w_1 - w_4) - 0.5 - d_{14}^+ + d_{14}^- = 0 \\ 0.3 - 1.5 \times (w_2 - w_3) - 0.5 - d_{23}^+ + d_{23}^- = 0 \\ 0.7 - 1.5 \times (w_2 - w_4) - 0.5 - d_{24}^+ + d_{24}^- = 0 \\ w_1 + w_2 + w_3 + w_4 = 1 \\ w_1, w_2, w_3, w_4, d_{13}^+, d_{13}^-, d_{14}^+, d_{14}^-, d_{23}^+, d_{23}^-, d_{24}^+, d_{24}^- \geq 0 \end{cases}$$

Solving the model, we obtain $w_1 = 0.3$, $w_2 = 0.233$, $w_3 = 0.3667$, and $w_4 = 0.1$, which is same as the result in Example 2.2, and we can get the same complete fuzzy reciprocal fitting relation $\bar{C}$.

2.5   Least Deviation Method

As Eq. (2.7) generally does not hold, we can also construct the following function (Xu & Da, 2009):

$$\min F(w) = \sum_{i=1}^{n} \sum_{j=1}^{n} \left[c_{ij} - \frac{n}{2}(w_i - w_j) - 0.5 \right]^2$$

It is called least deviation method (LVD).

Theorem 2.6 *Let $C = (c_{ij})_{n \times n}$ be an incomplete fuzzy reciprocal preference relation and $w = (w_1, w_2, \ldots, w_n)^T$ be its weighting vector; the weights are derived by the LVD, and then*

$$w_i = \frac{\sum_{j=1}^{n} c_{ij}}{\frac{n^2}{2}}, i \in N \tag{2.33}$$

Proof To prove the conclusion, we change $F(w)$ to the following form:

$$F'(w) = \sum_{i=1}^{n} \sum_{j=1}^{n} \left[c_{ij} - \beta(w_i - w_j) - 0.5 \right]^2$$

We can construct the Lagrange function

$$L(w, \lambda) = F'(w) + 2\lambda \left(\sum_{i=1}^{n} w_i - 1 \right) \tag{2.34}$$

where λ is the Lagrange multiplier. Since both functions $F'(w)$ and $L(w, \lambda)$ are differential for w_i, $i \in N$, differentiating (2.34) with respect to w_i, $i \in N$, and setting the partial derivatives equal to zero, we get the following set of equations:

$$\frac{\partial L}{\partial w_i} = 2 \sum_{j=1}^{n} \left[2\beta^2 (w_i - w_j) + \beta(c_{ji} - c_{ij}) \right] + 2\lambda = 0, i \in N$$

i.e.,

$$2n\beta^2 w_i - 2\beta^2 \sum_{j=1}^{n} w_j + \beta \sum_{j=1}^{n} (c_{ji} - c_{ij}) + \lambda = 0 \tag{2.35}$$

$$2n\beta^2 w_i - 2\beta^2 + \beta \sum_{j=1}^{n} (c_{ji} - c_{ij}) + \lambda = 0 \tag{2.36}$$

Summing on both sides of Eq. (2.36) with respect to i, $i \in N$, we have

$$2n\beta^2 \sum_{i=1}^{n} w_i - 2n\beta^2 + \beta \sum_{i=1}^{n} \sum_{j=1}^{n} (c_{ji} - c_{ij}) + n\lambda = 0 \tag{2.37}$$

Since

$$\sum_{i=1}^{n} \sum_{j=1}^{n} (c_{ji} - c_{ij}) = 0 \tag{2.38}$$

As a result, $\lambda = 0$. Hence, from (2.36) and $\lambda = 0$, it can be obtained that

$$w_i = \frac{1}{n} + \frac{1}{2n\beta} \sum_{j=1}^{n} (c_{ji} - c_{ij}) = \frac{1}{n} + \frac{1}{2n\beta} \left[2\sum_{j=1}^{n} c_{ij} - n \right] \qquad (2.39)$$

If $\beta = \frac{n}{2}$, then

$$w_i = \frac{2\sum_{j=1}^{n} c_{ij}}{n^2} \qquad (2.40)$$

which completes the proof Theorem 2.6. $\square$

If $\beta = \frac{n-1}{2}$, then

$$w_i = \frac{1}{n} + \frac{1}{2n \cdot \frac{n-1}{2}} \left[2\sum_{j=1}^{n} c_{ij} - n \right] = \frac{1}{n} + \frac{2\sum_{j=1}^{n} c_{ij} - n}{n(n-1)}$$

$$= \frac{2\sum_{j=1}^{n} c_{ij} - 1}{n(n-1)} = \frac{\sum_{j=1}^{n} c_{ij} - 0.5}{n(n-1)/2} = \frac{\sum_{j=1, j \neq i}^{n} c_{ij}}{\sum_{i=1}^{n} \sum_{j=1, j \neq i}^{n} c_{ij}} \qquad (2.41)$$

which is also same as the normalizing rank aggregation method when $\beta = (n - 1)/2$.

If $\beta = \frac{1}{2}$, then

$$w_i = \frac{1}{n} - 1 + \frac{2}{n} \sum_{j=1}^{n} c_{ij} \qquad (2.42)$$

If $\beta = 1$, then

$$w_i = \frac{1}{n} - \frac{1}{2} + \frac{1}{n} \sum_{j=1}^{n} c_{ij} \qquad (2.43)$$

From Theorem 2.6, we can know that the priority weighting vector derived by LVM is same as that by the normalizing rank aggregation method; the scientific and rational aspects of the normalizing rank aggregation method are also noted. From Eq. (2.40) or (2.41), if $\beta = n/2$ or $\beta = (n - 1)/2$, for all $i \in N$, it is always $w_i \geq 0$. Taking $\beta = 1/2$, if $\sum_{j=1}^{n} c_{ij} \leq \frac{n}{2} - \frac{1}{2}$, from (2.42), $w_i \leq 0$. Taking $\beta = 1$, if $\sum_{j=1}^{n} c_{ij} \leq \frac{n}{2} - 1$, it also will be $w_i \leq 0$; it is noted that it is unreasonable to take $\beta = 1/2$ or $\beta = 1$.

2.6 Quadratic Programming Method

As Eq. (2.7) generally does not hold, we can also construct the following function:

$$\min F(w) = \sum_{i=1}^{n} \sum_{j=1}^{n} \left[c_{ij} - \frac{n}{2}(w_i - w_j) - 0.5 \right]^2$$

$$\text{s.t.} \begin{cases} \sum_{i=1}^{n} w_i = 1 \\ w_i \geq 0, i \in N \end{cases} \tag{M-2.7}$$

This is quadratic programming problem. To solve this problem, we introduce the following lemma.

Lemma 2.1 (Kuhn-Tucher condition) (Wismer, 1978) *Consider the following general nonlinear programming problem:*

$$\min \ f(X)$$

$$\text{s.t.} \begin{cases} h_i(X) = 0, i = 1, 2, \ldots, m \\ g_j(X) \geq 0, j = 1, 2, \ldots, l \end{cases}$$

where X is a vector of n variables. Here, $f(X)$ is nonlinear and both constraints can be linear or nonlinear. Let X^* be the minimal point of nonlinear programming problem; the gradients $\nabla h_i(X^*)$ ($i = 1, 2, \ldots, m$) and $\nabla g_j(X^*)$ ($j = 1, 2, \ldots, l$) are linear independent, and the ∇ refers to the first-order partial derivatives with respect to X; then there exists the vector $\Lambda^* = (\lambda_1^*, \lambda_2^*, \ldots, \lambda_m^*)^T$ and $\Gamma^* = (\gamma_1^*, \gamma_2^*, \ldots, \gamma_l^*)^T$, such that

$$\begin{cases} \nabla f(X^*) - \sum_{i=1}^{m} \lambda_i^* \nabla h_i(X^*) \sum_{j=1}^{l} \gamma_j^* \nabla g_j(X^*) = 0 \\ \gamma_j^* g_j(X^*) = 0, j = 1, 2, \ldots, l \\ \gamma_j^* \geq 0, j = 1, 2, \ldots, l \end{cases}$$

where $\lambda_1^*, \lambda_2^*, \ldots, \lambda_m^*$ and $\gamma_1^*, \gamma_2^*, \ldots, \gamma_l^*$ are generalized Lagrange multipliers.

As (M-2.7) is a convex programming problem, by Lemma 2.1, we can obtain the following result.

Theorem 2.7 *The necessary condition of quadratic programming problem (M-2.7) is*

$$\begin{cases} n^3 w_i - 2n \sum_{j=1}^{n} \bar{c}_{ij} - \lambda - \gamma_i = 0, i \in N \\ \sum_{i=1}^{n} w_i = 1 \\ \gamma_i w_i = 0, i \in N \\ w_i \geq 0, \gamma_i \geq 0, i \in N \end{cases} \qquad \text{(M-2.8)}$$

As λ is a free variable, let $\lambda = \lambda' - \lambda''$, and $\lambda', \lambda'' \geq 0$, $\lambda'\lambda'' = 0$; introduce a variable v, and then we can establish the following (M-2.8) linear programming model:

$$\min z = v$$

$$\text{s.t.} \begin{cases} n^3 w_i - \lambda' + \lambda'' - \gamma_i = 2n \sum_{j=1}^{n} \bar{c}_{ij}, i \in N \\ \sum_{i=1}^{n} w_i + v = 1 \\ \gamma_i w_i = 0, i \in N \\ w_i \geq 0, \gamma_i \geq 0, i \in N \\ \lambda'\lambda'' = 0 \\ \lambda', \lambda'' \geq 0, v \geq 0 \end{cases} \qquad \text{(M-2.9)}$$

As C is an incomplete fuzzy reciprocal preference relation, in (M-2.7) and (M-2.8), $\bar{c}_{jk}$ should be in Eq. (2.8).

To prove Theorem 2.7, we first set the quadratic problem as

$$\min F(w) = \sum_{i=1}^{n} \sum_{j=1}^{n} \left[\bar{c}_{ij} - \beta(w_i - w_j) - 0.5 \right]^2$$

$$\text{s.t.} \begin{cases} \sum_{i=1}^{n} w_i = 1 \\ w_i \geq 0, i \in N \end{cases} \qquad \text{(M-2.10)}$$

According to Lemma 2.1, the necessary condition of quadratic programming problem (M-2.10) is

$$\begin{cases} 2\sum_{j=1}^{n}\left[2\beta^2\left(w_i-w_j\right)+\beta\left(\overline{c}_{ji}-\overline{c}_{ij}\right)\right]-\lambda-\gamma_i=0, i \in N \\[2mm] \sum_{i=1}^{n} w_i=1 \\[2mm] \gamma_i w_i=0, i \in N \\[1mm] w_i \geq 0, \gamma_i \geq 0, i \in N \end{cases} \qquad \text{(M-2.11)}$$

(M-2.11) can be simplified as

$$\begin{cases} 4\beta^2 n w_i-4\beta^2+2n\beta-4\beta\sum_{j=1}^{n}\overline{c}_{ij}-\lambda-\gamma_i=0, i \in N \\[2mm] \sum_{i=1}^{n} w_i=1 \\[2mm] \gamma_i w_i=0, i \in N \\[1mm] w_i \geq 0, \gamma_i \geq 0, i \in N \end{cases} \qquad \text{(M-2.12)}$$

If $\beta=\frac{n}{2}$, (M-2.12) becomes

$$\begin{cases} n^3 w_i-\lambda-\gamma_i=2n\sum_{j=1}^{n}\overline{c}_{ij}, i \in N \\[2mm] \sum_{i=1}^{n} w_i=1 \\[2mm] \gamma_i w_i=0, i \in N \\[1mm] w_i \geq 0, \gamma_i \geq 0, i \in N \end{cases} \qquad \text{(M-2.13)}$$

which completes proof of Theorem 2.7. □

It can be further equivalent to (M-2.9).
If $\beta=\frac{n-1}{2}$, (M-2.12) becomes

$$\begin{cases} (n-1)^2 n w_i+(n-1)-\lambda-\gamma_i=2(n-1)\sum_{j=1}^{n}\overline{c}_{ij}, i \in N \\[2mm] \sum_{i=1}^{n} w_i=1 \\[2mm] \gamma_i w_i=0, i \in N \\[1mm] w_i \geq 0, \gamma_i \geq 0, i \in N \end{cases} \qquad \text{(M-2.14)}$$

As λ is a free variable, let $\lambda=\lambda'-\lambda''$, and $\lambda', \lambda'' \geq 0$, $\lambda'\lambda''=0$; introduce a variable v, and then we can establish the following (M-2.15) linear programming model:

$$\min z = v$$

$$\begin{cases} (n-1)^2 nw_i + (n-1) - \lambda' + \lambda'' - \gamma_i = 2(n-1) \sum_{j=1}^{n} \bar{c}_{ij}, i \in N \\[2mm] \sum_{i=1}^{n} w_i + v = 1 \\[2mm] \gamma_i w_i = 0, i \in N \\[1mm] w_i \geq 0, \gamma_i \geq 0, i \in N \\[1mm] \lambda' \lambda'' = 0 \\[1mm] \lambda', \lambda'' \geq 0, v \geq 0 \end{cases} \qquad \text{(M-2.15)}$$

To verify the effectiveness of the proposed method, we illustrate the following example:

Example 2.7 Example 2.1 continued (where $\beta = n/2 = 1.5$):

To solve Example 2.1 by (M-2.9), we construct the following model:

$$\min \quad z = v$$

$$\text{s.t.} \begin{cases} 27w_1 - \lambda' + \lambda'' - \gamma_1 = 6(0.5 + 0.4 + 1.5(w_1 - w_3) + 0.5) \\[1mm] 27w_2 - \lambda' + \lambda'' - \gamma_2 = 6(0.6 + 0.5 + 0.7) \\[1mm] 27w_3 - \lambda' + \lambda'' - \gamma_3 = 6(1.5(w_3 - w_1) + 0.5 + 0.3 + 0.5) \\[1mm] w_1 + w_2 + w_3 + v = 1 \\[1mm] \lambda' \lambda'' = 0 \\[1mm] w_i \gamma_i = 0, i = 1, 2, 3 \\[1mm] w_i \geq 0, \gamma_i \geq 0, i = 1, 2, 3 \\[1mm] v \geq 0 \end{cases}$$

Solving the problem, we obtain $w_1 = 1/3$, $w_2 = 2/5$, $w_3 = 4/15$, $v = 0$, $\lambda' = 0$, $\lambda'' = 0$, $\gamma_1 = 0$, $\gamma_2 = 0$, and $\gamma_3 = 0$, which is also same as the results in Example 2.1.

Example 2.8 Example 2.2 continued (where $\beta = (n-1)/2 = 1.5$):

To solve the problem of Example 2.2 by (M-2.15), we construct the following model:

$$\min z = v$$

$$
\begin{cases}
36w_1 + 3 - \lambda' + \lambda'' - \gamma_1 = 6(0.5 + 1.5(w_1 - w_2) + 0.4 + 0.8) \\
36w_2 + 3 - \lambda' + \lambda'' - \gamma_2 = 6(1.5(w_2 - w_1) + 0.5 + 0.3 + 0.7) \\
36w_3 + 3 - \lambda' + \lambda'' - \gamma_3 = 6(0.6 + 0.7 + 0.5 + 1.5(w_3 - w_4)) \\
36w_4 + 3 - \lambda' + \lambda'' - \gamma_4 = 6(0.2 + 0.3 + 1.5(w_4 - w_3) + 0.5) \\
w_1 + w_2 + w_3 + w_4 + v = 1; \\
\lambda'\lambda'' = 0; \\
w_i\gamma_i = 0, i = 1, 2, 3, 4
\end{cases}
$$

Solving the model, we obtain $w_1 = 0.3$, $w_2 = 0.2333$, $w_3 = 0.3667$, $w_4 = 0.1$, $v = 0$, $\lambda' = 0$, $\lambda'' = 0$, $\gamma_1 = 0$, $\gamma_2 = 0$, $\gamma_3 = 0$, and $\gamma_4 = 0$, which is also same as the results in Example 2.2.

2.7 Summary

In this chapter, we have presented the normalizing rank aggregation-based methods of fuzzy reciprocal preference relation. In Eq. (1.33), when $\beta = n/2$ or $\beta = (n-1)/2$, we obtain two normalizing rank aggregation methods to derive the weights from fuzzy reciprocal preference relations. This is also extended to the group decision-making with incomplete fuzzy reciprocal preference relations, goal programming method, least deviation method, and quadratic programming method to derive the weight from incomplete fuzzy reciprocal preference relations.

References

Wismer, D. A. (1978). *Introduction to nonlinear optimization: A problem solving approach*. North-Holland Company.

Xu, Y. J., & Da, Q. L. (2009). Methods for priority of incomplete complementary judgement matrices. *Systems Engineering and Electronics, 31*(1), 95–99.

Xu, Y. J., Da, Q. L., & Liu, L. H. (2009). Normalizing rank aggregation method for priority of a fuzzy preference relation and its effectiveness. *International Journal of Approximate Reasoning, 50*(8), 1287–1297.

Xu, Y. J., Da, Q. L., & Wang, H. M. (2011). A note on group decision-making procedure based on incomplete reciprocal relations. *Soft Computing, 15*(7), 1289–1300.

Xu, Z. S. (2004). Incomplete complementary judgement matrix. *Systems Engineering - Theory & Practice, 24*(6), 93–97.

Xu, Z. S., & Chen, J. (2008). Group decision-making procedure based on incomplete reciprocal relations. *Soft Computing, 12*(6), 515–521.

Chapter 3
Eigenvector Method

In this chapter, we propose the eigenvector method (EM) for priority from an incomplete fuzzy reciprocal preference relation. EM is well known for multiplicative preference relation, which was proposed by Saaty (1980). Lipovetsky and Conklin (2002) and Wang and Parkan (2005) investigated the eigenvector problem for complete fuzzy reciprocal preference relation. In the following, we show that the EM can also be used to derive the weights for incomplete fuzzy reciprocal preference relation.

3.1 EM for Priority from an Incomplete Fuzzy Reciprocal Preference Relation

Let $w = (w_1, w_2, \ldots, w_n)^T$ be the priority vector of a fuzzy reciprocal preference relation $R = (r_{ij})_{n \times n}$, where $w_i > 0$, $i \in N$, $\sum_{i=1}^{n} w_i = 1$. If $R = (r_{ij})_{n \times n}$ is a multiplicative consistent complete fuzzy reciprocal preference relation, then such a preference relation is given by

$$r_{ij} = \frac{w_i}{w_i + w_j}, \forall i, j \in N \tag{3.1}$$

In this case, R can be expressed as

Y. Xu, *Deriving Priorities from Incomplete Fuzzy Reciprocal Preference Relations*, https://doi.org/10.1007/978-981-99-3169-9_3

$$R = \begin{bmatrix} \dfrac{w_1}{w_1+w_2} & \dfrac{w_1}{w_1+w_2} & \cdots & \dfrac{w_1}{w_1+w_n} \\ \dfrac{w_2}{w_2+w_1} & \dfrac{w_2}{w_2+w_2} & \cdots & \dfrac{w_2}{w_2+w_n} \\ \vdots & \vdots & \cdots & \vdots \\ \dfrac{w_n}{w_n+w_1} & \dfrac{w_n}{w_n+w_2} & \cdots & \dfrac{w_n}{w_n+w_n} \end{bmatrix} \qquad (3.2)$$

Let us write the following equations:

$$\frac{w_i}{w_i+w_1}(w_i+w_1) + \frac{w_i}{w_i+w_2}(w_i+w_2) + \ldots + \frac{w_i}{w_i+w_n}(w_i+w_n) = nw_i, i$$
$$\in N \qquad (3.3)$$

Using the general complete fuzzy reciprocal preference relation $R = (r_{ij})_{n \times n}$ instead of the multiplicative consistent complete fuzzy reciprocal preference relation in Eq. (3.3) and using λ_{max} instead of n, it follows that

$$r_{i1}(w_i+w_1) + r_{i2}(w_i+w_2) + \ldots + r_{in}(w_i+w_n) = \lambda_{max}w_i, i \in N \qquad (3.4)$$

Also, we can rewrite Eq. (3.4) in the following form:

$$r_{i1}w_1 + r_{i2}w_2 + \ldots + \left(r_{ii} + \sum_{j=1}^{n} r_{ij} \right) w_i + \ldots + r_{in}w_n = \lambda_{max}w_i \qquad (3.5)$$

Equation (3.5) can be further expressed as the following eigenvalue problem:

$$Pw = \lambda_{max}w \qquad (3.6)$$

where

$$P = \begin{bmatrix} r_{11} + \displaystyle\sum_{j=1}^{n} r_{1j} & r_{12} & \cdots & r_{1n} \\ r_{21} & r_{22} + \displaystyle\sum_{j=1}^{n} r_{2j} & \cdots & r_{2n} \\ \vdots & \vdots & \vdots & \vdots \\ r_{n1} & r_{n2} & \cdots & r_{nn} + \displaystyle\sum_{j=1}^{n} r_{nj} \end{bmatrix} \qquad (3.7)$$

So, we can solve the eigenvalue problem of Eq. (3.7) to derive the priorities of multiplicative consistent complete fuzzy reciprocal preference relation R just as we do in the AHP. This priority method is called the EM, which Lipovetsky and Conklin (2002) investigated in the context of the AHP.

In the following, we extend the EM to the multiplicative consistent incomplete fuzzy reciprocal preference relation.

In order to estimate the priority vector $w = (w_1, w_2, \ldots, w_n)^T$ of the multiplicative consistent incomplete fuzzy reciprocal preference relation $C = (c_{ij})_{n \times n}$, we can replace the unknown element "$-$" in C with $\frac{w_i}{w_i + w_j}$, and then construct an auxiliary fuzzy reciprocal relation $\overline{C} = (\overline{c}_{ij})_{n \times n}$, where

$$
\overline{c}_{ij} = \begin{cases} \dfrac{w_i}{w_i + w_j}, & c_{ij} = - \\ c_{ij}, & c_{ij} \neq - \end{cases} \tag{3.8}
$$

Then we replace Eq. (3.4) with the following system of equations:

$$
\overline{c}_{i1}(w_i + w_1) + \overline{c}_{i2}(w_i + w_2) + \ldots + \overline{c}_{in}(w_i + w_n) = \lambda_{\max} w_i, \, i \in N \tag{3.9}
$$

where $w_i > 0$, $i \in N$, $\sum_{i=1}^{n} w_i = 1$.

Xu (2005) solved the above system to obtain the priority vector for the incomplete fuzzy reciprocal preference relations. In the following, we will further investigate the problem.

For the incomplete fuzzy reciprocal preference relation $C = (c_{ij})_{n \times n}$, if there is only one missing element (generally, $c_{ij} = -$) in the ith row and jth column of the relation C, then its auxiliary relation $\overline{C} = \left(\overline{c}_{ij} \right)_{n \times n}$ is

$$
\overline{C} = \begin{matrix} & & & i & & j & & \\ & \begin{bmatrix} 0.5 & c_{12} & \cdots & \cdots & \cdots & \cdots & \cdots & c_{1n} \\ c_{21} & 0.5 & \cdots & \cdots & \cdots & \vdots & \vdots & c_{2n} \\ \vdots & \vdots & \ddots & \vdots & \vdots & \vdots & \vdots & \vdots \\ i & c_{i1} & \cdots & \cdots & 0.5 & \cdots & \frac{w_i}{w_i + w_j} & \cdots & c_{in} \\ \vdots & \vdots & \cdots & \vdots & \vdots & \ddots & \vdots & \cdots & \vdots \\ j & \vdots & \cdots & \cdots & \frac{w_j}{w_i + w_j} & \cdots & 0.5 & \cdots & c_{jn} \\ \vdots & \vdots & \cdots & \cdots & \cdots & \cdots & \vdots & \ddots & \vdots \\ c_{n1} & c_{n2} & \cdots & \cdots & \cdots & \cdots & \cdots & 0.5 \end{bmatrix} \end{matrix} \tag{3.10}
$$

or we use Eq. (3.9) to express as follows:

$$
c_{i1}(w_i + w_1) + c_{i2}(w_i + w_2) + \ldots + \frac{w_i}{w_i + w_j}(w_i + w_j) + \ldots
$$
$$
+ c_{in}(w_i + w_n) = \lambda_{\max} w_i \tag{3.11}
$$

That is,

$$\begin{cases} 0.5(w_1+w_1)+c_{12}(w_1+w_2)+\ldots+c_{1n}(w_1+w_n)=\lambda_{\max}w_1 \\ \vdots \\ c_{i1}(w_i+w_1)+\ldots+0.5(w_i+w_i)+\ldots+\dfrac{w_i}{w_i+w_j}(w_i+w_j)+\ldots+c_{in}(w_i+w_n)=\lambda_{\max}w_i \\ \vdots \\ c_{j1}(w_j+w_1)+\ldots\dfrac{w_j}{w_i+w_j}(w_j+w_i)+\ldots+0.5(w_j+w_j)+\ldots+c_{jn}(w_j+w_n)=\lambda_{\max}w_j \\ \vdots \\ c_{n1}(w_n+w_1)+c_{n2}(w_n+w_2)+\ldots+c_{nn}(w_n+w_n)=\lambda_{\max}w_n \end{cases}$$

$$(3.12)$$

which can be further expressed as follows:

$$\overline{P}v = \lambda_{\max}w \tag{3.13}$$

where

$$\overline{P}= \begin{array}{c} \\ \\ i \\ \\ \\ j \\ \\ \\ \end{array} \begin{bmatrix} 0.5+\sum\limits_{j=1}^{n}c_{1j} & \cdots & \cdots & \cdots & \cdots & \cdots & c_{1n} \\ \vdots & \ddots & \vdots & \vdots & \vdots & \vdots & \vdots \\ c_{i1} & \cdots & 2+\sum\limits_{\substack{j=1 \\ j\neq i}}^{n}c_{ij} & \cdots & 0 & \cdots & c_{in} \\ \vdots & \cdots & \vdots & \cdots & \cdots & \cdots & \vdots \\ \vdots & \cdots & 0 & \cdots & 2+\sum\limits_{\substack{k=1 \\ k\neq j}}^{n}c_{jk} & \cdots & c_{jn} \\ \vdots & \cdots & \cdots & \cdots & \cdots & \ddots & \vdots \\ c_{n1} & \cdots & \cdots & \cdots & \cdots & \cdots & 0.5+\sum\limits_{j=1}^{n}c_{nj} \end{bmatrix}$$

$$(3.14)$$

We call $\overline{P}$ an equivalent relation of the incomplete fuzzy reciprocal preference relation C.

Generally, if there are m_i missing elements in the ith row of the incomplete fuzzy reciprocal preference relation C, then its equivalent relation $\overline{P} = (\overline{p}_{ij})_{n \times n}$ can be expressed as follows:

$$\overline{p}_{ij} = \begin{cases} c_{ij}, & \text{if } i \neq j \text{ and } c_{ij} \neq - \\ 0, & \text{if } c_{ij} = - \\ m_i + 1 + \sum_{j=1, j \neq i}^{n} c_{ij}, & \text{if } i = j \text{ and } c_{ij} \neq - \end{cases} \tag{3.15}$$

where m_i denotes the number of missing elements in the ith row of the incomplete fuzzy reciprocal preference relation C. Equation (3.15) denotes that the elements of equivalent relation $\overline{P}$ are equal to the following: if the elements are known in the incomplete fuzzy reciprocal preference relation C, then $\overline{p}_{ij} = c_{ij}$; if the elements are unknown, then $\overline{p}_{ij} = 0$; and the diagonal elements $\overline{p}_{ij}$ are equal to the sum of the known elements and the number of missing elements m_i adds to 1.

Thus, the multiplicative consistent incomplete fuzzy reciprocal preference relation is equivalent to solve the eigenvalue problem of Eqs. (3.13) and (3.15). We refer this method as EM, which can be used to derive the priority vector of incomplete fuzzy reciprocal preference relation C, and the method is similar to the auxiliary eigenvalue problem developed by Harker (1987) in the multiplicative framework.

Especially, if there are no missing elements in the fuzzy reciprocal preference relation, then Eq. (3.15) is equivalent to Eq. (3.7), so Eq. (3.13) is an extension of Eq. (3.6); it can be used not only for the incomplete fuzzy reciprocal preference relation, but also for the complete fuzzy reciprocal preference one. Therefore, it has broad application prospects.

Theorem 3.1 *In Eq.* (3.13), $\lambda_{\max} \equiv n$.

Proof Let $\lambda > 0$ be a nonnegative eigenvalue of matrix $\overline{P}$, and we have

$$\begin{cases} \overline{p}_{11} w_1 + \overline{p}_{12} w_2 + \ldots + \overline{p}_{1n} w_n = \lambda v_1 \\ \overline{p}_{21} w_1 + \overline{p}_{22} w_2 + \ldots + \overline{p}_{2n} v_n = \lambda v_2 \\ \vdots \\ \overline{p}_{n1} w_1 + \overline{p}_{n2} w_2 + \ldots + \overline{p}_{nn} w_n = \lambda v_n \end{cases} \tag{3.16}$$

Side-by-side summation of the above equations gives

$$\sum_{i=1}^{n} \overline{p}_{i1} w_1 + \sum_{i=1}^{n} \overline{p}_{i2} w_2 + \ldots + \sum_{i=1}^{n} \overline{p}_{in} w_n = \lambda \sum_{i=1}^{n} w_i \tag{3.17}$$

Assume that there are m_i missing elements in the ith row of the incomplete fuzzy reciprocal preference relation C; therefore, there are also m_i missing elements in the ith column of the incomplete fuzzy reciprocal preference relation C, and therefore, the sum of the ith row and the ith column should be $n - m_i$. And with Eq. (3.15), we have

$$\sum_{i=1}^{n} \overline{p}_{ij} = \sum_{i=1, i \neq j}^{n} \overline{p}_{ij} + \overline{p}_{jj} = \sum_{i=1, i \neq j}^{n} c_{ij} + m_i + 1 + \sum_{j=1, j \neq i}^{n} c_{ij}$$

$$= \sum_{i=1, i \neq j}^{n} \left(c_{ij} + c_{ji}\right) + m_i + 1 = \sum_{i=1}^{n} \left(c_{ij} + c_{ji}\right) - 1 + m_i + 1 = n - m_i - 1$$

$$+ m_i + 1 = n \tag{3.18}$$

From Eq. (3.18), we know that the sum of each column of the equivalent relation of the incomplete fuzzy reciprocal preference relation C is equal to n. Thus, Eq. (3.17) can be further written as follows:

$$nw_1 + nw_2 + \ldots + nw_n = \lambda \sum_{i=1}^{n} w_i \tag{3.19}$$

It is evident that as long as $\sum_{i=1}^{n} w_i \neq 0$ and λ are nonnegative, $\lambda = n$. Since $\overline{P}$ is nonnegative matrix, according to the Perron-Frobenius theorem (Wang & Xu, 1990), its maximal eigenvalue, λ_{max}, and the corresponding eigenvector w are both positive. Therefore,

$$\lambda_{\max} \equiv n \tag{3.20}$$

which completes the proof of Theorem 3.1.   □

Theorem 3.2 *Let w be the principal right eigenvector of matrix $\overline{P}$ corresponding to $\lambda_{max} \equiv n$; then $w \geq 0$.*

This theorem is a direct result of the general Perron-Frobenius theorem (Wang & Xu, 1990).   □

The above two theorems show that for any incomplete fuzzy reciprocal preference relation C, we can always find a nonnegative normalized eigenvector v satisfying $\overline{P}v = nv$, where the elements of matrix $\overline{P}$ are determined by Eq. (3.15). The principal right eigenvector w is calculated by the following iterative algorithm:

Step 1. Set $k = 1$ and $w^{(0)} = (1/n)e$ and $\varepsilon = 10^{-6}$, where ε is a specified precision coefficient and $w^{(0)} = (w_1^{(0)}, \ldots, w_n^{(0)})^T$.

Step 2. Compute $w^{(k)} = \overline{P}w^{(k-1)}$ and normalize it, where $w^{(k)} = (w_1^{(k)}, \ldots, w_n^{(k)})^T$ is a normalized vector.

Step 3. If $\|w^{(k)} - w^{(k-1)}\| \leq \varepsilon$, then $w = w^{(k)}$, where $\|w^{(k)} - w^{(k-1)}\|$ is a vector norm, which will take one of the three forms: absolute, square, or minimax. Otherwise, let $k = k + 1$ and go to Step 2.

3.2 Algorithms for Repairing the Inconsistency of the Incomplete Fuzzy Reciprocal Preference Relation

In Sect. 1.2, we have given the measurement of the consistency for the incomplete fuzzy reciprocal preference relation, which only needs to compute the consistency ratio (*CR*, for short) similar to the Saaty (1980)'s method in the AHP. If the incomplete fuzzy reciprocal preference relation is not of acceptable consistency, we need to regulate the incomplete fuzzy reciprocal preference relation until its consistency is acceptable. In order to do this, we first need to use some techniques to identify the UFE. Therefore, we introduce the following maximum absolute deviation (MAD) criterion to identify the UFE:

$$\text{MAD} = \max_{i,j} \left\{ \left| c_{ij} - \frac{w_i}{w_i + w_j} \right| \middle| i, j \in N; c_{ij} \neq - \right\} \tag{3.21}$$

where $d_{ij} = |c_{ij} - \frac{w_i}{w_i + w_j}|$ is the fitting error for the comparison element c_{ij} of the incomplete fuzzy reciprocal preference relation; all the fitting errors d_{ij} consist of the matrix D ($D = (d_{ij})_{n \times n}$). If the priority vector $w = (w_1, w_2, \ldots, w_n)^T$ is able to precisely fit the incomplete fuzzy reciprocal preference relation C, then $d_{ij} \equiv 0$; otherwise, $d_{ij} > 0$. It is easy to find that $d_{ij} = d_{ji}$. The bigger the discrepancy is between the comparison element c_{ij} and theoretical structure, Eq. (3.8), the higher is the value of the index, Eq. (3.21). The biggest deviation of the comparison elements from the theoretical values corresponds to maximum input, and such input indicates the coordinate of UFE in the incomplete fuzzy reciprocal preference relation. Once we have found the UFE, then we need to regulate the UFE until the incomplete fuzzy reciprocal preference relation is of acceptable consistency. Since the known element c_{ij} should be as far as approximate to $w_i/(w_i + w_j)$, and the known element c_{ij} which the expert provided is generally in the set $\Omega = \{0.1, 0.2, 0.3, 0.4, 0.5, 0.6, 0.7, 0.8, 0.9\}$, we propose a method for repairing the inconsistency of the fuzzy reciprocal preference relation; the resolution process presents the scheme in Fig. 3.1.

Algorithm 3.1

Step 1. Let $C = (c_{ij})_{n \times n}$ be an initial incomplete fuzzy reciprocal preference relation. Using Theorem 1.4 to judge whether the incomplete fuzzy reciprocal preference relation is acceptable, if the incomplete fuzzy reciprocal preference relation is not acceptable, we return it to the expert to give a new fuzzy reciprocal preference relation; otherwise, go to Step 2.

Step 2. Using Eq. (3.15) to construct the equivalent matrix $\overline{P}$ of the incomplete fuzzy reciprocal preference relation, compute the eigenvector w using Eq. (3.13).

Step 3. Use Eq. (1.13) to compute the consistency ratio of the incomplete fuzzy reciprocal preference relation. If FCR < 0.1, then go to Step 6. Otherwise, go to Step 4.

Fig. 3.1 Consistency
resolution process of an
incomplete fuzzy reciprocal
preference relation

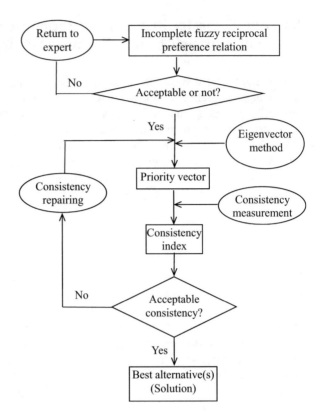

Step 4. Using Eq. (3.21) to compute the deviation between the comparison element
c_{ij} and theoretical structure, obtain the maximum deviation to find the
corresponding UFE.

Step 5. Change the initial UFE (c_{ij}) into the new one c'_{ij}, where $c'_{ij} = $ round
$(\frac{w_i}{w_i+w_j} \times 10) \times 10^{-1}$, and "round" is the usual round operation, and go to Step 2.

Step 6. Rank the alternatives according to the eigenvector w.

Step 7. End.

In Step 5 of Algorithm 3.1, we set the UFE (c_{ij}) by $c'_{ij} = \text{round}(\frac{w_i}{w_i+w_j} \times 10) \times 10^{-1}$
directly and C becomes C'. However, is it the most reasonable value of the UFE (c_{ij})?
That is, when the UFE (c_{ij}) is replaced by c'_{ij}, will the FCR be the minimum value
compared with other UFE (c_{ij}) values? In our deep investigation, the answer is
no. Thus, one important problem is to determine the most reasonable value of UFE
(c_{ij}). To derive the most reasonable value of the UFE (c_{ij}), we can look at the UFE
(c_{ij}) as an unknown element, and then C would be C'. Afterwards, we use Eq. (3.15)
to construct the equivalent relation $\overline{P}'$ of the incomplete fuzzy reciprocal preference
relation C', and then further use Eq. (3.13) to compute the eigenvector w' of the
equivalent $\overline{P}'$. Then, we propose the following Algorithm 3.2.

Algorithm 3.2
Step 1–Step 4 in Algorithm 3.1.
Step 5. Set the initial UFE (c_{ij}) as the incomplete element and C would be C'.
Step 6. Using Eq. (3.15) to construct the equivalent matrix $\overline{P}'$ of the incomplete fuzzy reciprocal preference relation C', compute the eigenvector w' of $\overline{P}'$ using Eq. (3.13).
Step 7. Change the initial UFE (c_{ij}) into the new one c'_{ij}, where $c'_{ij} = $ round $(\frac{w'_i}{w'_i+w'_j} \times 10) \times 10^{-1}$, and "round" is the usual round operation, C' would be C'', and go to Step 2.
Step 8. Rank the alternatives according to the eigenvector w.
Step 9. End.

Remark 3.1 The main difference between Algorithm 3.1 and Algorithm 3.2 is that we do not update the UFE (c_{ij}) by $c'_{ij} = $ round $(\frac{w_i}{w_i+w_j} \times 10) \times 10^{-1}$, but we first set it as unknown value, and then C would be C'. We use Eq. (3.13) to compute the eigenvector w' of the incomplete fuzzy reciprocal preference relation C'. Afterwards, we compute c'_{ij} by $c'_{ij} = $ round $(\frac{w'_i}{w'_i+w'_j} \times 10) \times 10^{-1}$. Here, we can also set $c'_{ij} = \frac{w'_i}{w'_i+w'_j}$, and C' becomes C''. Similarly, we can compute the eigenvector w'' of C''. It should be noted that $w' = w''$; this verifies that $c'_{ij} = \frac{w'_i}{w'_i+w'_j}$ is the most reasonable value, and it is very reasonable to set the initial UFE (c_{ij}) as the incomplete element in C in Step 5 of Algorithm 3.2. This can also be seen in Example 3.1.

3.3   Illustrative Example

Example 3.1 For a decision-making problem, there are six decision alternatives x_i $(i = 1, 2, \ldots, 6)$. The DM provides his/her preferences over these six decision alternatives and gives an incomplete fuzzy reciprocal preference relation as follows (adapted from Xu (2005)):

$$C = \begin{bmatrix} 0.5 & - & - & 0.3 & 0.8 & 0.3 \\ - & 0.5 & - & - & - & - \\ - & - & 0.5 & - & - & - \\ 0.7 & - & - & 0.5 & 0.4 & 0.8 \\ 0.2 & - & - & 0.6 & 0.5 & 0.7 \\ 0.7 & - & - & 0.2 & 0.3 & 0.5 \end{bmatrix}$$

First, we use Algorithm 3.1 to derive the weights.

Step 1. By Theorem 1.4, we know that C is not an acceptable incomplete fuzzy reciprocal preference relation, because there is no known element in the second and third row (or column) of C except for the diagonal elements ($c_{22} = 0.5$, $c_{33} = 0.5$). Thus, we return the incomplete fuzzy reciprocal preference relation $C = (c_{ij})_{n \times n}$ to the DM and ask him/her to provide more evaluation information and get an improved incomplete fuzzy reciprocal preference relation as follows:

$$C = \begin{bmatrix} 0.5 & 0.3 & - & 0.3 & 0.8 & 0.3 \\ 0.7 & 0.5 & 0.7 & - & 0.6 & - \\ - & 0.3 & 0.5 & 0.4 & - & - \\ 0.7 & - & 0.6 & 0.5 & 0.4 & 0.8 \\ 0.2 & 0.4 & - & 0.6 & 0.5 & 0.7 \\ 0.7 & - & - & 0.2 & 0.3 & 0.5 \end{bmatrix}$$

From Theorem 1.4, we know that the incomplete fuzzy reciprocal preference relation is acceptable and then go to Step 2.

Step 2. Using Eq. (3.15) to construct the equivalent matrix $\overline{P}$ of the incomplete fuzzy reciprocal preference relation C, we have

$$\overline{P} = \begin{bmatrix} 3.7 & 0.3 & 0 & 0.3 & 0.8 & 0.3 \\ 0.7 & 5 & 0.7 & 0 & 0.6 & 0 \\ 0 & 0.3 & 4.7 & 0.4 & 0 & 0 \\ 0.7 & 0 & 0.6 & 4.5 & 0.4 & 0.8 \\ 0.2 & 0.4 & 0 & 0.6 & 3.9 & 0.7 \\ 0.7 & 0 & 0 & 0.2 & 0.3 & 4.2 \end{bmatrix}$$

We compute its eigenvector and normalize it, and we have

$$w = (0.1310, 0.2756, 0.1275, 0.2077, 0.1578, 0.1003)^{T}$$

Step 3. Using Eq. (1.13) to compute the consistency ratio of the incomplete fuzzy reciprocal preference relation, we have

$$\text{FCI} = 0.1896, \text{FCR} = 0.1896/1.26 = 0.1505$$

Obviously, FCR > 0.1, so C is not of acceptable consistency, and we need to find the UFE and repair it.

Step 4. Using Eq. (3.21) to compute the deviation d_{ij} between the comparison element c_{ij} and theoretical structure, we have

$$D = \begin{bmatrix} 0 & 0.0222 & 0 & 0.0868 & 0.3463 & 0.2663 \\ 0.0222 & 0 & 0.0163 & 0 & 0.0360 & 0 \\ 0 & 0.0163 & 0 & 0.0196 & 0 & 0 \\ 0.0868 & 0 & 0.0196 & 0 & 0.1683 & 0.1257 \\ 0.3463 & 0.0360 & 0 & 0.1683 & 0 & 0.0887 \\ 0.2663 & 0 & 0 & 0.1257 & 0.0887 & 0 \end{bmatrix}$$

Obviously, the maximum deviations are d_{15} and d_{51}, so the UFEs are c_{15} and d_{51}.

Step 5. Change the initial UFE (c_{ij}) into the new one c'_{ij}, where $c'_{ij} = $ round $(\frac{w_i}{w_i+w_j} \times 10) \times 10^{-1}$; we have $c'_{15} = 0.5$, $c'_{51} = 0.5$.

Thus,

$$C' = \begin{bmatrix} 0.5 & 0.3 & - & 0.3 & 0.5 & 0.3 \\ 0.7 & 0.5 & 0.7 & - & 0.6 & - \\ - & 0.3 & 0.5 & 0.4 & - & - \\ 0.7 & - & 0.6 & 0.5 & 0.4 & 0.8 \\ 0.5 & 0.4 & - & 0.6 & 0.5 & 0.7 \\ 0.7 & - & - & 0.2 & 0.3 & 0.5 \end{bmatrix}$$

Using Eq. (3.15) to construct the equivalent matrix $\overline{P}$ of the incomplete fuzzy reciprocal preference relation, we have

$$\overline{P} = \begin{bmatrix} 3.4 & 0.3 & 0 & 0.3 & 0.5 & 0.3 \\ 0.7 & 5 & 0.7 & 0 & 0.6 & 0 \\ 0 & 0.3 & 4.7 & 0.4 & 0 & 0 \\ 0.7 & 0 & 0.6 & 4.5 & 0.4 & 0.8 \\ 0.5 & 0.4 & 0 & 0.6 & 4.2 & 0.7 \\ 0.7 & 0 & 0 & 0.2 & 0.3 & 4.2 \end{bmatrix}$$

By Eq. (3.13), we compute its eigenvector and normalize it, and we have

$$w = (0.1038, 0.2780, 0.1262, 0.2017, 0.1949, 0.0953)^T$$

Using Eq. (1.13) to compute the consistency ratio of the incomplete fuzzy reciprocal preference relation C', we have

$$\text{FCI} = 0.068, \text{FCR} = 0.068/1.26 = 0.054$$

Therefore, C' is acceptable consistent.

Table 3.1 The consistency ratio FCR values for different c_{15}

c_{15}	0.1	0.2	0.3	0.4	0.5	0.6	0.7	0.8	0.9
FCR	0.0539	0.0333	0.0336	0.0412	0.054	0.0727	0.1009	0.1504	0.2813

Step 6. Rank the alternatives according to the eigenvector w, and we have

$$x_2 \succ x_4 \succ x_5 \succ x_3 \succ x_1 \succ x_6$$

and thus, the most desirable alternative is x_2.

In the above Step 1, we use Theorem 1.4 to judge whether an incomplete fuzzy reciprocal preference relation is acceptable or not, and the judgment process is simple. Xu (2005) solved a series of equations to obtain the weighting vector, but he found that there exist infinite solutions to the equations. As we can see, it is difficult to find that whether there exist infinite solutions to a series of equations, and it requires careful analysis or complicated computation. Compared with Xu (2005)'s method, our method is effective and simple. Gong (2008) also gave an approach to judge whether an incomplete fuzzy reciprocal preference relation is acceptable or not; as we can see, his method is so complicated and cannot judge easily.

In Step 5, we only just set UFE (c_{15}) by $c'_{ij} = \mathrm{round}(\frac{w_1}{w_1+w_5} \times 10) \times 10^{-1} = 0.5$. To determine the most preferred value for UFE (c_{15}), one way is to update UFE (c_{15}) in a wide range of possible values and each time solve the eigenvector problem (3.13) to obtain the FCR (1.13). The results are given in Table 3.1.

From Table 3.1, we can see that the minimum value of FCR is reached when c_{15} is near 0.2 and 0.3. In real applications, it is not preferred to estimate c_{15} by setting all the values. It needs huge computation. Further, we still could not estimate c_{15} accurately. In the following, we use Algorithm 3.2 to estimate the approximate value of c_{15} directly and improve the consistency more accurately. The following steps are involved.

Step 5. We set c_{15} and c_{51} as the unknown elements, and we have

$$C' = \begin{bmatrix} 0.5 & 0.3 & - & 0.3 & - & 0.3 \\ 0.7 & 0.5 & 0.7 & - & 0.6 & - \\ - & 0.3 & 0.5 & 0.4 & - & - \\ 0.7 & - & 0.6 & 0.5 & 0.4 & 0.8 \\ - & 0.4 & - & 0.6 & 0.5 & 0.7 \\ 0.7 & - & - & 0.2 & 0.3 & 0.5 \end{bmatrix}$$

Step 6. Using Eq. (3.15) to construct the equivalent matrix $\overline{P}'$ of the incomplete fuzzy reciprocal preference relation C', we have

$$\overline{P}' = \begin{bmatrix} 3.9 & 0.3 & 0 & 0.3 & 0 & 0.3 \\ 0.7 & 5 & 0.7 & 0 & 0.6 & 0 \\ 0 & 0.3 & 4.7 & 0.4 & 0 & 0 \\ 0.7 & 0 & 0.6 & 4.5 & 0.4 & 0.8 \\ 0 & 0.4 & 0 & 0.6 & 4.7 & 0.7 \\ 0.7 & 0 & 0 & 0.2 & 0.3 & 4.2 \end{bmatrix}$$

By Eq. (3.13), we have

$$w' = (0.0811, 0.2800, 0.1251, 0.1967, 0.2260, 0.0911)^T$$

Step 7.

$$c_{15}' = \text{round}\left(\frac{w_1'}{w_1' + w_5'} \times 10\right) \times 10^{-1} = 0.3, c_{51}' = \text{round}\left(\frac{w_5'}{w_1' + w_5'} \times 10\right) \times 10^{-1}$$
$$= 0.7$$

Therefore,

$$C'' = \begin{bmatrix} 0.5 & 0.3 & - & 0.3 & 0.3 & 0.3 \\ 0.7 & 0.5 & 0.7 & - & 0.6 & - \\ - & 0.3 & 0.5 & 0.4 & - & - \\ 0.7 & - & 0.6 & 0.5 & 0.4 & 0.8 \\ 0.7 & 0.4 & - & 0.6 & 0.5 & 0.7 \\ 0.7 & - & - & 0.2 & 0.3 & 0.5 \end{bmatrix}$$

Using Eq. (3.15) to construct the equivalent matrix $\overline{P}''$ of the incomplete fuzzy reciprocal preference relation C'', we have

$$\overline{P}'' = \begin{bmatrix} 3.2 & 0.3 & 0 & 0.3 & 0.3 & 0.3 \\ 0.7 & 5 & 0.7 & 0 & 0.6 & 0 \\ 0 & 0.3 & 4.7 & 0.4 & 0 & 0 \\ 0.7 & 0 & 0.6 & 4.5 & 0.4 & 0.8 \\ 0.7 & 0.4 & 0 & 0.6 & 4.4 & 0.7 \\ 0.7 & 0 & 0 & 0.2 & 0.3 & 4.2 \end{bmatrix}$$

By Eq. (3.13), we have

$$w' = (0.0846, 0.2797, 0.1253, 0.1975, 0.2211, 0.0917)^T$$

Using Eq. (1.13) to compute the consistency ratio of the incomplete fuzzy reciprocal preference relation C'', we have

$$FCI = 0.0423, FCR = 0.0423/1.26 = 0.0336$$

Therefore, C'' is acceptably consistent.

Step 8. Rank the alternatives according to the eigenvector w, and we have

$$x_2 \succ x_5 \succ x_4 \succ x_3 \succ x_6 \succ x_1$$

and thus, the most desirable alternative is x_2.

In Step 7, if we set

$$c'_{15} = \frac{w'_1}{w'_1 + w'_5} = 0.2641, c'_{51} = \frac{w'_5}{w'_1 + w'_5} = 0.7359$$

then C' becomes

$$C'' = \begin{bmatrix} 0.5 & 0.3 & - & 0.3 & 0.2641 & 0.3 \\ 0.7 & 0.5 & 0.7 & - & 0.6 & - \\ - & 0.3 & 0.5 & 0.4 & - & - \\ 0.7 & - & 0.6 & 0.5 & 0.4 & 0.8 \\ 0.7359 & 0.4 & - & 0.6 & 0.5 & 0.7 \\ 0.7 & - & - & 0.2 & 0.3 & 0.5 \end{bmatrix}$$

Using Eq. (3.15) to construct the equivalent matrix $\overline{P}''$ of the incomplete fuzzy reciprocal preference relation C'', we have

$$\overline{P}'' = \begin{bmatrix} 3.1641 & 0.3 & 0 & 0.3 & 0.2641 & 0.3 \\ 0.7 & 5 & 0.7 & 0 & 0.6 & 0 \\ 0 & 0.3 & 4.7 & 0.4 & 0 & 0 \\ 0.7 & 0 & 0.6 & 4.5 & 0.4 & 0.8 \\ 0.7359 & 0.4 & 0 & 0.6 & 4.4359 & 0.7 \\ 0.7 & 0 & 0 & 0.2 & 0.3 & 4.2 \end{bmatrix}$$

By Eq. (3.13), we have

$$w'' = (0.0811, 0.2800, 0.1251, 0.1967, 0.2260, 0.0911)^T$$

Step 7. Using Eq. (1.13) to compute the consistency ratio of the incomplete fuzzy reciprocal preference relation C'', we have

$$FCI = 0.0408, FCR = 0.0408/1.26 = 0.0324$$

Therefore, C'' is acceptably consistent.

Ranking the alternatives according to the eigenvector w, we have

$$x_2 \succ x_5 \succ x_4 \succ x_3 \succ x_6 \succ x_1$$

and thus, the most desirable alternative is x_2.

Remark 3.2 From the above illustrative example, we can see that the results obtained by Algorithm 3.2 are different from Algorithm 3.1. Using Algorithm 3.1, the ranking is $x_2 \succ x_4 \succ x_5 \succ x_3 \succ x_1 \succ x_6$, while in Algorithm 3.2, it is $x_2 \succ x_5 \succ x_4 \succ x_3 \succ x_6 \succ x_1$. It is obvious that the ranking between x_4 and x_5, and x_1 and x_6, is reversed. However, if we check the original incomplete fuzzy reciprocal preference relation C, $c_{54} = 0.6$ and $c_{61} = 0.7$, denoting that x_5 is preferred to x_4 and x_6 is preferred to x_1. It also shows that the results obtained by Algorithm 3.2 are near the DM's original judgments.

Remark 3.3 In the illustrative example, as we can see, if we set the unknown elements (or UFE (c_{15})) by the estimated original value $c'_{15} = \frac{w'_1}{w'_1 + w'_5} = 0.2641$ and $c'_{51} = \frac{w'_5}{w'_1 + w'_5} = 0.7359$, and the obtained weight vector $w'' = w'$, it shows that the most reasonable values of UFE (c_{15}) and UFE (c_{51}) are 0.2641 and 0.7359, respectively. It demonstrates the effectiveness of Algorithm 3.2.

3.4 Summary

In this chapter, we have shown that the EM can also be used to derive the priority weights for incomplete fuzzy reciprocal preference relations. We also present two algorithms to improve the consistency of incomplete fuzzy reciprocal preference relations.

References

Gong, Z. W. (2008). Least-square method to priority of the fuzzy preference relations with incomplete information. *International Journal of Approximate Reasoning, 47*(2), 258–264.
Harker, P. T. (1987). Incomplete pairwise comparisons in the analytic hierarchy process. *Mathematical Modeling, 9*(11), 837–848.

Lipovetsky, S., & Conklin, W. M. (2002). Robust estimation of priorities in the AHP. *European Journal of Operational Research, 137*, 110–122.

Saaty, T. L. (1980). *The analytic hierarchy process*. McGraw-Hill Company.

Wang, L. F., & Xu, S. B. (1990). *The introduction to analytic hierarchy process*. China Renmin University.

Wang, Y. M., & Parkan, C. (2005). Multiple attribute decision making based on fuzzy preference information on alternatives: Ranking and weighting. *Fuzzy Sets and Systems, 153*(3), 331–346.

Xu, Z. S. (2005). A procedure for decision making based on incomplete fuzzy preference relation. *Fuzzy Optimization and Decision Making, 4*(3), 175–189.

Chapter 4
Logarithmic Least Squares Method

In this chapter, we present logarithmic least squares method (LLSM) for priority for incomplete fuzzy reciprocal preference relations. LLSM method is well known for multiplicative preference relation, which was investigated by Saaty and Vargas (1984). Wang and Fan (2007) used the LLSM to derive the weights from complete fuzzy preference relations. In the following, we show that the LLSM can be used to derive the priority for incomplete fuzzy reciprocal preference relations.

4.1 Logarithmic Least Squares Method for Priority from Incomplete Fuzzy Reciprocal Preference Relations

Let $E = \{e_1, e_2, \ldots, e_m\}$ ($m \geq 2$) be a finite set of DMs. Suppose that these m DMs provide their preferences over the set X and give m incomplete fuzzy reciprocal preference relations $C_k = (c_{ij}^{(k)})_{n \times n}$ ($k \in M$). Let $w = (w_1, w_2, \ldots, w_n)^T$ be the priority vector of the group incomplete multiplicative consistent fuzzy reciprocal preference relations $C_k = (c_{ij}^{(k)})_{n \times n}$; then these preference relations are given by

$$\delta_{ij}^{(k)} c_{ij}^{(k)} = \delta_{ij}^{(k)} \frac{w_i}{w_i + w_j}, i, j \in N \tag{4.1}$$

where $\delta_{ij}^{(k)}$ is a zero or one integer variable of the indicator matrix $\Delta_k = (\delta_{ij}^{(k)})_{n \times n}$, which is defined as in Eq. (1.10).

From Eq. (4.1), we have

$$\delta_{ij}^{(k)} c_{ij}^{(k)} w_j = \delta_{ij}^{(k)} c_{ji}^{(k)} w_i, i, j \in N, k \in M \tag{4.2}$$

© The Author(s), under exclusive license to Springer Nature Singapore Pte Ltd. 2023, corrected publication 2023
Y. Xu, *Deriving Priorities from Incomplete Fuzzy Reciprocal Preference Relations*, https://doi.org/10.1007/978-981-99-3169-9_4

If none of $c_{ij}^{(k)}$ is zero for $\forall i, j \in N, k \in M$, then Eq. (4.2) can be equivalently written as

$$\delta_{ij}^{(k)} \left(\ln w_i - \ln w_j - \ln c_{ij}^{(k)} + \ln c_{ji}^{(k)} \right) = 0 \tag{4.3}$$

However, in the general case, Eq. (4.3) does not hold. Let

$$\varepsilon_{ij}^{(k)} = \delta_{ij}^{(k)} \left(\ln w_i - \ln w_j - \ln c_{ij}^{(k)} + \ln c_{ji}^{(k)} \right) \tag{4.4}$$

where $\varepsilon_{ij}^{(k)}$ $(i, j \in N, k \in M)$ are deviation variables, whose absolute values should be kept as small as possible. Thus, we can construct the following LLSM model:

$$\min \; J = \sum_{k=1}^{m} \sum_{i=1}^{n} \sum_{j=1}^{n} \left(\varepsilon_{ij}^{(k)} \right)^2 = \sum_{k=1}^{m} \sum_{i=1}^{n} \sum_{j=1}^{n} \delta_{ij}^{(k)} \left(\ln w_i - \ln w_j - \ln c_{ij}^{(k)} + \ln c_{ji}^{(k)} \right)^2$$

$$\text{s.t.} \begin{cases} \sum_{i=1}^{n} w_i = 1 \\ w_i \geq 0, i \in N \end{cases}$$

$$\text{(M-4.1)}$$

The above model (M-4.1) is only suitable for $c_{ij}^{(k)} \neq 0$ or $c_{ij}^{(k)} \neq 1$. In order to avoid this problem, in the general case, we introduce the following model:

$$\min \; J = \sum_{k=1}^{m} \sum_{i=1}^{n} \sum_{j=1}^{n} \sigma_{ij}^{(k)} \delta_{ij}^{(k)} \left(\ln w_i - \ln w_j - \ln c_{ij}^{(k)} + \ln c_{ji}^{(k)} \right)^2$$

$$\text{s.t.} \begin{cases} \sum_{i=1}^{n} w_i = 1 \\ w_i \geq 0, i \in N \end{cases}$$

$$\text{(M-4.2)}$$

where $\delta_{ij}^{(k)}, \sigma_{ij}^{(k)}$ are zero or one integer variables defined as in Eqs. (1.10) and (1.14), respectively, which are introduced to avoid taking logarithm to zero. $\sigma_{ij}^{(k)} \delta_{ij}^{(k)}$ denotes that the element $c_{ij}^{(k)}$ is missing ($c_{ij}^{(k)} = -$) or equivalent to 1 or 0. $\sigma_{ij}^{(k)} \delta_{ij}^{(k)} = 1$ if and only if the element $c_{ij}^{(k)}$ is known and satisfies $0 < c_{ij}^{(k)} < 1$.

In order to solve the model (M-4.2), we construct the Lagrange function

$$L(w, \lambda) = \sum_{k=1}^{m} \sum_{i=1}^{n} \sum_{j=1}^{n} \sigma_{ij}^{(k)} \delta_{ij}^{(k)} \left(\ln w_i - \ln w_j - \ln c_{ij}^{(k)} + \ln c_{ji}^{(k)} \right)^2$$

$$+ 4\lambda \left(\sum_{i=1}^{n} w_i - 1 \right) \tag{4.5}$$

where λ is the Lagrange multiplier. Differentiating Eq. (4.5) with respect to w_i, $i \in N$, and setting the partial derivatives equal to zero, we get the following set of equations:

$$\sum_{j=1}^{n} \sum_{k=1}^{m} \sigma_{ij}^{(k)} \delta_{ij}^{(k)} \left(\ln w_i - \ln w_j - \ln c_{ij}^{(k)} + \ln c_{ji}^{(k)} \right) \cdot \frac{1}{w_i} + \lambda = 0, i \in N \tag{4.6}$$

which is equivalent to

$$\sum_{j=1}^{n} \sum_{k=1}^{m} \sigma_{ij}^{(k)} \delta_{ij}^{(k)} \left(\ln w_i - \ln w_j - \ln c_{ij}^{(k)} + \ln c_{ji}^{(k)} \right) + \lambda w_i = 0, i \in N \tag{4.7}$$

Summing on both sides of Eq. (4.7) with respect to i, $i \in N$, we have

$$\sum_{k=1}^{m} \sum_{i=1}^{n} \sum_{j=1}^{n} \sigma_{ij}^{(k)} \delta_{ij}^{(k)} \left(\ln w_i - \ln w_j - \ln c_{ij}^{(k)} + \ln c_{ji}^{(k)} \right) + \lambda \sum_{i=1}^{n} w_i = 0 \tag{4.8}$$

$\sum_{k=1}^{m} \sum_{i=1}^{n} \sum_{j=1}^{n} \sigma_{ij}^{(k)} \delta_{ij}^{(k)} \left(\ln w_i - \ln w_j - \ln c_{ij}^{(k)} + \ln c_{ji}^{(k)} \right) \equiv 0$ and $\sum_{i=1}^{n} w_i = 1$. As a result, $\lambda = 0$, and therefore Eq. (4.7) becomes

$$\sum_{j=1}^{n} \sum_{k=1}^{m} \sigma_{ij}^{(k)} \delta_{ij}^{(k)} \left(\ln w_i - \ln w_j - \ln c_{ij}^{(k)} + \ln c_{ji}^{(k)} \right) = 0, i \in N \tag{4.9}$$

That is,

$$\sum_{j=1}^{n} \sum_{k=1}^{m} \sigma_{ij}^{(k)} \delta_{ij}^{(k)} \ln w_i - \sum_{j=1}^{n} \sum_{k=1}^{m} \sigma_{ij}^{(k)} \delta_{ij}^{(k)} \ln w_j = \sum_{j=1}^{n}$$

$$\times \sum_{k=1}^{m} \sigma_{ij}^{(k)} \delta_{ij}^{(k)} \left(\ln c_{ij}^{(k)} - \ln c_{ji}^{(k)} \right), i \in N \tag{4.10}$$

which can be equivalently expressed in the form of matrix as

$$\overline{D}_n \overline{W}_n = \overline{Y}_n \tag{4.11}$$

where $\overline{W}_n = (\ln w_1, \ln w_2, \ldots, \ln w_n)^T$, $\overline{D}$ and $\overline{Y}$ are, respectively, the matrix and vector defined by

$$\overline{D}_n = \begin{bmatrix} \sum\limits_{j=2}^{n}\sum\limits_{k=1}^{m} \sigma_{1j}^{(k)}\delta_{1j}^{(k)} & -\sum\limits_{k=1}^{m}\sigma_{12}^{(k)}\delta_{12}^{(k)} & \cdots & -\sum\limits_{k=1}^{m}\sigma_{1n}^{(k)}\delta_{1n}^{(k)} \\ -\sum\limits_{k=1}^{m}\sigma_{21}^{(k)}\delta_{21}^{(k)} & \sum\limits_{j=1,j\neq2}^{n}\sum\limits_{k=1}^{m}\sigma_{2j}^{(k)}\delta_{2j}^{(k)} & \cdots & -\sum\limits_{k=1}^{m}\sigma_{2n}^{(k)}\delta_{2n}^{(k)} \\ \vdots & \vdots & \cdots & \vdots \\ -\sum\limits_{k=1}^{m}\sigma_{n1}^{(k)}\delta_{n1}^{(k)} & -\sum\limits_{k=1}^{m}\sigma_{n2}^{(k)}\delta_{n2}^{(k)} & \cdots & \sum\limits_{j=1}^{n-1}\sum\limits_{k=1}^{m}\sigma_{nj}^{(k)}\delta_{nj}^{(k)} \end{bmatrix} \tag{4.12}$$

$$\overline{Y}_n = \begin{bmatrix} \sum\limits_{k=1}^{m}\sum\limits_{j=1}^{n}\sigma_{1j}^{(k)}\delta_{1j}^{(k)}\left(\ln c_{1j}^{(k)} - \ln c_{j1}^{(k)}\right) \\ \sum\limits_{k=1}^{m}\sum\limits_{j=1}^{n}\sigma_{2j}^{(k)}\delta_{2j}^{(k)}\left(\ln c_{2j}^{(k)} - \ln c_{j2}^{(k)}\right) \\ \vdots \\ \sum\limits_{k=1}^{m}\sum\limits_{j=1}^{n}\sigma_{nj}^{(k)}\delta_{nj}^{(k)}\left(\ln c_{nj}^{(k)} - \ln c_{n1}^{(k)}\right) \end{bmatrix} \tag{4.13}$$

Obviously, the sum of each row or column of $\overline{D}_n$ is zero, that is, $|\overline{D}_n| = 0$, so $\overline{D}_n$ is a singular matrix. Therefore, there are infinitive solutions to Eq. (4.11), but there is only one solution that satisfies the constraint Eq. (4.11); letting $w_n = 1$, and solving the first $(n - 1)$ equations, we have

$$D_{n-1}W_{n-1} = Y_{n-1} \tag{4.14}$$

where

$\overline{D}_{n-1}$

$$= \begin{bmatrix} \sum\limits_{j=2}^{n}\sum\limits_{k=1}^{m} \sigma_{1j}^{(k)}\delta_{1j}^{(k)} & -\sum\limits_{k=1}^{m}\sigma_{12}^{(k)}\delta_{12}^{(k)} & \cdots & -\sum\limits_{k=1}^{m}\sigma_{1n}^{(k)}\delta_{1n}^{(k)} \\ -\sum\limits_{k=1}^{m}\sigma_{21}^{(k)}\delta_{21}^{(k)} & \sum\limits_{j=1,j\neq2}^{n}\sum\limits_{k=1}^{m}\sigma_{2j}^{(k)}\delta_{2j}^{(k)} & \cdots & -\sum\limits_{k=1}^{m}\sigma_{2n}^{(k)}\delta_{2n}^{(k)} \\ \vdots & \vdots & \cdots & \vdots \\ -\sum\limits_{k=1}^{m}\sigma_{n-1,1}^{(k)}\delta_{n-1,1}^{(k)} & -\sum\limits_{k=1}^{m}\sigma_{n-1,2}^{(k)}\delta_{n-1,2}^{(k)} & \cdots & \sum\limits_{j=1}^{n-1}\sum\limits_{k=1}^{m}\sigma_{n-1,j}^{(k)}\delta_{n-1,j}^{(k)} \end{bmatrix} \tag{4.15}$$

$$W_{n-1} = [\ln w_1,\ \ln w_2,\ \ldots,\ \ln w_{n-1}]^T \tag{4.16}$$

$$\overline{Y}_{n-1} = \begin{bmatrix} \sum\limits_{k=1}^{m} \sum\limits_{j=1}^{n} \sigma_{1j}^{(k)} \delta_{1j}^{(k)} \left(\ln c_{1j}^{(k)} - \ln c_{j1}^{(k)} \right) \\ \sum\limits_{k=1}^{m} \sum\limits_{j=1}^{n} \sigma_{2j}^{(k)} \delta_{2j}^{(k)} \left(\ln c_{2j}^{(k)} - \ln c_{j2}^{(k)} \right) \\ \vdots \\ \sum\limits_{k=1}^{m} \sum\limits_{j=1}^{n} \sigma_{n-1,j}^{(k)} \delta_{nj}^{(k)} \left(\ln c_{n-1,j}^{(k)} - \ln c_{n-1,1}^{(k)} \right) \end{bmatrix} \tag{4.17}$$

Because D_{n-1} is full rank, that is, $|D_{n-1}| \neq 0$, we have

$$W_{n-1} = D_{n-1}^{-1} Y_{n-1} \tag{4.18}$$

Thus,

$$w_i = \exp(W_i), i = 1, 2, \ldots, n-1 \tag{4.19}$$

and $w_n = 1$, and by normalizing the weighting vector, we have

$$w_i^* = \frac{\exp(W_i)}{\sum_{j=1}^{n-1} \exp(W_j) + 1}, i = 1, 2, \ldots, n-1 \tag{4.20}$$

$$w_i^* = \frac{1}{\sum_{j=1}^{n-1} \exp(W_j) + 1}, i = n \tag{4.21}$$

Thus, we get the following theorem:

Theorem 4.1 *Let* $w^* = (w_1^*, w_2^*, \ldots, w_n^*)^T$ *be the optimal solution to the model* (M-4.2), *and then*

$$w_i^* = \frac{\exp(W_i)}{\sum_{j=1}^{n-1} \exp(W_j) + 1}, i = 1, 2, \ldots, n-1 \tag{4.22}$$

$$w_i^* = \frac{1}{\sum_{j=1}^{n-1} \exp(W_j) + 1}, i = n \tag{4.23}$$

where W_i is determined by Eqs. (4.15)–(4.18).

Corollary 4.1 *If there is no* $c_{ij}^{(k)} = -$ *and there is no* $c_{ij}^{(k)} = 0$ *or 1, for any* $i, j \in N$ *and* $k \in M$, *then the optimal solution to the model* (M-4.2) *is*

$$w_i^* = \frac{\prod_{j=1}^{n}\prod_{k=1}^{m}\left(\frac{c_{ij}^{(k)}}{c_{ji}^{(k)}}\right)^{\frac{1}{nm}}}{\sum_{i=1}^{n}\prod_{j=1}^{n}\prod_{k=1}^{m}\left(\frac{c_{ij}^{(k)}}{c_{ji}^{(k)}}\right)^{\frac{1}{nm}}} \tag{4.24}$$

which denotes all the fuzzy reciprocal preference relations presented by multiple DMs with complete information. So, our model can deal with either complete or incomplete information.

Especially for a single complete fuzzy reciprocal preference relation, then

$$w_i^* = \frac{\prod_{j=1}^{n}\left(\frac{c_{ij}^{(k)}}{c_{ji}^{(k)}}\right)^{\frac{1}{n}}}{\sum_{i=1}^{n}\prod_{j=1}^{n}\left(\frac{c_{ij}^{(k)}}{c_{ji}^{(k)}}\right)^{\frac{1}{n}}} \tag{4.25}$$

which is same as described by Wang and Fan (2007) and Fedrizzi and Brunelli (2010). From the above analysis, we know that our model can be used to deal with incomplete or complete fuzzy reciprocal preference relations and single or group decision-making problems, while Wang and Fan (2007)'s method can only be used to deal with the complete fuzzy reciprocal preference relations. As a result, it has broad application prospects.

4.2   An Algorithm for Repairing the Inconsistency of an Incomplete Fuzzy Reciprocal Preference Relation

Similar with the algorithm for repairing the inconsistency of an incomplete fuzzy reciprocal preference relation in Sect. 3.2, we propose the following Algorithm 4.1 to repair the inconsistency of an incomplete fuzzy reciprocal preference relation.

Algorithm 4.1

Step 1. Let $C = (c_{ij})_{n \times n}$ be an initial incomplete fuzzy reciprocal preference relation. Using Theorem 1.4 to judge whether the incomplete fuzzy reciprocal preference relation is acceptable, if the incomplete fuzzy reciprocal preference relation is not acceptable, we return it to the expert to give a new fuzzy reciprocal preference relation; otherwise, go to Step 2.

Step 2. Use Eqs. (4.22)–(4.23) to derive the weight vector w for the incomplete fuzzy reciprocal preference relation.

Step 3. Use Eq. (1.13) to compute the consistency ratio of the incomplete fuzzy reciprocal preference relation. If FCR < 0.1, then go to Step 6. Otherwise, go to Step 4.

Step 4. Using Eq. (3.21) to compute the deviation between the comparison element c_{ij} and theoretical structure, obtain the maximum deviation to find the corresponding UFE (c_{ij}).

Step 5. Change the initial UFE (c_{ij}) into the new one c'_{ij}, where $c'_{ij} = $ round $(\frac{w_i}{w_i+w_j} \times 10) \times 10^{-1}$, and "round" is the usual round operation, and go to Step 2.

Step 6. Rank the alternatives according to the weight vector w.

Step 7. End.

Similar to Algorithm 3.1, we just set the UFE (c_{ij}) as $c'_{ij} = $ round$(\frac{w_i}{w_i+w_j} \times 10) \times 10^-$ [1]. It may not be the most reasonable value. Again, we look at the UFE (c_{ij}) as the unknown value, and C becomes C'; we use the LLSM to derive the weight vector w' for C', and then we can obtain the UFE (c_{ij}) by $c'_{ij} = $ round$(\frac{w'_i}{w'_i+w'_j} \times 10) \times 10^{-1}$. Further, if c'_{ij} can be the value in the interval [0, 1], we can set $c'_{ij} = \frac{w'_i}{w'_i+w'_j}$. Therefore, we propose the following Algorithm 4.2.

Algorithm 4.2

Step 1–Step 4 in Algorithm 4.1.

Step 5. Set the initial UFE (c_{ij}) as the unknown elements and C would be C'; go to Step 2 and compute the weights for C'.

Step 6. Rank the alternatives according to the weight vector w.

Step 7. End.

4.3 Numerical Examples

Example 4.1 For a decision-making problem, there are six decision alternatives x_i ($i = 1, 2, \ldots, 6$). The DM provides his/her preference over these six decision alternatives and gives an incomplete fuzzy reciprocal preference relation as follows (adapt from Xu (2004)):

$$
C = \begin{bmatrix}
0.5 & 0.4 & - & 0.3 & 0.8 & 0.3 \\
0.6 & 0.5 & 0.6 & 0.5 & - & 0.4 \\
- & 0.4 & 0.5 & 0.3 & 0.6 & - \\
0.7 & 0.5 & 0.7 & 0.5 & 0.4 & 0.8 \\
0.2 & - & 0.4 & 0.6 & 0.5 & 0.7 \\
0.7 & 0.6 & - & 0.2 & 0.3 & 0.5
\end{bmatrix}
$$

Step 1. By Theorem 1.4, we know that C is an acceptable incomplete fuzzy reciprocal preference relation.

Step 2. By Eqs. (4.15) and (4.17), we have (where $n = 6$)

$$
D_{n-1} = D_5 = \begin{bmatrix} 4 & -1 & 0 & -1 & -1 \\ -1 & 4 & -1 & -1 & 0 \\ 0 & -1 & 3 & -1 & -1 \\ -1 & -1 & -1 & 5 & -1 \\ -1 & 0 & -1 & -1 & 4 \end{bmatrix}
$$

$$
Y_{n-1} = Y_5 = \begin{bmatrix} \ln\dfrac{0.4}{0.6} + \ln\dfrac{0.3}{0.7} + \ln\dfrac{0.8}{0.2} + \ln\dfrac{0.3}{0.7} \\ \ln\dfrac{0.6}{0.4} + \ln\dfrac{0.6}{0.4} + \ln\dfrac{0.5}{0.5} + \ln\dfrac{0.4}{0.6} \\ \ln\dfrac{0.4}{0.6} + \ln\dfrac{0.3}{0.7} + \ln\dfrac{0.6}{0.4} \\ \ln\dfrac{0.7}{0.3} + \ln\dfrac{0.5}{0.5} + \ln\dfrac{0.7}{0.3} + \ln\dfrac{0.4}{0.6} + \ln\dfrac{0.8}{0.2} \\ \ln\dfrac{0.2}{0.8} + \ln\dfrac{0.4}{0.6} + \ln\dfrac{0.6}{0.4} + \ln\dfrac{0.7}{0.3} \end{bmatrix}
$$

Then, by Eqs. (4.18)–(4.21), we have

$$
W_{n-1} = W_5 = (0.0534, 0.2749, 0.0267, 0.6138, 0.0387)^T
$$

$$
w^* = \left(w_1^*, w_2^*, w_3^*, w_4^*, w_5^*, w_6^*\right)^T = (0.1448, 0.1807, 0.1410, 0.2536, 0.1427, 0.1373)^T
$$

Step 3. We use Eq. (1.13) to compute its consistency index, and we get FCR $= 0.1694 > 0.1$, so C is not an acceptable consistent preference relation.
Step 4.
   We set

$$
c'_{15} = \text{round}\left(\frac{w'_1}{w'_1 + w'_5} \times 10\right) \times 10^{-1} = 0.5, \, c'_{51} = \text{round}\left(\frac{w'_5}{w'_1 + w'_5} \times 10\right) \times 10^{-1}
$$

$$
= 0.5
$$

   Then,

$$
C = \begin{bmatrix} 0.5 & 0.4 & - & 0.3 & 0.5 & 0.3 \\ 0.6 & 0.5 & 0.6 & 0.5 & - & 0.4 \\ - & 0.4 & 0.5 & 0.3 & 0.6 & - \\ 0.7 & 0.5 & 0.7 & 0.5 & 0.4 & 0.8 \\ 0.5 & - & 0.4 & 0.6 & 0.5 & 0.7 \\ 0.7 & 0.6 & - & 0.2 & 0.3 & 0.5 \end{bmatrix}
$$

By Eqs. (4.18)–(4.21), we have

$$W_{n-1} = W_5 = (-0.2238, 0.2325, 0.1191, 0.6292, 0.3430)^T$$

$$w^* = \left(w_1^*, w_2^*, w_3^*, w_4^*, w_5^*, w_6^*\right)^T = (0.1070, 0.1688, 0.1507, 0.2511, 0.1886, 0.1338)^T$$

By Eq. (1.13), we get FCR $= 0.0869 > 0.1$, so C is an acceptable consistent preference relation.

By Algorithm 4.2, we have

Step 5. We set $c_{15} = c_{51} = -$, and we have

$$C' = \begin{bmatrix} 0.5 & 0.4 & - & 0.3 & - & 0.3 \\ 0.6 & 0.5 & 0.6 & 0.5 & - & 0.4 \\ - & 0.4 & 0.5 & 0.3 & 0.6 & - \\ 0.7 & 0.5 & 0.7 & 0.5 & 0.4 & 0.8 \\ - & - & 0.4 & 0.6 & 0.5 & 0.7 \\ 0.7 & 0.6 & - & 0.2 & 0.3 & 0.5 \end{bmatrix}$$

By Eqs. (4.18)–(4.21), we have

$$W_{n-1} = W_5 = (-0.4554, 0.1864, 0.1705, 0.6249, 0.5476)^T$$

$$w^* = \left(w_1^*, w_2^*, w_3^*, w_4^*, w_5^*, w_6^*\right)^T = (0.0832, 0.1581, 0.1556, 0.2451, 0.2268, 0.1321)^T$$

Then, by Eq. (1.13), we have

$$FCR = 0.0718 < 0.1$$

And

$$c_{15}' = \text{round}\left(\frac{w_1'}{w_1' + w_5'} \times 10\right) \times 10^{-1} = 0.3, \, c_{51}' = \text{round}\left(\frac{w_5'}{w_1' + w_5'} \times 10\right) \times 10^{-1}$$
$$= 0.7$$

By Eqs. (4.18)–(4.21), we have

$$W_{n-1} = W_5 = (-0.3993, 0.2066, 0.1756, 0.6386, 0.5289)^T$$

$$w^* = \left(w_1^*, w_2^*, w_3^*, w_4^*, w_5^*, w_6^*\right)^T = (0.0878, 0.1599, 0.1551, 0.2464, 0.2208, 0.1301)^T$$

$$FCR = 0.0719 < 0.1$$

Thus, C is of acceptable consistency.

Thus, the ranking of these six alternatives is

$$x_4 \succ x_5 \succ x_2 \succ x_3 \succ x_6 \succ x_1.$$

If we set

$$c'_{15} = \frac{w'_1}{w'_1 + w'_5} = 0.2684, c'_{51} = \frac{w'_5}{w'_1 + w'_5} = 0.7316,$$

then by Eqs. (4.18)–(4.21), we have

$$W_{n-1} = W_5 = (-0.4244, 0.2018, 0.1860, 0.6404, 0.5630)^T$$

$$w^* = (w_1^*, w_2^*, w_3^*, w_4^*, w_5^*, w_6^*)^T = (0.0846, 0.1582, 0.1557, 0.2453, 0.2270, 0.1293)^T$$

$$FCR = 0.0717 < 0.1$$

Thus, C is of acceptable consistency.

Thus, the ranking of these six alternatives is

$$x_4 \succ x_5 \succ x_2 \succ x_3 \succ x_6 \succ x_1.$$

Remark 4.1 We can see that when we look at the elements c_{15} and c_{51} as unknown, then the derived weights are very near the weights when $c'_{15} = \frac{w'_1}{w'_1 + w'_5} = 0.2684$, $c'_{51} = \frac{w'_5}{w'_1 + w'_5} = 0.7316$, and FCR are almost same. But when the value $c'_{15} = $ round $(\frac{w'_1}{w'_1 + w'_5} \times 10) \times 10^{-1} = 0.3$ and $c'_{51} = $ round$(\frac{w'_5}{w'_1 + w'_5} \times 10) \times 10^{-1} = 0.7$, the weights are slightly different. But, if we just compute c_{15} by the weights obtained from the original incomplete fuzzy reciprocal preference relation C using Algorithm 4.1, FCR is equal to 0.0869, which is larger than which is obtained in Algorithm 4.2. This also shows that it is more reasonable to set the UFE (c_{ij}) as the unknown element.

Example 4.2 Suppose that three DMs provide the following incomplete preference relations C_k ($k = 1, 2, 3$) on a set of three alternatives $X = \{x_1, x_2, x_3\}$:

$$C_1 = \begin{bmatrix} 0.5 & 0.5 & 0.6 \\ 0.5 & 0.5 & - \\ 0.4 & - & 0.6 \end{bmatrix}, C_2 = \begin{bmatrix} 0.5 & - & 0.6 \\ - & 0.5 & 0.6 \\ 0.4 & 0.4 & 0.6 \end{bmatrix}, C_2 = \begin{bmatrix} 0.5 & 0.5 & - \\ 0.5 & 0.5 & 0.6 \\ - & 0.4 & 0.6 \end{bmatrix}.$$

By Eqs. (4.15) and (4.17), we have (where $n = 3$)

$$D_{n-1} = D_2 = \begin{bmatrix} 4 & -2 \\ -2 & 4 \end{bmatrix}, Y_{n-2} = Y_2 = \begin{bmatrix} 2 \ln \frac{0.6}{0.4} \\ 2 \ln \frac{0.6}{0.4} \end{bmatrix}$$

Then, by Eqs. (4.18)–(4.21), we have

$$W_{n-1} = W_2 = (0.4055, 0.4055)^T$$
$$w^* = (0.375, 0.375, 0.25)^T$$

Then, by Eq. (1.13), we have

$$FCR_1 = FCR_2 = FCR_3 = 0 < 0.1$$

which means that all the three fuzzy reciprocal preference relations are perfectly multiplicative consistent and give the ranking of $x_1 \sim x_2 \succ x_3$, where the symbol "$\sim$" means "is equal to" and "$\succ$" means "is preferred to."

If we use Gong (2008)'s least square method to compute, we have

$$Q = \begin{bmatrix} 0.82 & -0.5 & -0.48 \\ -0.5 & 0.82 & -0.48 \\ -0.48 & -0.48 & 1.44 \end{bmatrix}$$

Because Q is a singular matrix, Q^{-1} does not exist; therefore, we cannot use Q^- $^1 e/e^T Q^{-1} e$ (Gong, 2008) to compute the priority vector. From above, we know that our method is robust.

Example 4.3 For a multi-attribute decision-making problem, there are four decision alternatives x_1, x_2, x_3, and x_4. The decision maker provides his/her preferences over these four decision alternatives and gives a fuzzy reciprocal preference relation as follows:

$$C = \begin{bmatrix} 0.5 & 0.7 & 0.6 & 0.8 \\ 0.3 & 0.5 & 0.4 & 0.6 \\ 0.4 & 0.6 & 0.5 & 0.7 \\ 0.2 & 0.4 & 0.3 & 0.5 \end{bmatrix}$$

By Eqs. (4.15) and (4.17), we have (where $n = 4$)

$$D_{n-1} = D_3 = \begin{bmatrix} 3 & -1 & -1 \\ -1 & 3 & -1 \\ -1 & -1 & 3 \end{bmatrix}, Y_{n-1} = Y_3 = \begin{bmatrix} \ln \dfrac{0.7}{0.3} + \ln \dfrac{0.6}{0.4} + \ln \dfrac{0.8}{0.2} \\ \ln \dfrac{0.3}{0.7} + \ln \dfrac{0.4}{0.6} + \ln \dfrac{0.6}{0.4} \\ \ln \dfrac{0.4}{0.6} + \ln \dfrac{0.6}{0.4} + \ln \dfrac{0.7}{0.3} \end{bmatrix}$$

Then, by Eqs. (4.18)–(4.21), we have

$$W_{n-1} = W_3 = (1.3195, 0.4479, 0.8716)^T$$

$$w^* = (0.4302, 0.1799, 0.2749, 0.1150)^T$$

Then, by Eq. (1.13), we have

$$FCR = 0.000897 < 0.1$$

Thus, C is of acceptable consistency and also gives the ranking of $x_1 \succ x_3 \succ x_2 \succ x_4$. Therefore, the most desirable alternative is x_1. If we use Eq. (4.25) to compute the weight vector, we will get the same result. Our weighting vector is approximate to Xu and Da (2005)'s least deviation method. And it also gets the same ranking. But you can see that Xu and Da (2005) used convergent iterative algorithm to derive the weighting vector, and the algorithm is so complicated, but our method is only to solve a series of equations, and it can be solved easily by the software of Matlab, Lingo, etc.

4.4   Summary

In this chapter, we have proposed the LLSM to priority for group decision-making with incomplete fuzzy reciprocal preference relations, which entries are not equal to 0 or 1. As we can see, our LLSM method and consistency test method can be used not only to derive the weighting vector for the incomplete fuzzy reciprocal preference relations, but also for the complete fuzzy reciprocal preference relations. Finally, some examples are illustrated; compared with the existing methods, our proposed approach has the following distinct characteristics.

Compared with Gong (2008)'s least square method, our method can be used to deal with the following two cases: (1) all the incomplete fuzzy reciprocal preference relations are perfectly multiplicative consistent and (2) at least one of the incomplete fuzzy reciprocal preference relations is not perfectly multiplicative consistent, while Gong's method can only do for the latter case.

The proposed method can deal with both the complete and incomplete fuzzy reciprocal preference relations, while Wang and Fan (2007) method is only suitable to deal with the complete fuzzy reciprocal preference relations. That is to say, Wang's method is only a special case of ours.

References

Fedrizzi, M., & Brunelli, M. (2010). On the priority vector associated with a reciprocal relation and a pairwise comparison matrix. *Soft Computing, 14*, 639–645.

Gong, Z. W. (2008). Least-square method to priority of the fuzzy preference relations with incomplete information. *International Journal of Approximate Reasoning, 47*(2), 258–264.

Saaty, T. L., & Vargas, L. G. (1984). Comparison of eigenvalue, logarithmic least squares and least squares methods in estimating ratios. *Mathematical Modeling, 5*(5), 309–324.

Wang, Y. M., & Fan, Z. P. (2007). Group decision analysis based on fuzzy preference relations: Logarithmic and geometric least squares methods. *Applied Mathematics and Computation, 194*, 108–119.

Xu, Z. S. (2004). Goal programming models for obtaining the priority vector of incomplete fuzzy preference relation. *International Journal of Approximate Reasoning, 36*(3), 261–270.

Xu, Z. S., & Da, Q. L. (2005). A least deviation method to obtain a priority vector of a fuzzy preference relation. *European Journal of Operational Research, 164*(1), 206–216.

Chapter 5
A Chi-Square Method

In Sect. 4.1, we have described the group decision-making problems with incomplete fuzzy reciprocal preference relations, where the relationship between the elements $c_{ij}^{(k)}$ and weights $w_i (i \in N)$ should satisfy Eq. (4.1). In the following, we propose another method called chi-square method.

5.1 Chi-Square Method for Priority from Group Incomplete Fuzzy Reciprocal Preference Relations

The following chi-square optimization model (M-5.1) is constructed (here, we assume that the DM's weight vector is $\lambda = (\lambda_1, \lambda_2, \ldots, \lambda_m)^T$):

$$
\min \quad F(w) = \sum_{k=1}^{m} \sum_{i=1}^{n} \sum_{j=1}^{n} \lambda_k \delta_{ij}^{(k)} \left[\frac{\left(c_{ij}^{(k)} - w_i / (w_i + w_j) \right)^2}{w_i / (w_i + w_j)} \right]
$$

(M-5.1)

$$
\text{s.t.} \begin{cases} \sum_{i=1}^{n} w_i = 1, \\ w_i \geq 0, \quad i \in N. \end{cases}
$$

$$
D_w = \left\{ w = (w_1, w_2, \ldots, w_n)^T \,\middle|\, \sum_{i=1}^{n} w_i = 1, \ w_i \geq 0, \quad i \in N \right\}.
$$

(5.1)

The idea is to minimize the overall deviation from Eq. (5.1). To solve this chi-square model (M-5.1), the following theorem is established:

Theorem 5.1 *$F(w)$ has a unique minimum point $w^* = (w_1, w_2, \ldots, w_n)^T \in D_w$, which is also the unique solution of the following system of equations in D_w:*

Y. Xu, *Deriving Priorities from Incomplete Fuzzy Reciprocal Preference Relations*, https://doi.org/10.1007/978-981-99-3169-9_5

$$\sum_{j=1}^{n}\sum_{k=1}^{m} \lambda_k \delta_{ji}^{(k)} c_{ji}^{2(k)} \frac{w_i}{w_j} = \sum_{j=1}^{n}\sum_{k=1}^{m} \lambda_k \delta_{ij}^{(k)} c_{ij}^{2(k)} \frac{w_j}{w_i} \tag{5.2}$$

Proof As D_w is a bounded vector space and $F(w)$ is continuous function in D_w, for $F(w) \geq 0$ and $w \in D_w$, $F(w)$ therefore has an infimum, namely there exists $w \in D_w$ such that function $F(w)$ reaches its minimum value.

In order to obtain the optimal priority vector $w^* = (w_1, w_2, \ldots, w_n)^T \in D_w$, the following Lagrangian function is constructed:

$$L(w, \rho) = F(w) + \rho \left(\sum_{i=1}^{n} w_i - 1 \right) \tag{5.3}$$

where ρ is the Lagrange multiplier. By setting the partial derivatives with respect to w_i to be zero, we obtain the following set of equations:

$$\frac{1}{w_i} \sum_{j=1}^{n}\sum_{k=1}^{m} \lambda_k \left(\delta_{ji}^{(k)} c_{ji}^{2(k)} \frac{w_i}{w_j} - \delta_{ij}^{(k)} c_{ij}^{2(k)} \frac{w_j}{w_i} \right) + \sum_{j=1}^{n}\sum_{k=1}^{m} \lambda_k \frac{w_j}{(w_i + w_j)^2}$$
$$\times \left(\delta_{ij}^{(k)} - \delta_{ji}^{(k)} \right) + \rho = 0, i \in N \tag{5.4}$$

Given that $\delta_{ij}^{(k)} = \delta_{ji}^{(k)}$, Eq. (5.4) can be further simplified as follows:

$$\frac{1}{w_i} \sum_{j=1}^{n}\sum_{k=1}^{m} \lambda_k \left(\delta_{ji}^{(k)} c_{ji}^{2(k)} \frac{w_i}{w_j} - \delta_{ij}^{(k)} c_{ij}^{2(k)} \frac{w_j}{w_i} \right) + \rho = 0, i \in N \tag{5.5}$$

which is equivalent to

$$\sum_{j=1}^{n}\sum_{k=1}^{m} \lambda_k \left(\delta_{ji}^{(k)} c_{ji}^{2(k)} \frac{w_i}{w_j} - \delta_{ij}^{(k)} c_{ij}^{2(k)} \frac{w_j}{w_i} \right) + \rho w_i = 0, i \in N \tag{5.6}$$

Summing up Eq. (5.6) with respect to w_i, $i \in N$, we have

$$\sum_{i=1}^{n}\sum_{j=1}^{n}\sum_{k=1}^{m} \lambda_k \left(\delta_{ji}^{(k)} c_{ji}^{2(k)} \frac{w_i}{w_j} - \delta_{ij}^{(k)} c_{ij}^{2(k)} \frac{w_j}{w_i} \right) + \rho \sum_{i=1}^{n} w_i = 0 \tag{5.7}$$

Since $\sum_{i=1}^{n}\sum_{j=1}^{n}\sum_{k=1}^{m} \lambda_k \left(\delta_{ji}^{(k)} c_{ji}^{2(k)} \frac{w_i}{w_j} - \delta_{ij}^{(k)} c_{ij}^{2(k)} \frac{w_j}{w_i} \right) \equiv 0$ and $\sum_{i=1}^{n} w_i = 1$, we have $\rho = 0$. Plugging $\rho = 0$ into Eq. (5.6), one has

$$\sum_{j=1}^{n}\sum_{k=1}^{m}\lambda_k\left(\delta_{ji}^{(k)}c_{ji}^{2(k)}\frac{w_i}{w_j}-\delta_{ij}^{(k)}c_{ij}^{2(k)}\frac{w_j}{w_i}\right)=0, i\in N \tag{5.8}$$

That is,

$$\sum_{j=1}^{n}\sum_{k=1}^{m}\lambda_k\delta_{ji}^{(k)}c_{ji}^{2(k)}\frac{w_i}{w_j}=\sum_{j=1}^{n}\sum_{k=1}^{m}\lambda_k\delta_{ij}^{(k)}c_{ij}^{2(k)}\frac{w_j}{w_i}, i\in N \tag{5.9}$$

It is clear that the minimum point w^* is a solution to Eq. (5.2); if the solution is unique in D_w, w^* can be uniquely determined. The uniqueness is proved by contradiction as follows:

Assume that $v=(v_1, v_2, \ldots, v_n)^T\in D_w$ and $w=(w_1, w_2, \ldots, w_n)^T\in D_w$ are two solutions to Eq. (5.2). Let $u_i=w_i/v_i$, $i\in N$, and $u_l=\max_{i\in N}\{u_i\}$. If there exists $j\in N$ such that $u_j<u_l$, then we have

$$\sum_{j=1}^{n}\sum_{k=1}^{m}\lambda_k\delta_{lj}^{(k)}c_{lj}^{2(k)}\frac{v_j}{v_l}>\sum_{j=1}^{n}\sum_{k=1}^{m}\lambda_k\delta_{lj}^{(k)}c_{lj}^{2(k)}\frac{v_j}{v_l}\cdot\frac{u_j}{u_l}=\sum_{j=1}^{n}\sum_{k=1}^{m}\lambda_k\delta_{lj}^{(k)}c_{lj}^{2(k)}\frac{w_j}{w_l} \tag{5.10}$$

$$\sum_{j=1}^{n}\sum_{k=1}^{m}\lambda_k\delta_{jl}^{(k)}c_{jl}^{2(k)}\frac{v_l}{v_j}<\sum_{j=1}^{n}\sum_{k=1}^{m}\lambda_k\delta_{jl}^{(k)}c_{jl}^{2(k)}\frac{v_l}{v_j}\cdot\frac{u_l}{u_j}=\sum_{j=1}^{n}\sum_{k=1}^{m}\lambda_k\delta_{jl}^{(k)}c_{jl}^{2(k)}\frac{w_l}{w_j} \tag{5.11}$$

According to Eqs. (5.2), (5.10), and (5.11), it can be deduced that

$$\sum_{j=1}^{n}\sum_{k=1}^{m}\lambda_k\delta_{lj}^{(k)}c_{lj}^{2(k)}\frac{w_j}{w_l}<\sum_{j=1}^{n}\sum_{k=1}^{m}\lambda_k\delta_{jl}^{(k)}c_{jl}^{2(k)}\frac{w_l}{w_j} \tag{5.12}$$

which contradicts Eq. (5.2), Thus, $u_j<u_l$ cannot hold. Therefore, for all $j\in N$, $u_j=u_l$, namely, $w_1/v_1=w_2/v_2=\ldots=w_n/v_n$. Due to the fact that $\sum_{i=1}^{n}v_i=1$ and $\sum_{i=1}^{n}w_i=1$, we have $w_i\equiv v_i$, $\forall i\in N$. This proves the uniqueness of the solution to Eq. (5.2). □

To solve Eq. (5.2), we put forward a simple convergent iterative algorithm as follows:

Algorithm 5.1

Let $C_k=(c_{ij}^{(k)})_{n\times n}$ $(k\in M)$ be the initial incomplete fuzzy reciprocal preference relations provided by the DMs.

Step 1. Use Theorem 1.4 to judge whether an incomplete fuzzy reciprocal preference relation C_k $(k\in M)$ given by the DM e_k is acceptable or not. If not, it is returned to expert e_k for an updated reciprocal preference relation; otherwise, go to Step 2.

Step 2. Initiate the iteration by giving an initial priority vector $w(0) = (w_1(0), w_2(0), \ldots, w_n(0))^T$ and specifying an error parameter ε $(0 < \varepsilon < 1)$, for example, $\varepsilon = 0.0001$, and setting $L = 0$.

Step 3. Calculate:

$$\eta_i(W(L)) = \sum_{j=1}^{n} \sum_{k=1}^{m} \lambda_k \delta_{ji}^{(k)} c_{ji}^{2(k)} \frac{w_i}{w_j} - \sum_{j=1}^{n} \sum_{k=1}^{m} \lambda_k \delta_{ij}^{(k)} c_{ij}^{2(k)} \frac{w_j}{w_i}, i \in N \quad (5.13)$$

If $|\eta_i(w(L)| \le \varepsilon$ holds for all $i \in N$, then $w^* = w(L)$ and stop; otherwise, continue to Step 4.

Step 4. Determine p such that $|\eta_p(w(L)| = \max_{i \in N}\{|\eta_i(w(L)|\}$ and compute:

$$T(L) = \sqrt{\frac{\sum_{j=1, j \ne p}^{n} \sum_{k=1}^{m} \lambda_k \delta_{pj}^{(k)} c_{pj}^{2(k)} \frac{w_j(L)}{w_p(L)}}{\sum_{j=1, j \ne p}^{n} \sum_{k=1}^{m} \lambda_k \delta_{jp}^{(k)} c_{jp}^{2(k)} \frac{w_p(L)}{w_j(L)}}} \quad (5.14)$$

$$f_i(L) = \begin{cases} T(L)w_p(L), & i = p, \\ w_i(L), & i \ne p, \end{cases} \quad (5.15)$$

$$w_i(L+1) = f_i(L) / \sum_{i=1}^{n} f_i(L), i \in N \quad (5.16)$$

Step 5. Let $L = L + 1$ and go to *Step 3*.

For Algorithm 5.1, we can establish the following theorem:

Theorem 5.2 *Algorithm 5.1 is convergent for any $\varepsilon > 0$.*

Proof We shall examine how $F(w)$ changes, when $w(L)$ progresses to $w(L + 1)$. Suppose that $t > 0$ and $S(t) = F(f(L)) = F(w_1(L), \ldots, w_{p-1}(L), tw_p(L), w_{p+1}(L), \ldots, w_n(L))$.

Then, we have

$$S(t) = \sum_{j=1, j \ne p}^{n} \sum_{k=1}^{m} \lambda_k \delta_{pj}^{(k)} \left[\left(c_{pj}^{(k)} - \frac{tw_p(L)}{tw_p(L) + w_j(L)} \right)^2 \right] \frac{tw_p(L) + w_j(L)}{tw_p(L)}$$

$$+ \sum_{i=1, i \ne p}^{n} \sum_{k=1}^{m} \lambda_k \delta_{ip}^{(k)} \left[\left(c_{ip}^{(k)} - \frac{w_i(L)}{w_i(L) + tw_p(L)} \right)^2 \right] \frac{w_i(L) + tw_p(L)}{w_i(L)}$$

$$+ \sum_{i=1, i \ne p}^{n} \sum_{j=1, j \ne p}^{n} \sum_{k=1}^{m} \lambda_k \delta_{ij}^{(k)} \left[\left(c_{ij}^{(k)} - \frac{w_i(L)}{w_i(L) + w_j(L)} \right)^2 \right] \frac{w_i(L) + w_j(L)}{w_i(L)} \quad (5.17)$$

which is equivalent to

$$S(t) = \sum_{j=1, j\neq p}^{n} \sum_{k=1}^{m} \lambda_k \delta_{pj}^{(k)} c_{pj}^{2(k)} \frac{w_j(L)}{w_p(L)} \cdot \frac{1}{t} + \sum_{j=1, j\neq p}^{n} \sum_{k=1}^{m} \lambda_k \delta_{jp}^{(k)} c_{jp}^{2(k)} \frac{w_p(L)}{w_j(L)} \cdot t$$

$$+ \sum_{j=1, j\neq p}^{n} \sum_{k=1}^{m} \lambda_k \left[\delta_{jp}^{(k)} c_{jp}^{2(k)} + \delta_{pj}^{(k)} c_{pj}^{2(k)} - 2\left(\delta_{jp}^{(k)} c_{jp}^{(k)} + \delta_{pj}^{(k)} c_{pj}^{(k)} \right) \right]$$

$$+ \sum_{j=1, j\neq p}^{n} \sum_{k=1}^{m} \lambda_k \left(\delta_{jp}^{(k)} \frac{t w_p(L)}{t w_p(L) + w_j(L)} + \delta_{pj}^{(k)} \frac{w_j(L)}{t w_p(L) + w_j(L)} \right)$$

$$+ \sum_{i=1, i\neq p}^{n} \sum_{j=1, j\neq p}^{n} \sum_{k=1}^{m} \lambda_k \delta_{ij}^{(k)} \left[\left(c_{ij}^{(k)} - \frac{w_i(L)}{w_i(L) + w_j(L)} \right)^2 \right] \frac{w_i(L) + w_j(L)}{w_i(L)} \quad (5.18)$$

Let

$$q_1 = \sum_{j=1, j\neq p}^{n} \sum_{k=1}^{m} \lambda_k \delta_{pj}^{(k)} c_{pj}^{2(k)} \frac{w_j(L)}{w_p(L)} \quad (5.19)$$

$$q_2 = \sum_{j=1, j\neq p}^{n} \sum_{k=1}^{m} \lambda_k \delta_{jp}^{(k)} c_{jp}^{2(k)} \frac{w_p(L)}{w_j(L)} \quad (5.20)$$

$$q_3 = \sum_{j=1, j\neq p}^{n} \sum_{k=1}^{m} \lambda_k \left[\delta_{jp}^{(k)} c_{jp}^{2(k)} + \delta_{pj}^{(k)} c_{pj}^{2(k)} - 2\left(\delta_{jp}^{(k)} c_{jp}^{(k)} + \delta_{pj}^{(k)} c_{pj}^{(k)} \right) \right]$$

$$+ \sum_{j=1, j\neq p}^{n} \sum_{k=1}^{m} \lambda_k \left(\delta_{jp}^{(k)} \frac{t w_p(L)}{t w_p(L) + w_j(L)} + \delta_{pj}^{(k)} \frac{w_j(L)}{t w_p(L) + w_j(L)} \right)$$

$$+ \sum_{i=1, i\neq p}^{n} \sum_{j=1, j\neq p}^{n} \sum_{k=1}^{m} \lambda_k \delta_{ij}^{(k)} \left[\left(c_{ij}^{(k)} - \frac{w_i(L)}{w_i(L) + w_j(L)} \right)^2 \right] \frac{w_i(L) + w_j(L)}{w_i(L)} \quad (5.21)$$

Since $\delta_{ij}^{(k)} = \delta_{ji}^{(k)}$, the second double summation term in Eq. (5.21) can be rewritten as

$$\sum_{j=1, j\neq p}^{n} \sum_{k=1}^{m} \lambda_k \left(\delta_{jp}^{(k)} \frac{t w_p(L)}{t w_p(L) + w_j(L)} + \delta_{pj}^{(k)} \frac{w_j(L)}{t w_p(L) + w_j(L)} \right)$$

$$= \begin{cases} (n-1) & \text{if } \delta_{jp}^{(k)} = \delta_{pj}^{(k)} = 1 \\ 0 & \text{if } \delta_{jp}^{(k)} = \delta_{pj}^{(k)} = 0 \end{cases} \quad (5.22)$$

Therefore, q_3 can be further simplified as

$$q_3 = \sum_{j=1,j\neq p}^{n} \sum_{k=1}^{m} \lambda_k \left[\delta_{jp}^{(k)} c_{jp}^{2(k)} + \delta_{pj}^{(k)} c_{pj}^{2(k)} - 2\left(\delta_{jp}^{(k)} c_{jp}^{(k)} + \delta_{pj}^{(k)} c_{pj}^{(k)} \right) \right]$$

$$+ \sum_{i=1,i\neq p}^{n} \sum_{j=1,j\neq p}^{n} \sum_{k=1}^{m} \lambda_k \delta_{ij}^{(k)} \left[\left(c_{ij}^{(k)} - \frac{w_i(L)}{w_i(L)+w_j(L)} \right)^2 \right] \frac{w_i(L)+w_j(L)}{w_i(L)}$$

$$+ \begin{cases} (n-1) & \text{if } \delta_{jp}^{(k)} = \delta_{pj}^{(k)} = 1, \\ 0 & \text{if } \delta_{jp}^{(k)} = \delta_{pj}^{(k)} = 0, \end{cases} \tag{5.23}$$

This indicates that q_3 is independent of t. Then, Eq. (5.18) can be equivalently expressed as

$$S(t) = q_1/t + q_2 \cdot t + q_3 \tag{5.24}$$

By setting $\frac{dS(t)}{dt}$ to be zero, we have

$$t^* = \sqrt{q_1/q_2} = \sqrt{\frac{\sum_{j=1,j\neq p}^{n} \sum_{k=1}^{m} \lambda_k \delta_{pj}^{(k)} c_{pj}^{2(k)} \frac{w_j(L)}{w_p(L)}}{\sum_{j=1,j\neq p}^{n} \sum_{k=1}^{m} \lambda_k \delta_{jp}^{(k)} c_{jp}^{2(k)} \frac{w_p(L)}{w_j(L)}}} \tag{5.25}$$

$$S(t^*) = 2\sqrt{q_1 q_2} + q_3 \tag{5.26}$$

where t^* stands for the minimum point, and $S(t^*)$ gives the minimum value of $S(t)$. If $t^* = 1$, Eq. (5.25) is equivalent to

$$\sum_{j=1,j\neq p}^{n} \sum_{k=1}^{m} \lambda_k \delta_{pj}^{(k)} c_{pj}^{2(k)} \frac{w_j(L)}{w_p(L)} = \sum_{j=1,j\neq p}^{n} \sum_{k=1}^{m} \lambda_k \delta_{jp}^{(k)} c_{jp}^{2(k)} \frac{w_p(L)}{w_j(L)} \tag{5.27}$$

which also holds for $j = p$; therefore, we have

$$\sum_{j=1}^{n} \sum_{k=1}^{m} \lambda_k \delta_{pj}^{(k)} c_{pj}^{2(k)} \frac{w_j(L)}{w_p(L)} = \sum_{j=1}^{n} \sum_{k=1}^{m} \lambda_k \delta_{jp}^{(k)} c_{jp}^{2(k)} \frac{w_p(L)}{w_j(L)} \tag{5.28}$$

That is,

$$\eta_p(W(L)) = \sum_{j=1}^{n} \sum_{k=1}^{m} \lambda_k \delta_{jp}^{(k)} c_{jp}^{2(k)} \frac{w_p(L)}{w_j(L)} - \sum_{j=1}^{n} \sum_{k=1}^{m} \lambda_k \delta_{pj}^{(k)} c_{pj}^{2(k)} \frac{w_j(L)}{w_p(L)} = 0.$$

By the definition of p in Step 3, we have $|\eta_p(w(L)| = 0$. Since p is the subscript such that $|\eta_i(w(L)|$ is maximized, we thus have $|\eta_i(w(L)| = 0$ for all $i \in N$. Therefore, the algorithm terminates and $w^* = w(L)$. □

If $t^* \neq 1$, then

$$F(w(L)) - F(f(L)) = S(1) - S(t^*) = q_1 + q_2 - 2\sqrt{q_1 q_2}$$
$$= \left(\sqrt{q_1} - \sqrt{q_2}\right)^2 > 0 \tag{5.29}$$

Since $F(w)$ is a homogenous function, $F(f(L) = F(w(L + 1))$. Inequality (5.29) shows that $F(w(L + 1)) < F(w(L))$, for any $L \geq 0$. Therefore, $F(w(L))$ is a monotonically decreasing sequence with an infimum in D_w and, hence, convergent.

5.2 A Method for Repairing Inconsistency of Incomplete Fuzzy Reciprocal Preference Relations

Algorithm 5.2

Let $C = (c_{ij})_{n \times n}$ be an incomplete fuzzy reciprocal preference relation given by the DM.

Step 1. Using Theorem 1.4 to judge whether the incomplete fuzzy reciprocal preference relation is acceptable, if the incomplete fuzzy reciprocal preference relation is not acceptable, we return it to the expert to give a new fuzzy reciprocal preference relation; otherwise, go to Step 2.

Step 2. Use the CSM algorithm in Sect. 5.1 to obtain the priority vector $w = (w_1, w_2, \ldots, w_n)^T$.

Step 3. Determine the consistency ratio of the incomplete fuzzy reciprocal preference relation as per Eq. (1.13); if FCR < 0.1, go to Step 5; otherwise, go to Step 3.

Step 4. Compute deviations d_{ij}'s by using Eq. (3.21) and identify the maximum deviation to find the corresponding UFEs (c_{ij}).

Step 5. Update the UFEs (c_{ij}) with c'_{ij}, where $c'_{ij} = \text{round}(\frac{w_i}{w_i + w_j} \times 10) \times 10^{-1}$, and go to Step 1.

Step 6. Rank the alternatives according to the priority vector w^*.

Step 7. End.

Similar as in Sect. 3.2, the UFEs (c_{ij}) should not be set directly by $c'_{ij} = \text{round}(\frac{w_i}{w_i + w_j} \times 10) \times 10^{-1}$ where the weight vector is generated from the original incomplete fuzzy reciprocal preference relation. We could look at them as unknown elements. Thus, we have the following Algorithm 5.3:

Algorithm 5.3
Step 1–Step 4 in Algorithm 5.2.
Step 5. Set the UFEs (c_{ij}) as the unknown elements and C would be C'; go to Step 1 and compute the weights for C'.
Step 6. Rank the alternatives according to the weight vector w.
Step 7. End.

5.3   Illustrative Examples

In this section, four numerical examples are examined to demonstrate the applications and advantages of the proposed CSM framework. Example 5.1 is a GDM problem with incomplete fuzzy reciprocal preference relations, and a comparative analysis is conducted between CSM and three existing methods. Example 5.2 is a single incomplete fuzzy reciprocal preference relation with unacceptable consistency, and Algorithm 5.2 is utilized to repair it until its consistency becomes acceptable. Example 5.3 considers a single incomplete fuzzy reciprocal preference relation with acceptable consistency. The purpose is to compare the result derived from CSM with those from EM, NRAM, GPM, LSM, and LLSM on three performance evaluation criteria: FCR, MAD, and MD. Example 5.4 discusses a GDM problem with incomplete fuzzy reciprocal preference relations with a purpose to show the advantages of CSM.

Example 5.1 For a GDM problem with four decision alternatives x_i ($i = 1, 2, 3, 4$) and three DMs e_k ($k = 1, 2, 3$), the DMs provide their preferences over the four decision alternatives as three incomplete fuzzy reciprocal preference relations (Xu, 2004):

$$C_1 = \begin{bmatrix} 0.5 & 0.6 & - & 0.7 \\ 0.4 & 0.5 & 0.2 & 0.8 \\ - & 0.8 & 0.5 & 0.4 \\ 0.3 & 0.2 & 0.6 & 0.5 \end{bmatrix}, C_2 = \begin{bmatrix} 0.5 & 0.8 & 0.4 & - \\ 0.2 & 0.5 & 0.3 & 0.6 \\ 0.6 & 0.7 & 0.5 & 0.3 \\ - & 0.4 & 0.7 & 0.5 \end{bmatrix},$$

$$C_3 = \begin{bmatrix} 0.5 & 0.3 & 0.4 & 0.6 \\ 0.7 & 0.5 & - & 0.5 \\ 0.6 & - & 0.5 & 0.7 \\ 0.4 & 0.5 & 0.3 & 0.5 \end{bmatrix}.$$

Xu (2004) employed goal programming (GP) models to derive a priority vector $w^* = (0.265, 0.236, 0.276, 0.223)^T$ from the aforesaid three incomplete fuzzy reciprocal preference relations. The research leads to a final ranking, $x_3 \succ x_1 \succ x_2 \succ x_4$, which is the same as the ranking generated by the LLSM (Xu et al., 2013) but slightly differs from the one obtained by the least square method (LSM) (Gong,

2008) with the order between x_2 and x_4 being reversed. We now examine the problem using the CSM. In order to offer a fair comparison with Xu (2004)'s method, we also set $\lambda_1 = \lambda_2 = \lambda_3 = 1/3$.

Step 1. According to Theorem 1.4, we know that C_k ($k = 1, 2, 3$) can all be completed by known elements.

Step 2. Given an initial priority vector $w(0) = (0.25, 0.25, 0.25, 0.25)^T$, specify the parameter $\varepsilon = 0.1$, and let $L = 0$.

Step 3. Calculate $\eta_i(w(0))$, and we have

$$|\eta_1(w(0))| = 0.2 > \varepsilon, \ |\eta_2(w(0))| = 0.2 > \varepsilon,$$

$$|\eta_3(w(0))| = 0.4 > \varepsilon, \ |\eta_4(w(0))| = 0.4 > \varepsilon.$$

As $|\eta_i(w(0)| > \varepsilon$ holds for all $i = 1, 2, 3, 4$, we continue to *Step* 4.

Step 4. Determine p such that $|\eta_p(w(L)| = \max_{i \in N}\{|\eta_i(w(L)|\}$; we can set $p = 3$, and compute $T(0), f(0)$, and $w(1)$:

$$T(0) = 1.3650, \quad f(0) = (0.2500, 0.2500, 0.3413, 0.2500)^T,$$

$$w(1) = (0.2291, 0.2291, 0.3127, 0.2291)^T.$$

Step 5. Let $L = L + 1 = 1$ and go to Step 3.

The computation processes are detailed in Table 5.1. It is clear that iterations terminate at $L = 3$, when $|\eta_1| = 0.0296 < 0.1$, $|\eta_2| = 0.0072 < 0.1$, $|\eta_3| = 0.0227 < 0.1$, and $|\eta_4| = 2.6357 \times 10^{-4} < 0.1$, indicating that the derived priority vector has reached an acceptable level of ε. The optimal priority vector is thus found to be $w^* = (0.2897, 0.2197, 0.3, 0.2007)^T$, resulting in a ranking of the four alternatives $x_3 \succ x_1 \succ x_2 \succ x_4$.

Remark 5.1 Computation results in Table 5.1 demonstrate that $F(w(L))$ decreases in iteration step L. However, for $|\eta_i(w(L)|$, this monotonicity does not hold any more and there may have ups and downs when L increases, but eventually $|\eta_i(w(L)|$ will decrease to a value below the threshold ε as ascertained by Theorem 5.2. As three of the four aforesaid methods derive an identical ranking with the other one yielding a slightly different order, this result demonstrates the robustness and credibility of the proposed CSM framework. To further compare the performances with the other three methods in fitting the three incomplete fuzzy reciprocal preference relations, the following evaluation criteria are introduced:

Maximum deviation (MD) for incomplete fuzzy reciprocal preference relations:

$$\text{MD} = \max_{i,j,k} \left\{ \delta_{ij}^{(k)} \left(\frac{c_{ij}}{c_{ji}} \frac{w_j}{w_i} + \frac{c_{ji}}{c_{ij}} \frac{w_i}{w_j} - 2 \right) \middle| i, j \in N, k \in M \right\} \quad (5.30)$$

Table 5.1 The iterative processes for Example 5.1

Iterative steps	$|\eta_l(w(L))|$				$w(L)$				
L	$|\eta_1|$	$|\eta_2|$	$|\eta_3|$	$|\eta_4|$	w_1	w_2	w_3	w_4	$F(w)$
0	0.2	0.2	0.4	0.4	0.25	0.25	0.25	0.25	0.7067
1	0.3031	0.0835	1.156×10^{-4}	0.2197	0.2291	0.2291	0.3127	0.2291	0.6449
2	6.197×10^{-5}	0.0571	0.0792	0.1362	0.2744	0.2256	0.2943	0.2156	0.6086
3	0.0296	0.0072	0.0227	2.6357×10^{-4}	0.2797	0.2197	0.3000	0.2007	0.6024

Table 5.2 Performance comparisons for Example 5.1

Methods	w^*	Ranking	MD	MAD
CSM	$(0.2797, 0.2197, 0.3000, 0.2007)^T$	$x_3 \succ x_1 \succ x_2 \succ x_4$	1.9277	0.2992
LSM (Gong, 2008)	$(0.2822, 0.1968, 0.3202, 0.2009)^T$	$x_3 \succ x_1 \succ x_4 \succ x_2$	2.3282	0.3145
GPM (Xu, 2004)	$(0.265, 0.236, 0.276, 0.223)^T$	$x_3 \succ x_1 \succ x_2 \succ x_4$	2.0442	0.2858
LLSM (Xu et al., 2013)	$(0.2806, 0.2105, 0.3189, 0.1900)^T$	$x_3 \succ x_1 \succ x_2 \succ x_4$	2.1717	0.3266

Maximum absolute deviation (MAD) for incomplete fuzzy reciprocal preference relations:

$$\mathrm{MAD} = \max_{i,j,k} \left\{ \delta_{ij}^{(k)} \left| c_{ij}^{(k)} - \frac{w_i}{w_i + w_j} \right| \middle| i,j \in N, \ k \in M \right\}. \tag{5.31}$$

where $\delta_{ij}^{(k)}$ is defined by Eq. (1.10). $d_{ij}^{(k)} = c_{ij}^{(k)} - w_i/(w_i + w_j)$ is the consistency deviation for $c_{ij}^{(k)}$ in the incomplete fuzzy reciprocal preference relation $C_k = (c_{ij}^{(k)})_{n \times n}$. If the priority vector $w = (w_1, \ldots, w_n)^T$ is able to precisely characterize the reciprocal preference relation C_k, then $|d_{ij}^{(k)}| \equiv 0$; otherwise, $|d_{ij}^{(k)}| > 0$.

Table 5.2 indicates that CSM results in an identical ranking as GPM and LLSM while the ranking derived by LSM is slightly different. CSM has a comparable MAD as GPM, which is smaller than both LSM and LLSM. In terms of MD, CSM outperforms all the other three methods as it yields the smallest deviation. This partly shows the advantage of the CSM.

Remark 5.2 To facilitate a comparative study with GPM, LSM, and LLSM, the weights of three reciprocal preference relations were set to be equal ($\lambda_1 = \lambda_2 = \lambda_3 = 1/3$). However, CSM allows an analyst to set different weights as per the practical situation, to properly reflect different experts' varying influences in the GDM problem at hand. It is worth noting that if $\delta_{ij} = 1$, for all $i, j \in N$, then the proposed CSM can still be utilized to derive a priority vector from reciprocal preference relations. This means that CSM can be used for both complete and incomplete fuzzy reciprocal preference relations. In addition, by setting $\lambda_1 = 1$ and $\lambda_k = 0$, for $k = 2, \ldots, m$, the CSM can be conveniently applied to derive a priority vector from a single incomplete fuzzy reciprocal preference relation. This allows CSM to be used for a single expert's decision-making problems in Examples 5.2 and 5.3.

Furthermore, by using Algorithm 5.1, we can get the values of L, w, and $F(w)$ and the ranking of alternatives for different ε's as listed in Table 5.3.

Example 5.2 Consider a single DM's decision problem with six alternatives x_i ($i = 1, 2, \ldots, 6$). The DM provides his/her preferences over the six decision

Table 5.3 The values of L, w, and $F(w)$ and ranking order for different ε in Example 5.1

ε	L	w	Ranking	$F(w)$	$|\eta_1|$	$|\eta_2|$	$|\eta_3|$	$|\eta_4|$
10^{-1}	3	$(0.2797, 0.2197, 0.3000, 0.2007)^T$	$x_3 \succ x_1 \succ x_2 \succ x_4$	0.6024	0.0001	0.0728	0.0868	0.0141
10^{-2}	15	$(0.2753, 0.2204, 0.3032, 0.2011)^T$	$x_3 \succ x_1 \succ x_2 \succ x_4$	0.6020	0.0031	0	0.0083	0.0052
10^{-3}	24	$(0.2746, 0.2201, 0.3041, 0.2012)^T$	$x_3 \succ x_1 \succ x_2 \succ x_4$	0.6019	3.6858×10^{-4}	0	9.8063×10^{-4}	6.1205×10^{-4}
10^{-4}	34	$(0.2745, 0.2201, 0.3043, 0.2012)^T$	$x_3 \succ x_1 \succ x_2 \succ x_4$	0.6019	5.9215×10^{-5}	2.6310×10^{-5}	8.5525×10^{-5}	0
10^{-5}	44	$(0.2746, 0.2201, 0.3041, 0.2012)^T$	$x_3 \succ x_1 \succ x_2 \succ x_4$	0.6019	1.1102×10^{-16}	6.4088×10^{-6}	8.2368×10^{-6}	1.8281×10^{-6}
10^{-6}	53	$(0.2746, 0.2201, 0.3041, 0.2012)^T$	$x_3 \succ x_1 \succ x_2 \succ x_4$	0.6019	1.1102×10^{-16}	6.4088×10^{-6}	8.2368×10^{-6}	1.8281×10^{-6}

alternatives, as an incomplete fuzzy reciprocal preference relation which is shown below (adapted from (Xu, 2005)):

$$C = \begin{bmatrix} 0.5 & - & - & 0.3 & 0.8 & 0.3 \\ - & 0.5 & - & - & - & - \\ - & - & 0.5 & - & - & - \\ 0.7 & - & - & 0.5 & 0.4 & 0.8 \\ 0.2 & - & - & 0.6 & 0.5 & 0.7 \\ 0.7 & - & - & 0.2 & 0.3 & 0.5 \end{bmatrix}$$

Step 1. According to Theorem 1.4, it is easy to tell that C cannot be completed as no non-diagonal elements are furnished in the second or third row (column) of C. Therefore, the initial judgment matrix has to be returned to the DM for an update, resulting in the following incomplete fuzzy reciprocal preference relation:

$$C = \begin{bmatrix} 0.5 & 0.3 & - & 0.3 & 0.8 & 0.3 \\ 0.7 & 0.5 & 0.7 & - & 0.6 & - \\ - & 0.3 & 0.5 & 0.4 & - & - \\ 0.7 & - & 0.6 & 0.5 & 0.4 & 0.8 \\ 0.2 & 0.4 & - & 0.6 & 0.5 & 0.7 \\ 0.7 & - & - & 0.2 & 0.3 & 0.5 \end{bmatrix}$$

Without loss of generality, let the original weight vector be $w(0) = (1/6, 1/6, 1/6, 1/6, 1/6, 1/6)^T$. Using Algorithm 5.1, one can get the values of L, w, $F(w)$, FCR, and $|\eta_i(w(L))|$ and ranking results by setting different ε values as listed in Table 5.4. When ε is sufficiently small, the weight vector approaches $w^* = (0.1301, 0.2714, 0.1281, 0.2090, 0.1509, 0.1106)^T$.

Step 2. Computing FCR by Eq. (1.13):

$$FCI = 0.1870, FCR = FCI/RI = 0.1870/1.26 = 0.1484 > 0.1.$$

Since FCR > 0.1, the incomplete fuzzy reciprocal preference relation C does not possess satisfactory consistency. We need to find its UFEs to repair this preference relation.

Step 3. Calculating the deviations between original judgment c_{ij} and its corresponding consistent representation, we have

Table 5.4 The values of L, w, $F(w)$, and FCR and rankings for different ε of C in Example 5.2

ε	L	w	Ranking	$F(w)$	FCR	$|\eta_i(w(L))|$
10^{-1}	26	$(0.1319, 0.2565,$ $0.1302, 0.2147,$ $0.1540, 0.1128)^T$	$x_2 \succ x_4$ $\succ x_5 \succ$ $x_1 \succ x_3$ $\succ x_6$	1.0276	0.1490	$4.4409 \times 10^{-16}, 0.098, 0.0256,$ $0.0093, 0.0291, 0.034$
10^{-2}	66	$(0.1305, 0.2699,$ $0.1280, 0.2094,$ $0.1511, 0.1110)^T$	$x_2 \succ x_4$ $\succ x_5 \succ$ $x_1 \succ x_3$ $\succ x_6$	1.0239	0.1484	$0.0041, 0.0095, 1.1102 \times 10^{-16},$ $0.0045, 2.2204 \times 10^{-16},$ 9.3303×10^{-4}
10^{-3}	107	$(0.1301, 0.2712,$ $0.1281, 0.2090,$ $0.1509, 0.1107)^T$	$x_2 \succ x_4$ $\succ x_5 \succ$ $x_1 \succ x_3$ $\succ x_6$	1.0239	0.1484	$4.2799 \times 10^{-4}, 9.7803 \times 10^{-4},$ $2.2542 \times 10^{-4}, 2.2980 \times 10^{-4},$ $2.2204 \times 10^{-16}, 9.4821 \times 10^{-5}$
10^{-4}	146	$(0.1301, 0.2714,$ $0.1281, 0.2090,$ $0.1509, 0.1106)^T$	$x_2 \succ x_4$ $\succ x_5 \succ$ $x_1 \succ x_3$ $\succ x_6$	1.0239	0.1484	$2.2204 \times 10^{-16}, 9.6242 \times 10^{-5},$ $2.2204 \times 10^{-16}, 3.3698 \times 10^{-5},$ $2.8917 \times 10^{-5}, 3.3627 \times 10^{-5}$
10^{-5}	187	$(0.1301, 0.2714,$ $0.1281, 0.2090,$ $0.1509, 0.1106)^T$	$x_2 \succ x_4$ $\succ x_5 \succ$ $x_1 \succ x_3$ $\succ x_6$	1.0239	0.1484	$2.2204 \times 10^{-16}, 9.6242 \times 10^{-5},$ $2.2204 \times 10^{-16}, 3.3698 \times 10^{-5},$ $2.8917 \times 10^{-5}, 3.3627 \times 10^{-5}$
10^{-6}	227	$(0.1301, 0.2714,$ $0.1281, 0.2090,$ $0.1509, 0.1106)^T$	$x_2 \succ x_4$ $\succ x_5 \succ$ $x_1 \succ x_3$ $\succ x_6$	1.0239	0.1484	$2.2204 \times 10^{-16}, 9.6242 \times 10^{-5},$ $2.2204 \times 10^{-16}, 3.3698 \times 10^{-5},$ $2.8917 \times 10^{-5}, 3.3627 \times 10^{-5}$

$$
D = \begin{bmatrix}
0 & 0.0241 & 0 & 0.0837 & 0.3369 & 0.2405 \\
0.0241 & 0 & 0.0206 & 0 & 0.0427 & 0 \\
0 & 0.0206 & 0 & 0.0201 & 0 & 0 \\
0.0837 & 0 & 0.0201 & 0 & 0.1808 & 0.1461 \\
0.3369 & 0.0427 & 0 & 0.1808 & 0 & 0.1231 \\
0.2405 & 0 & 0 & 0.1461 & 0.1231 & 0
\end{bmatrix}.
$$

Obviously, the maximum deviations are d_{15} and d_{51}, so the UFEs are c_{15} and c_{51}.

Step 4. Update the UFEs c_{15} and c_{51} with $c'_{15} = \text{round}\left(\frac{w_1}{w_1+w_5} \times 10\right) \times 10^{-1}$ and c'_{51}
$= \text{round}\left(\frac{w_5}{w_1+w_5} \times 10\right) \times 10^{-1}$, one has $c'_{15} = 0.5$ and $c'_{51} = 0.5$.

Thus, C is updated as

Table 5.5 The values of L, W, $F(W)$, and FCR and rankings for different ε of C' in Example 5.2

ε	L	w	Ranking	$F(w)$	FCR	$|\eta_i(w(L))|$
10^{-1}	22	$(0.1014, 0.2551, 0.1288, 0.2126, 0.1914, 0.1108)^T$	$x_2 \succ x_4$ $\succ x_5 \succ$ $x_3 \succ x_6$ $\succ x_1$	0.4193	0.0532	$0.0143, 0.0943, 0.0127, 0.0406, 0, 0.0267$
10^{-2}	61	$(0.0994, 0.2685, 0.1278, 0.2086, 0.1892, 0.1064)^T$	$x_2 \succ x_4$ $\succ x_5 \succ$ $x_3 \succ x_6$ $\succ x_1$	0.4154	0.0525	$2.2204 \times 10^{-16}, 0.0092, 0.003, 0.003, 0.0022, 0.001$
10^{-3}	97	$(0.0994, 0.2698, 0.1275, 0.2083, 0.1889, 0.1061)^T$	$x_2 \succ x_4$ $\succ x_5 \succ$ $x_3 \succ x_6$ $\succ x_1$	0.4154	0.0525	$2.2345 \times 10^{-4}, 8.7826 \times 10^{-4}, 0, 2.2196 \times 10^{-4}, 1.0941 \times 10^{-4}, 3.2344 \times 10^{-4}$
10^{-4}	133	$(0.0994, 0.2699, 0.1275, 0.2083, 0.1889, 0.1061)^T$	$x_2 \succ x_4$ $\succ x_5 \succ$ $x_3 \succ x_6$ $\succ x_1$	0.4154	0.0525	$2.1921 \times 10^{-5}, 9.2656 \times 10^{-5}, 1.1102 \times 10^{-16}, 3.8488 \times 10^{-5}, 2.2204 \times 10^{-16}, 3.2246 \times 10^{-5}$
10^{-5}	170	$(0.0994, 0.2699, 0.1275, 0.2082, 0.1889, 0.1061)^T$	$x_2 \succ x_4$ $\succ x_5 \succ$ $x_3 \succ x_6$ $\succ x_1$	0.4154	0.0525	$2.9494 \times 10^{-6}, 9.6250 \times 10^{-6}, 1.3882 \times 10^{-6}, 1.5475 \times 10^{-6}, 0, 3.7399 \times 10^{-6}$
10^{-6}	209	$(0.0994, 0.2699, 0.1275, 0.2082, 0.1889, 0.1061)^T$	$x_2 \succ x_4$ $\succ x_5 \succ$ $x_3 \succ x_6$ $\succ x_1$	0.4154	0.0525	$0, 9.2517 \times 10^{-7}, 2.4979 \times 10^{-7}, 1.9570 \times 10^{-7}, 3.6807 \times 10^{-7}, 1.1160 \times 10^{-7}$

$$C' = \begin{bmatrix} 0.5 & 0.3 & - & 0.3 & 0.5 & 0.3 \\ 0.7 & 0.5 & 0.7 & - & 0.6 & - \\ - & 0.3 & 0.5 & 0.4 & - & - \\ 0.7 & - & 0.6 & 0.5 & 0.4 & 0.8 \\ 0.5 & 0.4 & - & 0.6 & 0.5 & 0.7 \\ 0.7 & - & - & 0.2 & 0.3 & 0.5 \end{bmatrix}$$

Use Algorithm 5.1, one can obtain the values of L, w, $F(w)$, FCR, and $|\eta_i(w(L))|$ and ranking of alternatives with different ε's as listed in Table 5.5. When ε is sufficiently small, the final priority vector is obtained as

$$w^* = (0.0994, 0.2699, 0.1275, 0.2083, 0.1889, 0.1061)^T$$

Compute FCR by Eq. (1.13):

$$\text{FCI} = 0.0661, \text{FCR} = \text{FCI}/\text{RI} = 0.0661/1.26 = 0.0525 < 0.1.$$

Thus, this updated C is deemed to have acceptable consistency.
Step 5. Use the final priority vector w^* to rank the alternatives as

$$w^* = (0.0994, 0.2699, 0.1275, 0.2083, 0.1889, 0.1061)^T.$$

$$x_2 \succ x_4 \succ x_5 \succ x_3 \succ x_6 \succ x_1.$$

By changing only c_{15} and c_{51}, we were able to rectify an incomplete fuzzy reciprocal preference relation to derive one with acceptable consistency. This allows the analyst to avoid the hassle of returning the inconsistent preference relation to the DM for reconsideration.

In the above, we only just set UFEs c_{15} and c_{51} with $c'_{15} = $ round $(\frac{w_1}{w_1+w_5}$ $\times 10) \times 10^{-1}$ and $c'_{51} = $ round $(\frac{w_5}{w_1+w_5} \times 10) \times 10^{-1}$, where w is generated from the original C by CSM. However, if we look at UFEs c_{15} and c_{51} as unknown elements, and use Algorithm 5.3 to compute the weight vector and FCR, MD, and MAD values, we have

$$w'^* = (0.0749, 0.2635, 0.1245, 0.2034, 0.2327, 0.1009)^T$$

$$\text{FCR} = 0.0307, \text{MD} = 0.4886, \text{MAD} = 0.1316.$$

If we set $c'_{15} = \frac{w'_1}{w'_1+w'_5} = 0.2434$ and $c'_{51} = \frac{w'_5}{w'_1+w'_5} = 0.7566$, and use Algorithm 5.3 to compute the weight vector and FCR, MD, and MAD values, we have

$$w''^* = (0.0749, 0.2635, 0.1245, 0.2034, 0.2327, 0.1009)^T$$

$$\text{FCR} = 0.0307, \text{MD} = 0.4886, \text{and MAD} = 0.1316.$$

which are same as the above results when c_{15} and c_{51} are looked at as unknown values. This shows that $c_{15} = 0.2434$ and $c_{51} = 0.7566$ are most preferred.

If we want the values of c'_{15} and c'_{51} to be in the set U, i.e., $c'_{15} = $ round $(\frac{w'_1}{w'_1+w'_5}$ $\times 10) \times 10^{-1} = 0.2$ and $c'_{51} = $ round $(\frac{w'_5}{w'_1+w'_5} \times 10) \times 10^{-1} = 0.8$, then we have

$$w''^* = (0.0714, 0.2621, 0.1238, 0.2023, 0.2404, 0.1001)^T$$

$$\text{FCR} = 0.0318, \text{MD} = 0.4842, \text{and MAD} = 0.1310.$$

which are slightly different from the results when c_{15} and c_{51} are looked at as unknown values. This example is also examined by EM in Example 3.1, from the viewpoint of the value of FCR; in all the cases, the values of FCR generated by CSM are smaller than by EM, which denotes that CSM has better performances than EM.

Remark 5.3 Numerical results in Tables 5.4 and 5.5 demonstrate that iteration step L increases when error parameter ε decreases. In general, $F(w)$ and the consistency ratio of an incomplete fuzzy reciprocal preference relation C get smaller when ε

Table 5.6 Performance comparisons for Example 5.2

Method	w^*	Ranking	FCR	MD	MAD
CSM	$(0.0994, 0.2699, 0.1275, 0.2083,$ $0.1889, 0.1061)^T$	$x_2 \succ x_4 \succ x_5 \succ x_3 \succ$ $x_6 \succ x_1$	0.0525	0.6425	0.1836
EM	$(0.1038, 0.2780, 0.1262, 0.2017,$ $0.1949, 0.0953)^T$	$x_2 \succ x_4 \succ x_5 \succ x_3 \succ$ $x_1 \succ x_6$	0.054	0.9349	0.2213
LSM	$(0.1017, 0.3036, 0.1354, 0.1849,$ $0.1937, 0.0808)^T$	$x_2 \succ x_5 \succ x_4 \succ x_3 \succ$ $x_1 \succ x_6$	0.0607	1.2774	0.2573
LLSM	$(0.0965, 0.2682, 0.1288, 0.2166,$ $0.1901, 0.0998)^T$	$x_2 \succ x_4 \succ x_5 \succ x_3 \succ$ $x_6 \succ x_1$	0.0519	0.6994	0.1916

decreases. When the error parameter ε is sufficiently small, w, $F(w)$, FCR, and ranking results will converge to a set of values and remain unchanged.

In order to show the effectiveness of CSM, the other three methods EM (Xu & Wang, 2013), LSM (Gong, 2008), and LLSM (Xu et al., 2013) are also applied to the rectified C' and assessed in terms of the criteria FCR, MD, and MAD. Table 5.6 lists the ranking results by the four methods. It is clear that CSM and LLSM yield the same ranking $x_2 \succ x_4 \succ x_5 \succ x_1 \succ x_3 \succ x_6$, but EM and LSM generate slightly different rankings. Most notably, the EM and LSM reverse the order of x_1 and x_6, while the DM's original judgment points to $x_6 \succ x_1$ because $c_{61} = c'_{61} = 0.7$. It is apparent that this reverse is unwarranted and undesirable. Moreover, CSM produces the smallest MD and MAD among the four methods, and the FCR from CSM is marginally larger than that from LLSM but is smaller than those derived from EM and LSM. Across the three metrics, FCR, MD, and MAD, Table 5.6 shows that CSM overall performs better than the other three methods EM, LSM, and LLSM.

Example 5.3 Given a decision problem with six alternatives x_i ($i = 1, 2, \ldots, 6$), the DM provides his/her preferences over the six decision alternatives, as an incomplete fuzzy reciprocal preference relation (adapted from (Xu et al., 2013)):

$$C = \begin{bmatrix} 0.5 & 0.4 & - & 0.3 & 0.3 & 0.3 \\ 0.6 & 0.5 & 0.6 & 0.5 & - & 0.4 \\ - & 0.4 & 0.5 & 0.3 & 0.6 & - \\ 0.7 & 0.5 & 0.7 & 0.5 & 0.4 & 0.8 \\ 0.7 & - & 0.4 & 0.6 & 0.5 & 0.7 \\ 0.7 & 0.6 & - & 0.2 & 0.3 & 0.5 \end{bmatrix}$$

This incomplete fuzzy reciprocal preference relation was investigated by Xu et al. (2013), in which the optimal priority vector is derived by LLSM as $w^* = (0.0878, 0.1599, 0.1551, 0.2464, 0.2208, 0.1301)^T$. This yields a ranking of the six alternatives: $x_4 \succ x_5 \succ x_2 \succ x_3 \succ x_6 \succ x_1$. We now examine the problem using CSM as follows.

Table 5.7 Performance comparisons for Example 5.3

Method	w^*	Ranking	FCR	MD	MAD
CSM	$(0.0884, 0.1615, 0.1581,$ $0.2365, 0.2185, 0.1370)^T$	$x_4 \succ x_5 \succ x_2 \succ x_3$ $\succ x_6 \succ x_1$	0.0728	0.7487	0.1802
EM (Xu & Wang, 2013)	$(0.0896, 0.1671, 0.1594,$ $0.2355, 0.2225, 0.1258)^T$	$x_4 \succ x_5 \succ x_2 \succ x_3$ $\succ x_6 \succ x_1$	0.0729	0.6047	0.1826
NRAM (Xu & Da, 2009)	$(0.1204, 0.1681, 0.1648,$ $0.2000, 0.1931, 0.1537)^T$	$x_4 \succ x_5 \succ x_2 \succ x_3$ $\succ x_6 \succ x_1$	0.1014	1.3993	0.2345
GPM (Xu, 2004)	$(0.1091, 0.1636,$ $0.1091,0.2545, 0.2545,$ $0.1091)^T$	$x_4 \approx x_5 \succ x_2 \succ$ $x_3 \approx x_6 \approx x_1$	0.1033	1.7849	0.2999
LSM (Gong, 2008)	$(0.0978, 0.1765, 0.1591,$ $0.2263, 0.2220, 0.1183)^T$	$x_4 \succ x_5 \succ x_2 \succ x_3$ $\succ x_6 \succ x_1$	0.0778	0.6848	0.1987
LLSM (Xu et al., 2013)	$(0.0878, 0.1599, 0.1551,$ $0.2464, 0.2208, 0.1301)^T$	$x_4 \succ x_5 \succ x_2 \succ x_3$ $\succ x_6 \succ x_1$	0.0719	0.6037	0.1874

According to Theorem 1.4, we know that C can be completed. Without loss of generality, we set the original weight vector as $w(0) = (1/6, 1/6, 1/6, 1/6, 1/6, 1/6)^T$. When ε is set to 10^{-3}, the values of w, $F(w)$, and FCR and ranking of alternatives will stabilize and remain unchanged. At $L = 55$, one has $F(w) = 0.5860$, $|\eta_1| = 1.1863 \times 10^{-5} < \varepsilon$, $|\eta_2| = 0 < \varepsilon$, $|\eta_3| = 1.2503 \times 10^{-5} < \varepsilon$, $|\eta_4| = 9.6445 \times 10^{-5} < \varepsilon$, $|\eta_5| = 2.9292 \times 10^{-5} < \varepsilon$, $|\eta_6| = 4.2788 \times 10^{-5} < \varepsilon$, FCR $= 0.0728$, and $w^* = (0.0884, 0.1615, 0.1581, 0.2365, 0.2185, 0.1370)^T$, implying a ranking of these six alternatives as: $x_4 \succ x_5 \succ x_2 \succ x_3 \succ x_6 \succ x_1$.

For this single incomplete fuzzy reciprocal preference relation, it can also be solved by EM (Xu & Wang, 2013), NRAM (Xu & Da, 2009), LSM (Gong, 2008), LLSM (Xu et al., 2013), and GPM (Xu, 2004). The results are shown in Table 5.7, from which we can see that CSM achieves the same ranking as EM, NRAM, LSM, and LLSM, $x_4 \succ x_5 \succ x_2 \succ x_3 \succ x_6 \succ x_1$, while GPM yields a slightly different ranking, $x_4 \sim x_5 \succ x_2 \succ x_3 \sim x_6 \sim x_1$, which fails to discriminate x_4 and x_5, as well as x_1, x_3, and x_6. Furthermore, both NRAM and GPM lead to unacceptable consistency ratio FCR > 0.1 and have larger MD and MAD values than other methods. A further examination reveals that CSM results in the smallest MAD value among these six methods and outperforms NRAM, GPM, and LSM in all the three criteria.

Example 5.4 Consider a GDM problem with three DMs providing the following incomplete fuzzy reciprocal preference relations C_k ($k = 1, 2, 3$) for a set of four alternatives $X = \{x_1, x_2, x_3, x_4\}$:

Table 5.8 Performance comparisons for Example 5.4

Methods	w^*	Ranking	MD	MAD
CSM	$(0.1954, 0.4386, 0.2316, 0.1344)^T$	$x_2 \succ x_3 \succ x_1 \succ x_4$	0.7520	0.1672
LSM (Gong, 2008)	$(0.1822, 0.4611, 0.2160, 0.1408)^T$	$x_2 \succ x_3 \succ x_1 \succ x_4$	0.9909	0.1946
GPM (Xu, 2004)	$(0.2000, 0.4667, 0.2000, 0.1333)^T$	$x_2 \succ x_3 \approx x_1 \succ x_4$	1.0411	0.1999
LLSM (Xu et al., 2013)	$(0.1864, 0.4587, 0.2274, 0.1275)^T$	$x_2 \succ x_3 \succ x_1 \succ x_4$	0.8154	0.1825

$$C_1 = \begin{bmatrix} 0.5 & 0.3 & - & 0.5 \\ 0.7 & 0.5 & 0.6 & 0.6 \\ - & 0.4 & 0.5 & 0.7 \\ 0.5 & 0.4 & 0.3 & 0.5 \end{bmatrix}, C_2 = \begin{bmatrix} 0.5 & 0.2 & 0.6 & 0.7 \\ 0.8 & 0.5 & 0.8 & - \\ 0.4 & 0.2 & 0.5 & 0.8 \\ 0.3 & - & 0.4 & 0.5 \end{bmatrix},$$

$$C_3 = \begin{bmatrix} 0.5 & 0.2 & 0.5 & 0.6 \\ 0.8 & 0.5 & - & 0.7 \\ 0.5 & - & 0.5 & 0.8 \\ 0.4 & 0.3 & 0.2 & 0.5 \end{bmatrix}.$$

Let $\lambda_1 = \lambda_2 = \lambda_3 = 1/3$ and $\varepsilon = 0.0001$. After several iterations, $|\eta_1| = 5.7495 \times 10^{-5} < \varepsilon$, $|\eta_2| = 8.8394 \times 10^{-5} < \varepsilon$, $|\eta_3| = 3.0899 \times 10^{-5} < \varepsilon$, and $|\eta_4| = 1.1102 \times 10^{-5} < \varepsilon$, indicating that the derived priority vector has reached an acceptable error level. Therefore, the optimal priority vector is found to be $w^* = (0.1954, 0.4386, 0.2316, 0.1344)^T$.

The comparative result is shown in Table 5.8. It is clear that CSM preforms the best in both MD and MAD. CSM obtains the same ranking as LLSM and LSM, $x_2 \succ x_3 \succ x_1 \succ x_4$, while GPM yields a slightly different ranking $x_2 \succ x_3 \sim x_1 \succ x_4$, as it fails to discriminate x_1 and x_3 and underperforms the proposed CSM and the other two methods in both MD and MAD.

Comparative studies with existing methods reveal the following features of the proposed CSM:

1. In contrast to LSM, GPM, and LLSM where DM's weights are not considered, the proposed CSM allows the analyst to assign proper weights to different experts to reflect their varying influences in GDM problems.
2. By setting $\lambda_1 = 1$ and $\lambda_k = 0$ for $k = 2, 3, \ldots, m$, CSM can be conveniently applied to derive a priority vector from a single incomplete fuzzy reciprocal preference relation. This implies that the proposed CSM model can be employed to handle both group and individual decision problems.
3. By setting $\delta_{ij} = 1$, for all $i, j \in N$, CSM can be utilized to derive a priority vector from complete reciprocal preference relations. This indicates that it can be

flexibly used to handle decision problems with both complete and incomplete fuzzy reciprocal preference relations.

4. Numerical experiments demonstrate that CSM often outperforms the other methods such as EM, GPM, LSM, LLSM, and NRAM in terms of FCR, MD, and MAD when handling incomplete fuzzy reciprocal preference relations.
5. As illustrated in Example 5.2, CSM tends to have better rank preservation capability and discrimination power.

5.4   Summary

This chapter proposes a chi-square method to handle decision problems with incomplete fuzzy reciprocal preference relations and develops a convergent iterative algorithm to determine a priority vector. An adapted acceptable consistency ratio is employed to judge whether an incomplete fuzzy reciprocal preference relation is acceptably consistent. If its consistency is not acceptable, an algorithm is put forward to repair it until its consistency reaches threshold. This extended CSM not only improves the consistency level but also aims to preserve the initial preference information as much as possible.

References

Gong, Z. W. (2008). Least-square method to priority of the fuzzy preference relations with incomplete information. *International Journal of Approximate Reasoning, 47*(2), 258–264.

Xu, Y. J., & Da, Q. L. (2009). Methods for priority of incomplete complementary judgement matrices. *Systems Engineering and Electronics, 31*(1), 95–99.

Xu, Y. J., Patnayakuni, R., & Wang, H. M. (2013). Logarithmic least squares method to priority for group decision making with incomplete fuzzy preference relations. *Applied Mathematical Modelling, 37*(4), 2139–2152.

Xu, Y. J., & Wang, H. M. (2013). Eigenvector method, consistency test and inconsistency repairing for an incomplete fuzzy preference relation. *Applied Mathematical Modelling, 37*(7), 5171–5183.

Xu, Z. S. (2004). Goal programming models for obtaining the priority vector of incomplete fuzzy preference relation. *International Journal of Approximate Reasoning, 36*(3), 261–270.

Xu, Z. S. (2005). A procedure for decision making based on incomplete fuzzy preference relation. *Fuzzy Optimization and Decision Making, 4*(3), 175–189.

Chapter 6
A Least Deviation Method

In this chapter, we propose another method called least deviation method (LDM).

6.1 Least Deviation Method for Priority from Group Incomplete Fuzzy Reciprocal Preference Relations

Consider a GDM problem, where m DMs give their preferences in the form of reciprocal preference relations, i.e., expert e_k describes his/her preference information as $R_k = (r_{ij}^{(k)})_{n \times n}$ and let $w = (w_1, w_2, \ldots, w_n)^T$ be the priority of the fuzzy reciprocal preference relation $R_k = (r_{ij}^{(k)})_{n \times n}$, where $w_i > 0$, $i \in N$.

By Eqs. (1.1) and (1.9), we have $r_{ij}^{(k)} = (1 + \log_9(w_i/w_j))/2$, that is,

$$w_i/w_j = p\left(r_{ij}^{(k)}\right), i, j \in N \tag{6.1}$$

being $p\left(r_{ij}^{(k)}\right) = 9^{\left(2r_{ij}^{(k)} - 1\right)}$. Then, it is clear that

$$p\left(r_{ij}^{(k)}\right)(w_j/w_i) = p\left(r_{ji}^{(k)}\right)(w_i/w_j) = 1, \forall i, j \in N \tag{6.2}$$

Here, we introduce the following deviation element:

$$f_{ij} = p\left(r_{ij}^{(k)}\right)(w_j/w_i) + p\left(r_{ji}^{(k)}\right)(w_i/w_j) - 2, \forall i, j \in N \tag{6.3}$$

If some elements of R_k cannot be given by DM, then R_k is an incomplete fuzzy reciprocal preference relation. We extend Eq. (6.3) to the incomplete fuzzy reciprocal preference relation; for the convenience of computation, we construct an

Y. Xu, *Deriving Priorities from Incomplete Fuzzy Reciprocal Preference Relations*, https://doi.org/10.1007/978-981-99-3169-9_6

indication matrix $\Delta = (\delta_{ij})_{n \times n}$ of the incomplete fuzzy reciprocal preference relation $C_k = (c_{ij}^{(k)})_{n \times n}$, and the formulas are given as follows:

$$f_{ij} = \delta_{ij}^{(k)} \left(p\left(c_{ij}^{(k)}\right)\left(w_j/w_i\right) + p\left(c_{ji}^{(k)}\right)\left(w_i/w_j\right) - 2 \right), \forall i, j \in N \qquad (6.4)$$

where $\delta_{ij}^{(k)}$ is a zero or one integer variable of the indicator matrix $\Delta_k = (\delta_{ij}^{(k)})_{n \times n}$, which is defined as in Eq. (1.10). It is easy to find that $\delta_{ij}^{(k)} = \delta_{ji}^{(k)}$.

We turn to seeking a priority $w = (w_1, w_2, \ldots, w_n)^T$, where $\sum_{i=1}^{n} w_i = 1$, $w_i \geq 0$ has to satisfy Eq. (6.4) as much as possible. Thus, we can construct the following least deviation optimization model:

$$\min \quad F(w) = \sum_{k=1}^{m} \sum_{i=1}^{n} \sum_{j=1}^{n} \lambda_k \delta_{ij}^{(k)} \left[p\left(c_{ij}^{(k)}\right)\left(w_j/w_i\right) + p\left(c_{ji}^{(k)}\right)\left(w_i/w_j\right) - 2 \right]$$

$$\text{s.t.} \begin{cases} \sum_{i=1}^{n} w_i = 1 \\ w_i \geq 0, \qquad i \in N. \end{cases}$$

$$(\text{M-6.1})$$

$$D_w = \left\{ w = (w_1, w_2, \ldots, w_n)^T \; \middle| \; \sum_{i=1}^{n} w_i = 1, \; w_i > 0, \quad i \in N \right\} \qquad (6.5)$$

About the solution to the above least deviation model, we have the following theorem.

Theorem 6.1 *$F(w)$ has a unique minimum point* $w^* = (w_1, w_2, \ldots, w_n)^T \in D_w$, *which is also the unique solution of the following system of equation in D_w:*

$$\sum_{k=1}^{m} \sum_{j=1}^{n} \lambda_k \left(\delta_{ij}^{(k)} + \delta_{ji}^{(k)} \right) p\left(c_{ji}^{(k)}\right) \frac{w_i}{w_j} = \sum_{k=1}^{m} \sum_{j=1}^{n} \lambda_k \left(\delta_{ji}^{(k)} + \delta_{ij}^{(k)} \right) p\left(c_{ij}^{(k)}\right) \frac{w_j}{w_i} \qquad (6.6)$$

Proof Due to the fact that D_w is a bounded vector space and $F(w)$ is the continuous function in D_w, for $F(w) \geq 0$ and $w \in D_w$, $F(w)$ therefore has an infimum, namely there exists such $w \in D_w$ that can make function $F(w)$ get minimum value.

In order to obtain the priority vector $w^* = (w_1, w_2, \ldots, w_n)^T \in D_w$, we construct the following Lagrange function:

$$L(w, \rho) = F(w) + \rho \left(\sum_{i=1}^{n} w_i - 1 \right) \qquad (6.7)$$

where ρ is the Lagrange multiplier. Setting the partial derivatives with respect to w_i equal to zero, we can get the following set of equations:

$$\sum_{k=1}^{m} \sum_{j=1}^{n} \lambda_k \left(\delta_{ij}^{(k)} + \delta_{ji}^{(k)} \right) p \left(c_{ji}^{(k)} \right) \frac{1}{w_j} - \sum_{k=1}^{m} \sum_{j=1}^{n} \lambda_k \left(\delta_{ji}^{(k)} + \delta_{ij}^{(k)} \right) p \left(c_{ij}^{(k)} \right) \frac{w_j}{w_i^2}$$

$$+ \rho = 0, i \in N \tag{6.8}$$

Multiplying the above equation by w_i and summing up them lead to the following:

$$\sum_{k=1}^{m} \sum_{i=1}^{n} \sum_{j=1}^{n} \lambda_k \left(\delta_{ij}^{(k)} + \delta_{ji}^{(k)} \right) p \left(c_{ji}^{(k)} \right) \frac{w_i}{w_j} - \sum_{k=1}^{m} \sum_{i=1}^{n}$$

$$\times \sum_{j=1}^{n} \lambda_k \left(\delta_{ji}^{(k)} + \delta_{ij}^{(k)} \right) p \left(c_{ij}^{(k)} \right) \frac{w_j}{w_i} + \rho \sum_{i=1}^{n} w_i = 0 \tag{6.9}$$

Due to the fact that

$$\sum_{k=1}^{m} \sum_{i=1}^{n} \sum_{j=1}^{n} \lambda_k \left(\delta_{ij}^{(k)} + \delta_{ji}^{(k)} \right) p \left(c_{ji}^{(k)} \right) \frac{w_i}{w_j}$$

$$\equiv \sum_{k=1}^{m} \sum_{i=1}^{n} \sum_{j=1}^{n} \lambda_k \left(\delta_{ji}^{(k)} + \delta_{ij}^{(k)} \right) p \left(c_{ij}^{(k)} \right) \frac{w_j}{w_i} \tag{6.10}$$

and $\sum_{i=1}^{n} w_i \neq 0$, we therefore get from Eq. (6.9) that $\rho \equiv 0$. Accordingly, Eq. (6.8) becomes

$$\sum_{k=1}^{m} \sum_{j=1}^{n} \lambda_k \left(\delta_{ij}^{(k)} + \delta_{ji}^{(k)} \right) p \left(c_{ji}^{(k)} \right) \frac{1}{w_j} - \sum_{k=1}^{m} \sum_{j=1}^{n} \lambda_k \left(\delta_{ji}^{(k)} + \delta_{ij}^{(k)} \right) p \left(c_{ij}^{(k)} \right) \frac{w_j}{w_i^2}$$

$$= 0 \tag{6.11}$$

which can be further simplified as Eq. (6.6).

It is clear that the minimum point w^* is a solution to Eq. (6.6), and if the solution proves to be unique in D_w, w^* can be uniquely determined.

Assume that $v = (v_1, v_2, \ldots, v_n)^T \in D_w$ and $w = (w_1, w_2, \ldots, w_n)^T \in D_w$ are two solutions of Eq. (6.6). Let $u_i = w_i/v_i$, $i \in N$, and $u_l = \max_{i \in N} \{u_i\}$. If there exists $j \in N$ such that $u_j < u_l$, then we have

$$\sum_{k=1}^{m}\sum_{j=1}^{n}\lambda_k\left(\delta_{lj}^{(k)}+\delta_{jl}^{(k)}\right)p\left(c_{lj}^{(k)}\right)\frac{v_j}{v_l} > \sum_{k=1}^{m}\sum_{j=1}^{n}\lambda_k\left(\delta_{lj}^{(k)}+\delta_{jl}^{(k)}\right)p\left(c_{lj}^{(k)}\right)\frac{v_j}{v_l}\cdot\frac{u_j}{u_l}$$

$$=\sum_{k=1}^{m}\sum_{j=1}^{n}\lambda_k\left(\delta_{lj}^{(k)}+\delta_{jl}^{(k)}\right)p\left(c_{lj}\right)\frac{w_j}{w_l} \tag{6.12}$$

and

$$\sum_{k=1}^{m}\sum_{j=1}^{n}\lambda_k\left(\delta_{jl}^{(k)}+\delta_{lj}^{(k)}\right)p\left(c_{jl}^{(k)}\right)\frac{v_l}{v_j} < \sum_{k=1}^{m}\sum_{j=1}^{n}\lambda_k\left(\delta_{jl}^{(k)}+\delta_{lj}^{(k)}\right)p\left(c_{jl}^{(k)}\right)\frac{v_l}{v_j}\cdot\frac{u_l}{u_j}$$

$$=\sum_{k=1}^{m}\sum_{j=1}^{n}\lambda_k\left(\delta_{jl}^{(k)}+\delta_{lj}^{(k)}\right)p\left(c_{jl}^{(k)}\right)\frac{w_l}{w_j} \tag{6.13}$$

According to Eqs. (6.6), (6.12), and (6.13), it can be deducted that

$$\sum_{k=1}^{m}\sum_{j=1}^{n}\lambda_k\left(\delta_{lj}^{(k)}+\delta_{jl}^{(k)}\right)p\left(c_{lj}^{(k)}\right)\frac{w_j}{w_l} < \sum_{k=1}^{m}\sum_{j=1}^{n}\lambda_k\left(\delta_{jl}^{(k)}+\delta_{lj}^{(k)}\right)p\left(c_{jl}^{(k)}\right)\frac{w_l}{w_j} \tag{6.14}$$

which contradicts Eq. (6.6). Thus, $u_j < u_l$ could not hold. That is to say, for all $j \in N$, $u_j = u_l$, namely, $w_1/v_1 = w_2/v_2 = \ldots = w_n/v_n$. Due to the fact that $\sum_{i=1}^{n}v_i = 1$ and $\sum_{i=1}^{n}w_i = 1$, we have $w_i \equiv v_i$ and $\forall i \in N$, which means that the solution of Eq. (6.6) is unique. $\qquad\square$

To solve Eq. (6.6), we put forward a simple convergent iterative algorithm, which is detailed in the following.

Algorithm 6.1

Step 1. Use Theorem 1.4 to judge whether the incomplete fuzzy reciprocal preference relation C_k ($k \in M$) given by the DM could be completed or not. If it could not be completed, we return it to expert e_k to give a new reciprocal preference relation; otherwise, go to Step 2.

Step 2. Given an initial priority vector $w(0) = (w_1(0), w_2(0), \ldots, w_n(0))^T$, specify a parameter ε ($0 < \varepsilon < 1$), for example, $\varepsilon = 0.08$, and let $L = 0$.

Step 3. Calculate

$$\eta_i(W(L)) = \sum_{k=1}^{m} \sum_{j=1}^{n} h_k\left(\delta_{ij}^{(k)} + \delta_{ji}^{(k)}\right) p\left(c_{ji}^{(k)}\right) \frac{w_i}{w_j} - \sum_{k=1}^{m}$$

$$\times \sum_{j=1}^{n} h_k\left(\delta_{ji}^{(k)} + \delta_{ij}^{(k)}\right) p\left(c_{ij}^{(k)}\right) \frac{w_j}{w_i}, i \in N \tag{6.15}$$

If $|\eta_i(w(L)| \leq \varepsilon$ holds for all $i \in N$, then $w^* = w(L)$ and stop; otherwise, continue to Step 4.

Step 4. Determine the number q such that $|\eta_q(w(L)| = \max_{i \in N}\{|\eta_i(w(L)|\}$ and compute

$$T(L) = \sqrt{\frac{\sum_{k=1}^{m}\sum_{j=1,j\neq q}^{n} h_k\left(\delta_{qj}^{(k)} + \delta_{jq}^{(k)}\right) p\left(c_{qj}^{(k)}\right) \frac{w_j(L)}{w_q(L)}}{\sum_{k=1}^{m}\sum_{j=1,j\neq q}^{n} h_k\left(\delta_{jq}^{(k)} + \delta_{qj}^{(k)}\right) p\left(c_{jq}^{(k)}\right) \frac{w_q(L)}{w_j(L)}}} \tag{6.16}$$

$$f_i(L) = \begin{cases} T(L)w_q(L), & i = q, \\ w_i(L), & i \neq q, \end{cases} \tag{6.17}$$

$$w_i(L+1) = f_i(L)/\sum_{i=1}^{n} f_i(L), i \in N \tag{6.18}$$

Step 5. Let $L = L + 1$ and go to Step 3.

For the above algorithm, we have the following theorem:

Theorem 6.2 *The above algorithm is convergent for any $\varepsilon > 0$.*

Proof Consider the change of $F(w)$, when $w(L)$ is transformed into $w(L + 1)$. Suppose that $t > 0$ and $S(t) = F(f(L)) = F(w_1(L), \ldots, w_{p-1}(L), tw_p(L), w_{p+1}(L), \ldots, w_n(L))$, and then we have

$$S(t) = \sum_{k=1}^{m} \sum_{j=1,j\neq q}^{n} \lambda_k \delta_{qj}^{(k)} \left[p\left(c_{qj}^{(k)}\right) \frac{w_j(L)}{tw_q(L)} + p\left(c_{jq}^{(k)}\right) \frac{tw_q(L)}{w_j(L)} - 2\right]$$

$$= \sum_{k=1}^{m} \sum_{j=1,j\neq q}^{n} \lambda_k \delta_{iq}^{(k)} \left[p\left(c_{iq}^{(k)}\right) \frac{tw_q(L)}{w_i(L)} + p\left(c_{qi}^{(k)}\right) \frac{w_i(L)}{tw_q(L)} - 2\right]$$

$$= \sum_{k=1}^{m} \sum_{i=1,i\neq q}^{n} \sum_{j=1,j\neq q}^{n} \lambda_k \delta_{ij}^{(k)} \left[p\left(c_{ij}^{(k)}\right) \frac{w_j(L)}{w_i(L)} + p\left(c_{ji}^{(k)}\right) \frac{w_i(L)}{w_j(L)} - 2\right] \tag{6.19}$$

which is equivalent to

$$S(t) = \sum_{k=1}^{m} \sum_{j=1,j\neq q}^{n} \lambda_k \left(\delta_{qj}^{(k)} + \delta_{jq}^{(k)} \right) p \left(c_{qj}^{(k)} \right) \frac{w_j(L)}{w_q(L)} \cdot \frac{1}{t} + \sum_{k=1}^{m}$$

$$\times \sum_{j=1,j\neq q}^{n} \lambda_k \left(\delta_{jq}^{(k)} + \delta_{qj}^{(k)} \right) p \left(c_{jq}^{(k)} \right) \frac{w_q(L)}{w_j(L)} \cdot t$$

$$+ \sum_{k=1}^{m} \sum_{i=1,i\neq q}^{n} \sum_{j=1,j\neq q}^{n} \lambda_k \delta_{ij}^{(k)} \left[p \left(c_{ij}^{(k)} \right) \frac{w_j(L)}{w_i(L)} + p \left(c_{ji}^{(k)} \right) \frac{w_i(L)}{w_j(L)} - 2 \right]$$

$$- \sum_{k=1}^{m} \sum_{j=1,j\neq q}^{n} 2h_k \left(\delta_{qj}^{(k)} + \delta_{jq}^{(k)} \right) \tag{6.20}$$

Let

$$b_1 = \sum_{k=1}^{m} \sum_{j=1,j\neq q}^{n} \lambda_k \left(\delta_{qj}^{(k)} + \delta_{jq}^{(k)} \right) p \left(c_{qj}^{(k)} \right) \frac{w_j(L)}{w_q(L)} \tag{6.21}$$

$$b_2 = \sum_{k=1}^{m} \sum_{j=1,j\neq q}^{n} \lambda_k \left(\delta_{jq}^{(k)} + \delta_{qj}^{(k)} \right) p \left(c_{jq}^{(k)} \right) \frac{w_q(L)}{w_j(L)} \tag{6.22}$$

$$b_0 = \sum_{k=1}^{m} \sum_{i=1,i\neq q}^{n} \sum_{j=1,j\neq q}^{n} \lambda_k \delta_{ij}^{(k)} \left[p \left(c_{ij}^{(k)} \right) \frac{w_j(L)}{w_i(L)} + p \left(c_{ji}^{(k)} \right) \frac{w_i(L)}{w_j(L)} - 2 \right]$$

$$- \sum_{k=1}^{m} \sum_{j=1,j\neq q}^{n} 2\lambda_k \left(\delta_{qj}^{(k)} + \delta_{jq}^{(k)} \right) \tag{6.23}$$

Then, Eq. (6.20) can be equivalently expressed as

$$S(t) = b_1/t + b_2 \cdot t + b_0 \tag{6.24}$$

Setting derivative $\frac{dS(t)}{dt}$ equal to zero, we have

$$t^* = \sqrt{b_1/b_2} = \sqrt{\frac{\sum_{k=1}^{m}\sum_{j=1,j\neq q}^{n} \lambda_k \left(\delta_{qj}^{(k)} + \delta_{jq}^{(k)} \right) p \left(c_{qj}^{(k)} \right) \frac{w_j(L)}{w_q(L)}}{\sum_{k=1}^{m}\sum_{j=1,j\neq q}^{n} \lambda_k \left(\delta_{jq}^{(k)} + \delta_{qj}^{(k)} \right) p \left(c_{jq}^{(k)} \right) \frac{w_q(L)}{w_j(L)}}} \tag{6.25}$$

$$S(t^*) = 2\sqrt{b_1 b_2} + b_0 \tag{6.26}$$

where t^* means the minimum point and $S(t^*)$ means minimum value of $S(t)$. If $t^* = 1$, Eq. (6.25) is equivalent to the following:

$$\sum_{k=1}^{m} \sum_{\substack{j=1 \\ j \neq q}}^{n} \lambda_k \left(\delta_{qj}^{(k)} + \delta_{jq}^{(k)}\right) p\left(c_{qj}^{(k)}\right) \frac{w_j(L)}{w_q(L)} = \sum_{k=1}^{m} \sum_{\substack{j=1 \\ j \neq q}}^{n} \lambda_k \left(\delta_{jq}^{(k)} + \delta_{qj}^{(k)}\right) p\left(c_{jq}^{(k)}\right)$$

$$\times \frac{w_q(L)}{w_j(L)} \tag{6.27}$$

which also holds for $j = q$; therefore, we have

$$\sum_{k=1}^{m} \sum_{j=1}^{n} \lambda_k \left(\delta_{qj}^{(k)} + \delta_{jq}^{(k)}\right) p\left(c_{qj}^{(k)}\right) \frac{w_j(L)}{w_q(L)} = \sum_{k=1}^{m} \sum_{j=1}^{n} \lambda_k \left(\delta_{jq}^{(k)} + \delta_{qj}^{(k)}\right) p\left(c_{jq}^{(k)}\right)$$

$$\times \frac{w_q(L)}{w_j(L)} \tag{6.28}$$

That is,

$$\eta_q(W(L)) = \sum_{k=1}^{m} \sum_{j=1}^{n} \lambda_k \left(\delta_{qj}^{(k)} + \delta_{jq}^{(k)}\right) p\left(c_{qj}^{(k)}\right) \frac{w_j(L)}{w_q(L)}$$

$$- \sum_{k=1}^{m} \sum_{j=1}^{n} \lambda_k \left(\delta_{jq}^{(k)} + \delta_{qj}^{(k)}\right) p\left(c_{jq}^{(k)}\right) \frac{w_q(L)}{w_j(L)} = 0 \tag{6.29}$$

And by the definition of q in *Step* 3, we have $|\eta_q(w(L)| = 0$. Since q is the subscript that makes $|\eta_i(w(L))|$ maximal, we therefore have $|\eta_i(w(L))| = 0$ for all $i \in N$. According to Theorem 4, the algorithm terminates and $w^* = w(L)$. $\square$

If $t^* \neq 1$, then

$$F(w(L)) - F(f(L)) = S(1) - S(t^*) = b_1 + b_2 - 2\sqrt{b_1 b_2}$$

$$= \left(\sqrt{b_1} - \sqrt{b_2}\right)^2 > 0 \tag{6.30}$$

Since $F(w)$ is a homogenous function, $F(f(L)) = F(w(L + 1))$. The above inequality shows that $F(w(L + 1)) < F(w(L))$, for any $L \geq 0$. That is to say, $F(w(L))$ is a monotone decreasing sequence with an infimum in D_w. From the principle of mathematical analysis, we can learn that a monotonically decreasing and bounded sequence is certain to converge.

6.2   A Method for Repairing Inconsistency of an Incomplete Fuzzy Reciprocal Preference Relation

Algorithm 6.2

Let $C = (c_{ij})_{n \times n}$ be an incomplete fuzzy reciprocal preference relation given by the DM.

Step 1. Use Theorem 1.4 to judge whether the incomplete fuzzy reciprocal preference relation is acceptable, if the incomplete fuzzy reciprocal preference relation is not acceptable, we return it to the expert to give a new fuzzy reciprocal preference relation; otherwise, go to Step 2.

Step 2. Use the LDM algorithm in Sect. 6.1 to obtain the priority vector $w = (w_1, w_2, \ldots, w_n)^T$.

Step 3. Determine the consistency ratio of the incomplete fuzzy reciprocal preference relation as per Eq. (1.13), if FCR < 0.1, go to Step 5; otherwise, go to Step 3.

Step 4. Compute deviations d_{ij}'s by using Eq. (3.21), and identify the maximum deviation to find the corresponding UFEs (c_{ij}).

Step 5. Update the UFEs (c_{ij}) with c'_{ij}, where $c'_{ij} = \mathrm{round}(\frac{w_i}{w_i + w_j} \times 10) \times 10^{-1}$, and go to Step 1.

Step 6. Rank the alternatives according to the priority vector w^*.

Step 7. End.

Similar as in Sect. 3.2, the UFEs (c_{ij}) should not be set directly by $c'_{ij} = \mathrm{round}(\frac{w_i}{w_i + w_j} \times 10) \times 10^{-1}$ where the weight vector is generated from the original incomplete fuzzy reciprocal preference relation. We could look at them as unknown elements. Thus, we have the following Algorithm 6.3.

Algorithm 6.3

Step 1–Step 4 in Algorithm 6.2.

Step 5. Set the UFEs (c_{ij}) as the unknown elements and C would be C'; go to Step 1 and compute the weights for C'.

Step 6. Rank the alternatives according to the weight vector w.

Step 7. End.

6.3   Illustrative Examples

In this section, we examine three numerical examples to show the applications of the LDM in deriving priorities from different kinds of preference relations. Example 6.1 is a group decision-making problem with three incomplete fuzzy reciprocal preference relations, Example 6.2 is a single incomplete fuzzy reciprocal preference relation, and Example 6.3 is three complete reciprocal preference relations. The algorithm is applied to all the three examples. Furthermore, comparative analyses with the existing methods are also given.

Example 6.1 For a group decision-making problem, suppose that there are four decision alternatives x_i $(i = 1, 2, 3, 4)$ and three DMs e_k $(k = 1, 2, 3)$. The DMs provide their preferences over these four decision alternatives and give three incomplete fuzzy reciprocal preference relations as follows (adapted from (Xu, 2004)), respectively:

$$C_1 = \begin{bmatrix} 0.5 & 0.6 & - & 0.7 \\ 0.4 & 0.5 & 0.2 & 0.8 \\ - & 0.8 & 0.5 & 0.4 \\ 0.3 & 0.2 & 0.6 & 0.5 \end{bmatrix}, \quad C_2 = \begin{bmatrix} 0.5 & 0.8 & 0.4 & - \\ 0.2 & 0.5 & 0.3 & 0.6 \\ 0.6 & 0.7 & 0.5 & - \\ - & 0.4 & - & 0.5 \end{bmatrix},$$

$$C_3 = \begin{bmatrix} 0.5 & 0.3 & 0.4 & 0.6 \\ 0.7 & 0.5 & - & 0.5 \\ 0.6 & - & 0.5 & 0.7 \\ 0.4 & 0.5 & 0.3 & 0.5 \end{bmatrix}.$$

Algorithm 6.1 is employed to obtain priority from group incomplete fuzzy reciprocal preference relations. In order to compare the performances with existing methods, we also set $\lambda_1 = \lambda_2 = \lambda_3 = 1/3$.

Step 1. According to Theorem 1.4, we know that C_k $(k = 1, 2, 3)$ all could be completed.

Step 2. Given an initial priority vector $w(0) = (0.25, 0.25, 0.25, 0.25)^T$, specify the parameter $\varepsilon = 0.8$, and let $L = 0$.

Step 3. Calculate $\eta_i(w(0))$, and we have

$$|\eta_1(w(0))| = 2.3131, |\eta_2(w(0))| = 2.3131,$$
$$|\eta_3(w(0))| = 5.5754, |\eta_4(w(0))| = 5.5754.$$

Since $|\eta_i(w(0)| > \varepsilon$ $(i = 1, 2, 3, 4)$, we continue to *Step 4*.

Step 4. Determine the number q such that $|\eta_q(w(L)| = \max_{i \in N}\{|\eta_i(w(L)|\}$; we can set $q = 3$, and compute $T(0)$, $f(0)$, and $w(1)$:

$$T(0) = 1.7673, f(0) = (0.2500, 0.2500, 0.4418, 0.2500)^T,$$
$$w(1) = (0.2098, 0.2098, 0.3707, 0.2098)^T.$$

Step 5. Let $L = L + 1 = 1$ and go to Step 3.

This procedure terminates after three iterations, and the detailed iterative processes are depicted in Table 6.1.

Table 6.1 The iterative process for $\varepsilon = 0.8$ in Example 6.1

L	$w(L)$	$|\eta_i(w(L))|$	q	$T(L)$	$f_i(L)$
0	$(0.2500, 0.2500,$ $0.2500, 0.2500)^T$	2.3131, 2.3131, 5.5754, 5.5754	3	1.7673	0.2500, 0.2500, 0.4418, 0.2500
1	$(0.2098, 0.2098,$ $0.3707, 0.2098)^T$	3.8701, 0.1857, 0.0019, 3.6863	1	1.3950	0.2927, 0.2098, 0.3707, 0.2098
2	$(0.2702, 0.1937,$ $0.3423, 0.1937)^T$	8.4836×10^{-4}, 1.7656, 0.8929, 2.6594	4	0.7953	0.2702, 0.1937, 0.3423, 0.1541
3	$(0.2814, 0.2017,$ $0.3565, 0.1604)^T$	0.6415, 0.5803, 0.0591, 0.0021	1	0.9447	0.2658, 0.2017, 0.3565, 0.1604

Table 6.2 Performance comparisons for Example 6.1

Methods	w^*	Ranking	MD	MAD
LDM	$(0.2710, 0.2080, 0.3595,$ $0.1615)^T$	$x_3 \succ x_1 \succ x_2 \succ x_4$	1.6385	0.2900
LSM (Gong, 2008)	$(0.2652, 0.1814, 0.3798,$ $0.1736)^T$	$x_3 \succ x_1 \succ x_2 \succ x_4$	2.0892	0.2938
GPM (Xu, 2004)	$(0.2642, 0.1698, 0.3962,$ $0.1698)^T$	$x_3 \succ x_1 \succ x_2 \approx x_4$	2.2500	0.3088
LLSM (Xu et al., 2013)	$(0.2723, 0.2015, 0.3677,$ $0.1585)^T$	$x_3 \succ x_1 \succ x_2 \succ x_4$	1.7672	0.2988
CSM (Xu et al., 2015)	$(0.2772, 0.2302, 0.2889,$ $0.2027)^T$	$x_3 \succ x_1 \succ x_2 \succ x_4$	1.9277	0.2992

Table 6.1 shows that after three iterations, $|\eta_1(w(3))| = 0.6415 < \varepsilon$, $|\eta_2(w(3))|$ $= 0.5803 < \varepsilon$, $|\eta_3(w(3))| = 0.0591 < \varepsilon$, and $|\eta_4(w(3))| = 0.0021 < \varepsilon$, indicating that the priority vector obtained has reached an acceptable level of initial parameter ε. Therefore, the optimal priority vector is found to be $w^* = (0.2814, 0.2017, 0.3565,$ $0.1604)^T$, resulting in a ranking of the four alternatives $x_3 \succ x_1 \succ x_2 \succ x_4$.

To further compare the performance with the other three methods in fitting the three incomplete fuzzy reciprocal preference relations, the criteria MD and MAD in Eqs. (5.29) and (5.30) are also used.

From Table 6.2, it is observed that the LDM achieves an identical ranking as LSM (Gong, 2008), CSM (Xu et al., 2015), and LLSM (Xu et al., 2013), while the ranking derived by GPM (Xu, 2004) is slightly different. The GPM fails to discriminate x_2 and x_4. The LDM outperforms all the other four prioritization methods in terms of two performance evaluation criteria: MD and MAD, which partly shows the advantage of the LDM.

Furthermore, by using the Algorithm 6.1, we can get the values of L, w, and $F(w)$ and the ranking of alternatives for different ε as listed in Table 6.3.

From Table 6.3, it is clear that, after nine iterations ($\varepsilon = 10^{-2}$), the values of w and $F(w)$ and ranking of alternatives will stabilize and remain unchanged. However, for CSM, 44 iterations ($\varepsilon = 10^{-2}$) are needed. It shows that the extended LDM needs less computation efforts, and this partly shows the advantages of LDM.

Table 6.3 The values of L, W, and $F(W)$ and ranking order for different ε in Example 6.1

ε	L	w	Ranking	$F(w)$	$|\eta_1|$	$|\eta_2|$	$|\eta_3|$	$|\eta_4|$
0.8	3	$(0.2814, 0.2017, 0.3565, 0.1604)^T$	$x_3 \succ x_1 \succ x_2 \succ x_4$	4.5030	0.6415	0.5803	0.0591	0.0021
0.3	4	$(0.2700, 0.2049, 0.3621, 0.1630)^T$	$x_3 \succ x_1 \succ x_2 \succ x_4$	4.4848	1.2944×10^{-15}	0.2501	0.0935	0.1566
0.1	6	$(0.2709, 0.2073, 0.3599, 0.1620)^T$	$x_3 \succ x_1 \succ x_2 \succ x_4$	4.4821	3.0182×10^{-16}	0.0539	0.0118	0.0421
10^{-2}	9	$(0.2710, 0.2080, 0.3595, 0.1615)^T$	$x_3 \succ x_1 \succ x_2 \succ x_4$	4.4819	1.3388×10^{-15}	0.0010	0.0031	0.0042
10^{-3}	11	$(0.2710, 0.2080, 0.3595, 0.1615)^T$	$x_3 \succ x_1 \succ x_2 \succ x_4$	4.4819	5.1789×10^{-4}	1.7053×10^{-4}	3.3517×10^{-16}	6.8842×10^{-4}
10^{-4}	14	$(0.2710, 0.2080, 0.3595, 0.1615)^T$	$x_3 \succ x_1 \succ x_2 \succ x_4$	4.4819	4.0435×10^{-5}	1.1466×10^{-5}	5.7243×10^{-16}	2.8969×10^{-5}

Example 6.2 Consider a single DM's decision problem with six decision alternatives x_i ($i = 1, 2, \ldots, 6$). The DM provides his/her preferences over these six decision
alternatives and gives an incomplete fuzzy reciprocal preference relation as follows
(adapted from (Xu & Wang, 2013)):

$$C = \begin{bmatrix} 0.5 & 0.3 & - & 0.3 & 0.5 & 0.3 \\ 0.7 & 0.5 & 0.7 & - & 0.6 & - \\ - & 0.3 & 0.5 & 0.4 & - & - \\ 0.7 & - & 0.6 & 0.5 & 0.4 & 0.8 \\ 0.5 & 0.4 & - & 0.6 & 0.5 & 0.7 \\ 0.7 & - & - & 0.2 & 0.3 & 0.5 \end{bmatrix}$$

Xu and Wang (2013) employed EM to derive a priority vector $w^* = (0.1038, 0.2780,$
$0.1262, 0.2017, 0.1949, 0.0953)^T$ from the aforesaid incomplete fuzzy reciprocal
preference relation. The research leads to a final ranking: $x_2 \succ x_4 \succ x_5 \succ x_3 \succ x_1 \succ x_6$.
We now examine the problem using the LDM as follows.

According to Theorem 1.4, we know that C could be completed. Without loss of
generality, we let the original weight vector $w(0) = (1/6, 1/6, 1/6, 1/6, 1/6, 1/6)^T$.
When ε is set to 10^{-3}, the values of w and $F(w)$ and ranking of alternatives will
stabilize and remain unchanged. The results are displayed in Table 6.4. At $L = 25$,
one has $F(w) = 3.9564$, $|\eta_1| = 2.3587 \times 10^{-4} < \varepsilon$, $|\eta_2| = 3.2312 \times 10^{-4} < \varepsilon$,
$|\eta_3| = 4.1525 \times 10^{-16} < \varepsilon$, $|\eta_4| = 2.7599 \times 10^{-4} < \varepsilon$, $|\eta_5| = 4.6256 \times 10^{-4} < \varepsilon$,
$|\eta_6| = 8.3498 \times 10^{-16} < \varepsilon$, and $w^* = (0.0945, 0.2727, 0.1250, 0.2140, 0.1909,$
$0.1028)^T$, implying a ranking of these six alternatives: $x_2 \succ x_4 \succ x_5 \succ x_3 \succ x_6 \succ x_1$.

For this single incomplete fuzzy reciprocal preference relation, it can also be
solved by the EM (Xu & Wang, 2013), NRAM (Xu et al., 2009), LSM (Gong, 2008),
LLSM (Xu et al., 2013), CSM (Xu et al., 2015), and GPM (Xu, 2004). The results
are shown in Table 6.5, from which we can see that LDM achieves the same ranking
$x_2 \succ x_4 \succ x_5 \succ x_1 \succ x_3 \succ x_6$ as LLSM, GPM, NRAM, and CSM. Moreover, LDM
has the smallest MD and MAD among these seven methods. However, EM and LSM
give different ranking. Compared with LDM, LLSM, GPM, CSM, and NRAM, the
EM and LSM reverse the order of x_1 and x_6, while the DM's original judgment is x_6
$\succ x_1$ because $c_{61} = 0.6$. Evidently, both the EM and the LSM suffer from the rank
reversal phenomenon. This shows another advantage of the LDM. Moreover, from
Table 6.4 in this chapter and Table 6 in the work of Xu et al. (2015)), it is clear that
LDM has a faster convergence speed than CSM.

In Example 6.2, the value $c_{15} = c_{51} = 0.5$, if $c_{15} = 0.8$ and $c_{51} = 0.2$, and it will be
Example 3.1 and Example 5.2. In this case, if we use LDM to derive its optimal
weights and improve its consistency, the following steps are involved:

Step 1. From Theorem 1.4, we know that the incomplete fuzzy reciprocal preference
relation is acceptable and then go to Step 2.
Step 2. Use the Algorithm 6.2 to obtain the priority vector, we have

Table 6.4 The values of L, w, and $F(w)$ and ranking order for different ε in Example 6.2

ε	L	w	Ranking	$F(w)$	$|\eta_i(w(L))|$
0.8	8	$(0.0911, 0.2718, 0.1304,$ $0.2173, 0.1879, 0.1014)^T$	$x_2 \succ x_4 \succ x_5$ $\succ x_3 \succ x_6 \succ$ x_1	3.9771	$0.5778, 2.5097 \times 10^{-16},$ 0.2956 $0.3777, 0.0956,$ 1.3049×10^{-15}
0.3	9	$(0.0937, 0.2710, 0.1300,$ $0.2167, 0.1874, 0.1011)^T$	$x_2 \succ x_4 \succ x_5$ $\succ x_3 \succ x_6 \succ$ x_1	3.9680	$3.3836 \times 10^{-17}, 0.1279,$ $0.2956, 0.2523, 0.2537,$ 0.1663
0.1	11	$(0.0947, 0.2710, 0.1250,$ $0.2148, 0.1912, 0.1033)^T$	$x_2 \succ x_4 \succ x_5$ $\succ x_3 \succ x_6 \succ$ x_1	3.9568	$0.0922, 0.0202, 0.0925,$ $1.1506 \times 10^{-15}, 0.1461,$ 0.0589
10^{-2}	17	$(0.0945, 0.2729, 0.1251,$ $0.2140, 0.1908, 0.1028)^T$	$x_2 \succ x_4 \succ x_5$ $\succ x_3 \succ x_6 \succ$ x_1	3.9564	$0.0038, 0.0060, 0.0073,$ $6.4207 \times 10^{-16}, 0.0129,$ 0.0034
10^{-3}	25	$(0.0945, 0.2727, 0.1250,$ $0.2140, 0.1909, 0.1028)^T$	$x_2 \succ x_4 \succ x_5$ $\succ x_3 \succ x_6 \succ$ x_1	3.9564	$2.3587 \times 10^{-4},$ $3.2312 \times 10^{-4},$ 4.1525×10^{-16} $2.7599 \times 10^{-4},$ $4.6256 \times 10^{-4},$ 8.3498×10^{-16}
10^{-4}	29	$(0.0945, 0.2727, 0.1250,$ $0.2140, 0.1909, 0.1028)^T$	$x_2 \succ x_4 \succ x_5$ $\succ x_3 \succ x_6 \succ$ x_1	3.9564	$8.2745 \times 10^{-6},$ $2.2917 \times 10^{-5},$ $2.4746 \times 10^{-16},$ $1.7050 \times 10^{-5},$ $3.9811 \times 10^{-16},$ 3.1692×10^{-5}

Table 6.5 Performance comparisons for Example 6.2

Method	w^*	Ranking	FCR	MD	MAD
LDM	$(0.0945, 0.2727, 0.1250,$ $0.2140, 0.1909, 0.1028)^T$	$x_2 \succ x_4 \succ x_5 \succ x_3$ $\succ x_6 \succ x_1$	0.0520	0.6112	0.1790
EM (Xu & Wang, 2013)	$(0.1038, 0.2780, 0.1262,$ $0.2017, 0.1949, 0.0953)^T$	$x_2 \succ x_4 \succ x_5 \succ x_3$ $\succ x_1 \succ x_6$	0.0540	0.9349	0.2213
LSM (Gong, 2008)	$(0.1017, 0.3036, 0.1354,$ $0.1849, 0.1937, 0.0808)^T$	$x_2 \succ x_5 \succ x_4 \succ x_3$ $\succ x_1 \succ x_6$	0.0607	1.2774	0.2573
LLSM (Xu et al., 2013)	$(0.0965, 0.2682, 0.1288,$ $0.2166, 0.1901, 0.0998)^T$	$x_2 \succ x_4 \succ x_5 \succ x_3$ $\succ x_6 \succ x_1$	0.0519	0.6994	0.1916
GPM (Xu, 2004)	$(0.0835, 0.3031, 0.1299,$ $0.1948, 0.2021, 0.0866)^T$	$x_2 \succ x_4 \succ x_5 \succ x_3$ $\succ x_6 \succ x_1$	0.0583	0.8335	0.2076
NRAM (Xu et al., 2009)	$(0.1299, 0.2101, 0.1507,$ $0.1913, 0.1832, 0.1348)^T$	$x_2 \succ x_4 \succ x_5 \succ x_3$ $\succ x_6 \succ x_1$	0.0850	1.1734	0.2134
CSM (Xu et al., 2015)	$(0.0994, 0.2698, 0.1275,$ $0.2083, 0.1889, 0.1061)^T$	$x_2 \succ x_4 \succ x_5 \succ x_3$ $\succ x_6 \succ x_1$	0.0525	0.6434	0.1837

$$w^* = (0.1326, 0.2769, 0.1264, 0.2155, 0.1410, 0.1077)^T$$

Step 3. Compute FCR by Eq. (1.13):

$$FCR = 0.146 > 0.1.$$

Since FCR > 0.1, the incomplete fuzzy reciprocal preference relation C does not possess satisfactory consistency. We need to find its UFEs to repair this preference relation.

Step 4. Calculate the deviations between original judgment c_{ij} and its corresponding consistent representation, we have

$$D = \begin{bmatrix} 0 & 0.0238 & 0 & 0.0809 & 0.3153 & 0.2518 \\ 0.0238 & 0 & 0.0133 & 0 & 0.0626 & 0 \\ 0 & 0.0133 & 0 & 0.0304 & 0 & 0 \\ 0.0809 & 0 & 0.0304 & 0 & 0.2045 & 0.1332 \\ 0.3153 & 0.0626 & 0 & 0.2045 & 0 & 0.1331 \\ 0.2518 & 0 & 0 & 0.1332 & 0.1331 & 0 \end{bmatrix}.$$

Obviously, the maximum deviations are d_{15} and d_{51}, so the UFEs are c_{15} and c_{51}.

Step 5. Update the UFEs c_{15} and c_{51} with $c'_{15} = $ round $(\frac{w_1}{w_1 + w_5} \times 10) \times 10^{-1}$ and $c'_{51} = $ round $(\frac{w_5}{w_1 + w_5} \times 10) \times 10^{-1}$, one has $c'_{15} = 0.5$ and $c'_{51} = 0.5$.

In this case, it will be Example 6.1, and it is consistent.

Similarly, if we look at UFEs c_{15} and c_{51} as unknown elements, and use Algorithm 6.3 to compute the weight vector and FCR, MD, and MAD values, we have

$$w'^* = (0.0724, 0.2645, 0.1214, 0.2081, 0.2353, 0.0983)^T$$

$$FCR = 0.0305, MD = 0.4188, \text{ and } MAD = 0.0305.$$

If we set $c'_{15} = \frac{w'_1}{w'_1 + w'_5} = 0.2354$ and $c'_{51} = \frac{w'_5}{w'_1 + w'_5} = 0.7646$, and use Algorithm 6.3 to compute the weight vector and FCR, MD, and MAD values, we have

$$w'^* = (0.0727, 0.2646, 0.1214, 0.2082, 0.2347, 0.0984)^T$$

$$FCR = 0.0305, MD = 0.4188, \text{ and } MAD = 0.0305.$$

The weights are slightly different from c_{15} and c_{51} that are looked at as unknown values, while FCR, MD, and MAD values are same, and this shows that $c_{15} = 0.2354$ and $c_{51} = 0.7646$ are preferred.

If we want the values of c'_{15} and c'_{51} to be in the set U, i.e., $c'_{15} = $ round $(\frac{w'_1}{w'_1+w'_5}$
$\times 10) \times 10^{-1} = 0.2$ and $c'_{51} = $ round $(\frac{w'_5}{w'_1+w'_5} \times 10) \times 10^{-1} = 0.8$, we have

$$w''^* = (0.0702, 0.2633, 0.1208, 0.2072, 0.2408, 0.0978)^T$$

$$FCR = 0.0318, MD = 0.4172, \text{ and } MAD = 0.1206.$$

which are slightly different from the results when c_{15} and c_{51} are looked at as unknown values. This example is also examined by EM in Example 3.1 and CSM in Example 5.2, from the viewpoint of the value of FCR; in all the cases, the values of FCR generated by LDM are smaller than by EM, and almost same as CSM, which denotes that LDM has better performances than EM.

Example 6.3 Consider a GDM problem with three DMs providing the following complete fuzzy reciprocal preference relations C_k ($k = 1, 2, 3, 4$) for a set of four alternatives $X = \{x_1, x_2, x_3, x_4\}$:

$$C_1 = \begin{bmatrix} 0.5 & 0.3 & 0.7 & 0.1 \\ 0.7 & 0.5 & 0.6 & 0.6 \\ 0.3 & 0.4 & 0.5 & 0.2 \\ 0.9 & 0.4 & 0.8 & 0.5 \end{bmatrix}, C_2 = \begin{bmatrix} 0.5 & 0.4 & 0.6 & 0.2 \\ 0.6 & 0.5 & 0.7 & 0.4 \\ 0.4 & 0.3 & 0.5 & 0.1 \\ 0.8 & 0.6 & 0.9 & 0.5 \end{bmatrix},$$

$$C_3 = \begin{bmatrix} 0.5 & 0.4 & 0.7 & 0.2 \\ 0.6 & 0.5 & 0.4 & 0.3 \\ 0.3 & 0.6 & 0.5 & 0.1 \\ 0.8 & 0.7 & 0.9 & 0.5 \end{bmatrix}.$$

For these three complete reciprocal preference relations, we can use LDM to solve. Without loss of generality, we let the original weight vector $w(0) = (1/4, 1/4, 1/4, 1/4)^T$. When ε is set to 10^{-2}, the values of w and $F(w)$ and ranking of alternatives will stabilize and remain unchanged. At $L = 10$, one has $F(w) = 3.1984$, $|\eta_1| = 0.0043 < \varepsilon$, $|\eta_2| = 5.7473 \times 10^{-16} < \varepsilon$, $|\eta_3| = 3.9884 \times 10^{-4} < \varepsilon$, $|\eta_4| = 0.0039 < \varepsilon$, and $w^* = (0.1538, 0.2459, 0.1129, 0.4873)^T$, implying a ranking of these four alternatives: $x_4 \succ x_2 \succ x_1 \succ x_3$.

Table 6.6 shows the priority vectors and ranking obtained by the LDM along with LSM (Gong, 2008), GPM (Fan et al., 2006), CSM (Xu et al., 2015), and LLSM (Xu et al., 2013). The performance evaluation criteria MD and MAD are also given in Table 6.6. It is clear that the LDM achieves the same ranking as all the other priority methods, which shows that the ranking is robust and credible. LDM still performs better than the LSM, GPM, and LLSM according to MD and MAD. The LDM is based on the transfer relationship between reciprocal preference relation and multiplicative preference relation. It could be applied to handle both incomplete

Table 6.6 Performance comparisons for Example 6.3

Methods	w^*	Ranking	MD	MAD
LDM	$(0.1538, 0.2459, 0.1129, 0.4873)^T$	$x_4 \succ x_2 \succ x_1 \succ x_3$	1.5731	0.2853
LSM (Gong, 2008)	$(0.1437, 0.2781, 0.1111, 0.4671)^T$	$x_4 \succ x_2 \succ x_1 \succ x_3$	2.0211	0.3145
GPM (Fan et al., 2006)	$(0.1544, 0.2667, 0.0772, 0.5018)^T$	$x_4 \succ x_2 \succ x_1 \succ x_3$	3.3750	0.3755
LLSM (Xu et al., 2013)	$(0.1386, 0.2322, 0.0977, 0.5315)^T$	$x_4 \succ x_2 \succ x_1 \succ x_3$	1.8455	0.3038
CSM (Xu et al., 2015)	$(0.1564, 0.2452, 0.1155, 0.4829)^T$	$x_4 \succ x_2 \succ x_1 \succ x_3$	1.4984	0.2798

fuzzy reciprocal preference relations and incomplete multiplicative preference relations, while LLSM, LSM, GPM, and CSM can only be employed to incomplete fuzzy reciprocal preference relations.

In order to compare the performances with existing methods, we directly set $\lambda = (1/n, 1/n, \ldots, 1/n)^T$ in Examples 6.1, 6.2, and 6.3. According to the actual conditions, we can assign proper weights to different experts to reflect their varying influences in GDM problems. The weight of each expert can be determined by the method of AHP according to appraisal index (academic level, technical title, professional expertise, professional ethics, etc.).

While there is no specific rule to determine ε, it can be set to sufficiently small values to ensure accuracy. In this chapter, we set $\varepsilon = 0.8, 0.3, 0.1, 10^{-2}, 10^{-3}$, and 10^{-4} to derive the ranking. After our detailed computation experiment, it is noteworthy that when ε is set to be 10^{-3}, the w, $F(w)$, and FCR and ranking results will converge to a set of values and remain unchanged in most situations. That is to say, generally, we can set $\varepsilon = 10^{-3}$, and the weight vector can be obtained.

6.4   Statistical Comparative Study

Given a GDM problem with incomplete fuzzy reciprocal relations, different priority methods used to derive priorities from the group preference relations play an important role in finding the best alternative(s) from a set of feasible ones. It is therefore worth conducting research to ascertain whether or not the use of different priority methods could affect the ranking results.

For continuous data and two related samples, the main nonparametric tests available are the sign test and the Wilcoxon signed-rank test (Chiclana et al., 2013). In this chapter, we apply the Wilcoxon signed-rank test in our experimental study, because it incorporates more information about the data. The hypothesis we are testing in this chapter can be stated as follows:

The application of the CSM, LSM, LLSM, GPM, and LDM in GDM problems does not produce significant differences in ranking results. To test it, 12 sets of preference relations were randomly generated for each combination expert ($m = 4$, 6, 8, 10, 12) and alternative ($n = 4$, 6, 8), and the different priority methods were applied in turn to obtain the ranking results. Each one of these random GDM problems was executed five times, each time using one of the five different priority methods. There is no significant difference among five priority methods to obtain the priority vectors and ranking results in most GDM problems on the whole, but for a certain GDM problem, the results are different.

6.5   Complexity of Computation of Different Algorithms

Once we have developed an algorithm for solving a computational problem and analyzed its worst-case time requirements as a function of the size of its input (most usually, in terms of the O-notation), we analyze the complexity of computation of different methods, and the analysis results are listed in Table 6.7.

From Table 6.7, we can find that the LDM and CSM have the same time complexity and space complexity. The time complexity of LLSM, LSM, and GPM depends on the parameter n (the number of alternatives), while the time complexity of LDM and CSM depends on the product of n and m (the number of experts). LDM, CSM, LLSM, and LSM have the same space complexity $O(n \times m)$.

The LDM possesses some attractive properties that make it an appealing alternative to the other prioritization methods:

1. By setting $\lambda_1 = 1$ and $\lambda_k = 0$ for $k = 2, \ldots, m$, the LDM can also be conveniently applied to derive a priority vector from a single incomplete fuzzy reciprocal preference relation. This implies that the proposed LDM model can be employed to handle both group and individual decision problems. Other methods such as EM and NRAM can only be applied to a single incomplete fuzzy reciprocal preference relation. This advantage makes it a natural choice for handling GDM.
2. The LDM is convenient in considering different DMs' weights in the decision process, while this issue has been largely omitted by other methods.
3. By setting $\delta_{ij} = 1$, for all $i, j \in N$, LDM can be utilized to derive a priority vector from complete reciprocal preference relations. This indicates that it can be flexibly used to handle decision problems with both complete and incomplete fuzzy reciprocal preference relations.

Table 6.7 Time complexity and space complexity of five methods

Methods	Time complexity	Space complexity
LDM	$O(n \times m)$	$O(n \times m)$
CSM	$O(n \times m)$	$O(n \times m)$
LLSM	$O(n^2)$	$O(n \times m)$
LSM	$O(n^{5/2})$	$O(n \times m)$
GPM	$O(2^n)$	$O(1)$

4. Compared with other methods, the LDM is known for its better fitting performance, rank preservation capability, and discrimination power.

6.6   Summary

We have proposed a least deviation method to handle decision problems with incomplete fuzzy reciprocal preference relations and developed a convergent iterative algorithm to determine a priority vector. The main idea of the LDM is to utilize the transfer relationship between fuzzy reciprocal preference relation and multiplicative reciprocal preference relation.

References

Chiclana, F., Garcia Tapia, J. M., Del Moral, M. J., & Herrera-Viedma, E. (2013). A statistical comparative study of different similarity measures of consensus in group decision making. *Information Sciences, 221*, 110–123.

Fan, Z. P., Ma, J., Jiang, Y. P., Sun, Y. H., & Ma, L. (2006). A goal programming approach to group decision making based on multiplicative preference relations and fuzzy preference relations. *European Journal of Operational Research, 174*(1), 311–321.

Gong, Z. W. (2008). Least-square method to priority of the fuzzy preference relations with incomplete information. *International Journal of Approximate Reasoning, 47*(2), 258–264.

Xu, Y. J., Chen, L., Li, K. W., & Wang, H. M. (2015). A chi-square method for priority derivation in group decision making with incomplete reciprocal preference relations. *Information Sciences, 306*, 166–179.

Xu, Y. J., Da, Q. L., & Liu, L. H. (2009). Normalizing rank aggregation method for priority of a fuzzy preference relation and its effectiveness. *International Journal of Approximate Reasoning, 50*(8), 1287–1297.

Xu, Y. J., Patnayakuni, R., & Wang, H. M. (2013). Logarithmic least squares method to priority for group decision making with incomplete fuzzy preference relations. *Applied Mathematical Modelling, 37*(4), 2139–2152.

Xu, Y. J., & Wang, H. M. (2013). Eigenvector method, consistency test and inconsistency repairing for an incomplete fuzzy preference relation. *Applied Mathematical Modelling, 37*(7), 5171–5183.

Xu, Z. S. (2004). Goal programming models for obtaining the priority vector of incomplete fuzzy preference relation. *International Journal of Approximate Reasoning, 36*(3), 261–270.

Chapter 7
Priorities from Fuzzy Best-Worst Method Matrix

In 2015, Rezaei (2015) proposed the best-worst method (BWM). A nonlinear minmax model is used to derive the weights. The minmax model may result in multiple optimal solutions. Later, Rezaei (2016) proposed a linear model for BWM, which yields a unique solution. On the one hand, this method has been widely used to solve various decision-making problems (Badri Ahmadi et al., 2017; Gupta & Barua, 2016; Gupta et al., 2017; Salimi & Rezaei, 2016, 2018). On the other hand, BWM has been further extended to combine with other types of fuzzy sets. Recently, Xu et al. (2021) proposed the fuzzy BWM (FBWM), which incorporates the fuzzy preference into BWM.

7.1 FBWM and Its Structure

In the following, the steps of FBWM to obtain the priority are presented.

Step 1. For an MCDM problem, a set of criteria $C = \{c_1, c_2, \ldots, c_n\}$ are given.

Step 2. The DM identifies his best criterion (c_B) and worst criterion (c_W).

Step 3. The DM gives his fuzzy comparison values between the best criterion (c_B) and other criteria. The fuzzy best-to-others vector (FBV) is elicited:

$$R_B = (r_{B1}, r_{B2}, \ldots, r_{Bn}) \tag{7.1}$$

where $0.5 \leq r_{Bj} \leq 1$, and $r_{BB} = 0.5$.

Step 4. The DM gives his fuzzy comparison values between the worst criterion (c_B) and other criteria. The fuzzy others-to-worst vector (FWV) is elicited:

$$R_W = (r_{1W}, r_{2W}, \ldots, r_{nW})^T \tag{7.2}$$

where $0.5 \leq r_{jW} \leq 1$, and $r_{WW} = 0.5$.

Y. Xu, *Deriving Priorities from Incomplete Fuzzy Reciprocal Preference Relations*, https://doi.org/10.1007/978-981-99-3169-9_7

Step 5. Calculate the optimal fuzzy weights w_j^* $(j \in N)$.

The optimal weights will satisfy the following requirements:

$$r_{Bj} = \frac{w_B}{w_B + w_j} \tag{7.3}$$

and

$$r_{jW} = \frac{w_j}{w_j + w_W} \tag{7.4}$$

However, Eqs. (7.3) and (7.4) do not always hold. The following optimization problem would be formulated:

$$\min \quad \max_j \left\{ \left| \frac{w_B}{w_B + w_j} - r_{Bj} \right|, \left| \frac{w_j}{w_j + w_W} - r_{jW} \right| \right\}$$

$$\text{s.t.} \begin{cases} \sum_{j=1}^{n} w_j = 1 \\ w_j \geq 0, \ j \in N \end{cases} \tag{M-7.1}$$

Problem (M-7.1) is equivalent to the following problem (M-7.2):

$$\min \ \xi$$

$$\text{s.t.} \begin{cases} \left| \dfrac{w_B}{w_B + w_j} - r_{Bj} \right| \leq \xi, j \in N \\ \left| \dfrac{w_j}{w_j + w_W} - r_{jW} \right| \leq \xi, j \in N \\ \sum_{j=1}^{n} w_j = 1 \\ w_j \geq 0, j \in N \end{cases} \tag{M-7.2}$$

Solving (M-7.2), the optimal fuzzy weights w_j^* $(j \in N)$ are obtained.

From the point of view of the matrix, we can find that FBV and FWV can construct two incomplete fuzzy reciprocal preference relations, respectively. In each incomplete fuzzy reciprocal preference relations, there is only one line and one column vector. The two incomplete fuzzy reciprocal preference relations R_1 and R_2 can be established as follows:

$$
R_1 = \begin{array}{c} c_1 \\ \vdots \\ c_B \\ \vdots \\ c_{W'} \\ \vdots \\ c_n \end{array}
\begin{pmatrix}
0.5 & & & 1-r_{B1} & & & \\
& \ddots & & \vdots & & & \\
r_{B1} & \cdots & 0.5 & \cdots & r_{BW'} & \cdots & r_{Bn} \\
& & & \vdots & \ddots & & \\
& & & 1-r_{BW'} & & 0.5 & \\
& & & \vdots & & & \ddots \\
& & & 1-r_{Bn} & & & 0.5
\end{pmatrix}
$$
$$
\begin{array}{ccccccc} c_1 & \cdots & c_B & \cdots & c_{W'} & \cdots & c_n \end{array}
$$

$$
R_2 = \begin{array}{c} c_1 \\ \vdots \\ c_{B'} \\ \vdots \\ c_W \\ \vdots \\ c_n \end{array}
\begin{pmatrix}
0.5 & & & & r_{1W} & & \\
& \ddots & & & \vdots & & \\
& & 0.5 & & r_{B'W} & & \\
& & & \ddots & \vdots & & \\
1-r_{1W} & \cdots & 1-r_{B'W} & \cdots & 0.5 & \cdots & 1-r_{nW} \\
& & & & \vdots & \ddots & \\
& & & & r_{nW} & & 0.5
\end{pmatrix}
$$
$$
\begin{array}{ccccccc} c_1 & \cdots & c_{B'} & \cdots & c_W & \cdots & c_n \end{array}
$$

Obviously, there is a best-to-worst fuzzy comparison $r_{BW'}$ in R_1 and a best-to-worst fuzzy comparison $r_{B'W}$ in R_2. Generally, the two comparisons should be equal when a DM gives these two values, i.e., $r_{BW'} = r_{B'W}$. Otherwise, the information given by the DM would be contradictory. For simplicity, r_{BW} is used to represent the identical comparison. In this regard, R_1 and R_2 can constitute one incomplete fuzzy reciprocal preference relation R as follows:

$$
R = \begin{array}{c} c_1 \\ \vdots \\ c_B \\ \vdots \\ c_W \\ \vdots \\ c_n \end{array}
\begin{pmatrix}
0.5 & & 1-r_{B1} & & r_{1W} & & \\
& \ddots & \vdots & & \vdots & & \\
r_{B1} & \cdots & 0.5 & \cdots & r_{BW} & \cdots & r_{Bn} \\
& & \vdots & \ddots & \vdots & & \\
1-r_{1W} & \cdots & 1-r_{BW} & \cdots & 0.5 & \cdots & 1-r_{nW} \\
& & \vdots & & \vdots & \ddots & \\
& & 1-r_{Bn} & & r_{nW} & & 0.5
\end{pmatrix}
$$
$$
\begin{array}{ccccccc} c_1 & \cdots & c_B & \cdots & c_W & \cdots & c_n \end{array} .
$$

As mentioned above, we can construct an incomplete fuzzy reciprocal preference relation R by FBV and FWV. We call R an FBWM matrix. Then, the problem of FBWM can be transformed to derive the optimal weights from R, which is the focus of this chapter.

To obtain the priorities from a fuzzy reciprocal preference relation, the distances between $\frac{w_i}{w_i+w_j}$ and all the known pairwise values r_{ij} should be minimized. Therefore, the following least absolute error (LAE) model can be established:

$$D = \min \sum_{i=1}^{n} \sum_{j=1}^{n} \left| \frac{w_i}{w_i + w_j} - r_{ij} \right| \tag{7.5}$$

As R is an incomplete fuzzy reciprocal preference relation, the absolute distances $\left| \frac{w_B}{w_B+w_j} - r_{Bj} \right|$, $\left| \frac{w_j}{w_j+w_W} - r_{jW} \right|$, and $\left| \frac{w_W}{w_W+w_j} - r_{Wj} \right|$ for all j should be minimized. Therefore, the model (7.5) can be transferred into the following model (7.6):

$$\min \sum_{j=1}^{n} \left(\left| \frac{w_B}{w_B + w_j} - r_{Bj} \right| + \left| \frac{w_j}{w_j + w_B} - r_{jB} \right| \right) + \sum_{j=1,j\neq i}^{n}$$
$$\times \left(\left| \frac{w_j}{w_j + w_W} - r_{jW} \right| + \left| \frac{w_W}{w_W + w_j} - r_{Wj} \right| \right) \tag{7.6}$$

Given that $r_{Bj} = 1 - r_{jB}$ and $r_{jW} = 1 - r_{Wj}$,

$$\left| \frac{w_B}{w_B + w_j} - r_{Bj} \right| = \left| \frac{w_j}{w_j + w_B} - r_{jB} \right| \tag{7.7}$$

and

$$\left| \frac{w_j}{w_j + w_W} - r_{jW} \right| = \left| \frac{w_W}{w_W + w_j} - r_{Wj} \right| \tag{7.8}$$

Therefore, model (7.6) can be simplified to model (7.9):

$$\min \sum_{j=1}^{n} \left(\left| \frac{w_B}{w_B + w_j} - r_{Bj} \right| \right) + \sum_{j=1,j\neq i}^{n} \left(\left| \frac{w_j}{w_j + w_W} - r_{jW} \right| \right) \tag{7.9}$$

Additionally, the following general least absolute error (GLAE) optimization model for metric $1 \leq \lambda \leq \infty$ can be formulated:

$$\min \left[\sum_{j=1}^{n} \left(\left| \frac{w_B}{w_B + w_j} - r_{Bj} \right| + \left| \frac{w_j}{w_j + w_W} - r_{jW} \right| \right)^{\lambda} \right]^{\frac{1}{\lambda}} \tag{7.10}$$

Obviously, when $\lambda = 1$, Eq. (7.10) reduces to Eq. (7.9). When $\lambda = \infty$, Eq. (7.10) leads to the following minmax (Chebyshev) model:

$$\lim_{\lambda \to \infty} \min \left[\sum_{j=1}^{n} \left(\left| \frac{w_B}{w_B + w_j} - r_{Bj} \right| + \left| \frac{w_j}{w_j + w_W} - r_{jW} \right| \right)^{\lambda} \right]^{\frac{1}{\lambda}}$$

$$= \min \quad \max_{j} \left\{ \left| \frac{w_B}{w_B + w_j} - r_{Bj} \right|, \left| \frac{w_j}{w_j + w_W} - r_{jW} \right| \right\} \tag{7.11}$$

which is (M-7.1). Therefore, the FBWM is one of the special cases of Eq. (7.10), which means that FBWM is one kind of the methods to derive the weights from the incomplete fuzzy reciprocal preference relation R.

7.2   Methods for Priorities from FBWM Matrix

As we have discussed above, FBWM is one of the methods to derive the weights from FBV and FWV. And FBV and FWV can formulate an incomplete fuzzy reciprocal preference relations R; we call the matrix an FBWM matrix R. In this section, we present some methods to derive the priorities based on the FBWM matrix R.

7.2.1   Methods for Priorities from an FBWM Matrix

Here, we elaborate various methods for the priority of FBWM with a single DM based on the FBWM matrix P.

1. **Least absolute error method (LAEM)**

    Based on Eq. (7.9), we can construct the following model:

$$\min \sum_{j=1}^{n} \left(\left| \frac{w_B}{w_B + w_j} - r_{Bj} \right| \right) + \sum_{j=1, j \neq B}^{n} \left(\left| \frac{w_j}{w_j + w_W} - r_{jW} \right| \right)$$

$$\text{s.t.} \begin{cases} \sum_{j=1}^{n} w_j = 1 \\ w_j \geq 0, \ j \in N \end{cases} \tag{M-7.3}$$

2. **Least square method (LSM-I)**

Liu and He (2012) proposed LSM for obtaining priority from an incomplete fuzzy reciprocal preference relation. In FBWM, only the FBV and FWV need to be considered. Based on Eqs. (7.7) and (7.8), we put forward the following LSM-I of FBWM, as shown in (M-7.4):

$$\min \ F(w) = \sum_{j=1}^{n} \left(\frac{w_B}{w_B + w_j} - r_{Bj} \right)^2 + \sum_{j=1, j \neq B}^{n} \left(\frac{w_j}{w_j + w_W} - r_{jW} \right)^2$$

$$\text{s.t.} \begin{cases} \sum_{j=1}^{n} w_j = 1 \\ w_j \geq 0, \ j \in N \end{cases} \tag{M-7.4}$$

3. **Least square method (LSM-II)**

Gong (2008) proposed another form of LSM. Similarly, if only the FBV and FWV are considered, we put forward the following LSM-II of FBWM, as shown in (M-7.5):

$$\min \ F(w) = \sum_{j=1}^{n} \left(r_{Bj} w_j - r_{jB} w_B \right)^2 + \sum_{j=1, j \neq B}^{n} \left(r_{jW} w_W - r_{Wj} w_j \right)^2$$

$$\text{s.t.} \begin{cases} \sum_{j=1}^{n} w_j = 1 \\ w_j \geq 0, \ j \in N \end{cases} \tag{M-7.5}$$

As we have pointed out, FBWM matrix is a special incomplete fuzzy reciprocal preference relation. Gong (2008) proposed the LSM of incomplete fuzzy reciprocal preference relation. Thus, we have the following result:

Theorem 7.1 *Let* $w = (w_1, w_2, \ldots, w_n)^T$ *be the optimal solution to the model* (M-7.5); *then*

$$w = Q^{-1} e / e^T Q^{-1} e \tag{7.12}$$

where

$$
Q = \begin{bmatrix}
r_{B1}^2 + (1-r_{1W})^2 & \cdots & -(1-r_{B1})r_{B1} & \cdots & -r_{1W}(1-r_{1W}) & \cdots & \cdots \\
\vdots & \ddots & \vdots & \vdots & \vdots & \vdots & \vdots \\
-r_{B1}(1-r_{B1}) & \cdots & \sum_{i=1,i\neq B}^{n}(1-r_{Bi})^2 & \cdots & -r_{BW}(1-r_{BW}) & \cdots & -r_{Bn}(1-r_{Bn}) \\
\vdots & \vdots & \ddots & \vdots & \vdots & \vdots & \vdots \\
-(1-r_{1W})r_{1W} & \cdots & -(1-r_{BW})r_{BW} & \cdots & \sum_{i=1,i\neq W}^{n} r_{iW}^2 & \cdots & -(1-r_{nW})r_{nW} \\
\vdots & \vdots & \vdots & \vdots & \vdots & \ddots & \vdots \\
\cdots & \cdots & -(1-r_{Bn})r_{Bn} & \cdots & -r_{nW}(1-r_{nW}) & \cdots & r_{Bn}^2 + (1-r_{nW})^2
\end{bmatrix}
$$

$e = (1, 1, \ldots, 1)^T.$

Remark 7.1 Obviously, Q is irreducible, and (M-7.5) has unique solution Eq. (7.12).

4. **Logarithmic least square method (LLSM)**

Xu et al. (2013) presented the LLSM to priority for incomplete fuzzy reciprocal preference relation. According to FBV and FWV, the LLSM of FBWM can be formulated in (M-7.6):

$$
\begin{aligned}
\min \ F(w) = &\sum_{j=1}^{n}\left(\ln w_B - \ln w_j - \ln r_{Bj} + \ln r_{jB}\right)^2 \\
&+ \sum_{j=1,j\neq B}^{n}\left(\ln w_j - \ln w_W - \ln r_{jW} + \ln r_{Wj}\right)^2 \\
\text{s.t.} &\begin{cases} \sum_{j=1}^{n} w_j = 1 \\ w_j \geq 0, \ j \in N \end{cases}
\end{aligned}
\tag{M-7.6}
$$

As we have pointed out, FBWM matrix is a special incomplete fuzzy reciprocal preference relation, and Xu et al. (2013) proposed the LLSM to priority ranking method. Thus, it could be extended to derive the weights from the FBWM matrix. Thus, we have the following result:

Theorem 7.2 (Xu et al., 2013) *Let* $w^* = (w_1^*, w_2^*, \ldots, w_n^*)^T$ *be the optimal solution to the model* (M-7.6); *then*

$$
w_i^* = \frac{\exp(w_i)}{\sum_{j=1}^{n-1}\exp(w_j) + 1}, i = 1, 2, \ldots, n-1
\tag{7.13}
$$

$$
w_i^* = \frac{1}{\sum_{j=1}^{n-1}\exp(w_j) + 1}, i = n
\tag{7.14}
$$

where w_i is determined by the following Eqs. (7.15)–(7.18):

$$D_{n-1} = \begin{bmatrix} 2 & \cdots & -1 & \cdots & -1 & \cdots & \cdots \\ \vdots & \ddots & \vdots & \vdots & \vdots & \vdots & \vdots \\ -1 & \cdots & n-1 & \cdots & -1 & \cdots & -1 \\ \vdots & \vdots & \vdots & \ddots & \vdots & \vdots & \vdots \\ -1 & \cdots & -1 & \cdots & n-1 & \cdots & -1 \\ \vdots & \vdots & \vdots & \vdots & \vdots & \ddots & \vdots \\ \cdots & \cdots & -1 & \cdots & -1 & \cdots & 2 \end{bmatrix} \tag{7.15}$$

$$w_{n-1} = \begin{bmatrix} \ln w_1 \\ \ln w_2 \\ \vdots \\ \ln w_{n-1} \end{bmatrix} \tag{7.16}$$

$$Y_{n-1} = \begin{bmatrix} (\ln(1 - r_{B1}) - \ln r_{B1}) + (\ln(r_{1W}) - \ln(1 - r_{1W})) \\ \vdots \\ \sum_{j=1}^{n} \left(\ln r_{Bj} - \ln(1 - r_{Bj}) \right) \\ \vdots \\ \sum_{j=1}^{n} \left(\ln(1 - r_{jW}) - \ln r_{jW} \right) \\ \vdots \\ (\ln(1 - r_{B,n-1}) - \ln r_{B,n-1}) + (\ln(r_{n-1,W}) - \ln(1 - r_{n-1,W})) \end{bmatrix} \tag{7.17}$$

$$w_{n-1} = D_{n-1}^{-1} Y_{n-1} \tag{7.18}$$

5. Chi-square method (CSM)

In 2015, Xu et al. (2015a) provided a CSM to priority for incomplete fuzzy reciprocal preference relations. According to FBV, FWV, and Eq. (7.6), the CSM of FBWM can be described in (M-7.7):

$$\min \ F(w) = \sum_{j=1}^{n} \left(\frac{\left(r_{Bj} - \frac{w_B}{w_B + w_j} \right)^2}{\frac{w_B}{w_B + w_j}} \right) + \sum_{j=1, j \neq B}^{n} \left(\frac{\left(r_{jW} - \frac{w_j}{w_j + w_W} \right)^2}{\frac{w_j}{w_j + w_W}} \right) +$$

$$\sum_{j=1}^{n} \left(\frac{\left(r_{jB} - \frac{w_j}{w_j + w_B} \right)^2}{\frac{w_j}{w_j + w_B}} \right) + \sum_{j=1, j \neq B}^{n} \left(\frac{\left(r_{Wj} - \frac{w_W}{w_W + w_j} \right)^2}{\frac{w_W}{w_W + w_j}} \right)$$

$$\text{s.t.} \begin{cases} \sum_{j=1}^{n} w_j = 1 \\ w_j \geq 0, \ j \in N \end{cases}$$

$$(\text{M-7.7})$$

Different from the models (M-7.3), (M-7.4), and (M-7.5), the four items in the objective function of the CSM are needed, due to

$$\frac{\left(r_{Bj} - \frac{w_B}{w_B + w_j} \right)^2}{\frac{w_B}{w_B + w_j}} \neq \frac{\left(r_{jB} - \frac{w_j}{w_j + w_B} \right)^2}{\frac{w_j}{w_j + w_B}}, \quad \frac{\left(r_{jW} - \frac{w_j}{w_j + w_W} \right)^2}{\frac{w_j}{w_j + w_W}} \neq \frac{\left(r_{Wj} - \frac{w_W}{w_W + w_j} \right)^2}{\frac{w_W}{w_W + w_j}}.$$

6. **Least deviation method (LDM)**

When the fuzzy reciprocal preference relation is additively consistent, we have $r_{ij} = (1 + \log_9(w_i/w_j))/2$, that is, $w_i/w_j = h(r_{ij})$, $i, j \in N$, being $h(r_{ij}) = 9^{(2r_{ij} - 1)}$. Obviously, $h(r_{ij}) (w_j/w_i) = h(r_{ji})(w_i/w_j) = 1$, $i, j \in N$. Xu et al. (2015b) introduced the deviation element $f_{ij} = h(r_{ij}) (w_j/w_i) + h(r_{ji})(w_i/w_j) - 2$, $i, j \in N$, and extended it to the incomplete fuzzy reciprocal preference relations. Then, the LDM of FBWM is given in (M-7.8):

$$\min \ F(w) = \sum_{j=1}^{n} \left(\frac{r_{Bj} \ w_j}{r_{jB} \ w_B} + \frac{r_{jB} \ w_B}{r_{Bj} \ w_j} - 2 \right) + \sum_{j=1, j \neq B}^{n} \left(\frac{r_{jW} \ w_W}{r_{Wj} \ w_j} + \frac{r_{Wj} \ w_j}{r_{jW} \ w_W} - 2 \right)$$

$$\text{s.t.} \begin{cases} \sum_{j=1}^{n} w_j = 1 \\ w_j \geq 0, \ j \in N \end{cases}$$

$$(\text{M-7.8})$$

7. **Goal programming model (GPM)**

Xu (2004) suggested a GPM to calculate the priority vector of an incomplete fuzzy reciprocal preference relation. Similarly, the GPM of FBWM is formulated in (M-7.9):

$$\min \ J = \sum_{j=1}^{n} \left(d_{Bj}^{+} + d_{Bj}^{-} \right) + \sum_{j=1, j \neq B}^{n} \left(d_{jW}^{+} + d_{jW}^{-} \right)$$

$$\text{s.t.} \begin{cases} \left(r_{Bj} w_j - r_{jB} w_B \right) - d_{Bj}^{+} + d_{Bj}^{-} = 0, j \in N \\ \left(r_{jW} w_W - r_{Wj} w_j \right) - d_{jW}^{+} + d_{jW}^{-} = 0, j \in N, j \neq B \\ \sum_{j=1}^{n} w_j = 1 \\ w_j \geq 0, d_{Bj}^{+} \geq 0, \ d_{Bj}^{-} \geq 0, d_{jW}^{+} \geq 0, \ d_{jW}^{-} \geq 0, \ j \in N \end{cases} \tag{M-7.9}$$

8. Eigenvector method (EM)

Generally, for an incomplete fuzzy reciprocal preference relation R, if there are m_i unknown values in the ith row, then its auxiliary relation $\bar{L} = (\bar{l}_{ij})_{n \times n}$ can be expressed as follows:

$$\bar{l}_{ij} = \begin{cases} r_{ij}, & \text{if } i \neq j \text{ and } r_{ij} \neq - \\ 0, & \text{if } r_{ij} = - \\ m_i + 1 + \sum_{j=1, j \neq i}^{n} r_{ij}, & \text{if } i = j \text{ and } r_{ij} \neq - \end{cases} \tag{7.19}$$

According to the equivalent relation $\bar{L} = (\bar{l}_{ij})_{n \times n}$, the eigenvalue problem of multiplicative consistent incomplete fuzzy reciprocal preference relation can be solved by the following equation:

(M-7.10)

$$\bar{L}\omega = \lambda_{\max} \omega \tag{7.20}$$

It is obvious that this method can be used to derive the priority vector of incomplete fuzzy reciprocal preference relation constructed by FBWM as well, and the auxiliary matrix $\bar{L} = (\bar{l}_{ij})_{n \times n}$ is

$$\bar{l}_{ij} = \begin{cases} r_{ij}, & i \neq j, i, j = B \text{ or } i, j = W \\ 0, & r_{ij} = - \\ 0.5, & i = j, i = B \text{ or } i = W \\ n - 1 - r_{Bj} + r_{jW}, i = j, i \neq B \text{ or } i \neq W \end{cases} \tag{7.21}$$

Remark 7.2 In the above, we propose eight models to derive the weights from FBWM matrix. It should be noted that the above models are nonlinear problems except (M-7.9). The original FBWM model (M-7.1) can be transformed into (M-7.2), which further can be transformed into a linear programming model. (M-7.3) is LAEM, which can also be transformed into a linear programming model. (M-7.4) and (M-7.5) are two least square methods. As we can see, (M-7.5) can finally be solved by Eq. (7.12); it is easier than (M-7.4). (M-7.6) is an extension of the LLSM and can be solved by Eqs. (7.13)–(7.14). (M-7.7) and (M-7.8) can be solved by CSM (Xu et al., 2015a) and LDM (Xu et al., 2015b) model, respectively. (M-7.9) is a linear programming model, and (M-10) can be solved by eigenvalue problem. Further, we can use the software such as Matlab and Lingo to solve these problems.

7.2.2 Priority Methods from FBWM Matrices in Group Decision-Making

In fact, most decision problems are involved in multiple DMs. Let $E = \{e_1, e_2, \ldots, e_m\}$ ($k \in M$) be the set of DMs. According to the steps of FBWM, the FBV $R_{B_k}^k = (r_{B_k 1}^k, r_{B_k 2}^k, \ldots, r_{B_k n}^k)$ and FWV $R_{W_k}^k = (r_{1W_k}^k, r_{2W_k}^k \ldots, r_{nW_k}^k)^T$ can be given by different DMs. Each DM's FBV and FWV can constitute an FBWM matrix P. In the following, we give some methods to derive the priorities from $R_{B_k}^k$ and $R_{W_k}^k$ ($k \in M$) given by a group of DMs.

1. **FBWM**

   According to the model (M-7.2) for a single matrix, it is easy to extend (M-7.2) to deal with the group $R_{B_k}^k$ and $R_{W_k}^k$ ($k \in M$), and the following (M-7.11) can be formulated:

   $$\min\ \xi$$
   $$\text{s.t.}\ \begin{cases} \left| \dfrac{w_{B_k}}{w_{B_k} + w_j} - r_{B_k j}^k \right| \leq \xi, j \in N, k \in M \\[3mm] \left| \dfrac{w_j}{w_j + w_{W_k}} - r_{jW_k}^k \right| \leq \xi, j \in N, k \in M \\[3mm] \sum\limits_{j=1}^{n} w_j = 1 \\[3mm] w_j \geq 0, j \in N \end{cases} \qquad \text{(M-7.11)}$$

2. **LAEM**

   For a group of FBWM matrix R^k, the optimal weights can be obtained by minimizing all the sum of the distances $\left| \dfrac{w_{B_k}}{w_{B_k} + w_j} - r_{B_k j}^k \right|$ and $\left| \dfrac{w_j}{w_{j+w_{W_k}}} - r_{jW_k}^k \right|$. The model (7.6) can be transformed as

$$\min \sum_{k=1}^{m} \left(\sum_{j=1}^{n} \left(\left| \frac{w_{B_k}}{w_{B_k} + w_j} - r_{B_k j}^{k} \right| \right) + \sum_{j=1, j \neq B_k}^{n} \left(\left| \frac{w_j}{w_j + w_{W_k}} - r_{jW_k}^{k} \right| \right) \right)$$

$$\text{s.t.} \begin{cases} \sum_{j=1}^{n} w_j = 1 \\ w_j \geq 0, \ j \in N \end{cases}$$

$$(\text{M-7.12})$$

According to model (7.9), the group decision-making methods for priority of FBWM can also be given. Here, some methods such as LSM and LLSM are exhibited.

3. **LSM-I**

$$\min F(w) = \sum_{k=1}^{m} \left(\sum_{j=1}^{n} \left(\frac{w_{B_k}}{w_{B_k} + w_j} - r_{B_k j}^{k} \right)^2 + \sum_{j=1, j \neq B_k}^{n} \left(\frac{w_j}{w_j + w_{W_k}} - r_{jW_k}^{k} \right)^2 \right)$$

$$\text{s.t.} \begin{cases} \sum_{j=1}^{n} w_j = 1 \\ w_j \geq 0, \ j \in N \end{cases}$$

$$(\text{M-7.13})$$

4. **LSM-II**

$$\min F(w) = \sum_{k=1}^{m} \left(\sum_{j=1}^{n} \left(r_{B_k j}^{k} w_j - r_{jB_k}^{k} w_{B_k} \right)^2 + \sum_{j=1, j \neq B_k}^{n} \left(r_{jW_k}^{k} w_{W_k} - r_{W_k j}^{k} w_j \right)^2 \right)$$

$$\text{s.t.} \begin{cases} \sum_{j=1}^{n} w_j = 1 \\ w_j \geq 0, \ j \in N \end{cases}$$

$$(\text{M-7.14})$$

5. **LLSM**

$$\min F(w) = \sum_{k=1}^{m} \left(\sum_{j=1}^{n} \left(\ln w_{B_k} - \ln w_j - \ln r_{B_k j}^{k} + \ln r_{jB_k}^{k} \right)^2 \right.$$

$$\left. + \sum_{j=1, j \neq B_k}^{n} \left(\ln w_j - \ln w_{W_k} - \ln r_{jW_k}^{k} + \ln r_{W_k j}^{k} \right)^2 \right) \qquad (\text{M-7.15})$$

$$\text{s.t.} \begin{cases} \sum_{j=1}^{n} w_j = 1 \\ w_j \geq 0, \ j \in N \end{cases}$$

6. **CSM**

$$\min \ F(w) = \sum_{k=1}^{m} \left(\begin{array}{l} \sum_{j=1}^{n} \left(\dfrac{\left(r_{B_kj}^{k} - \dfrac{w_{B_k}}{w_{B_k} + w_j}\right)^2}{\dfrac{w_{B_k}}{w_{B_k} + w_j}} \right) + \sum_{j=1,j \neq B_k}^{n} \left(\dfrac{\left(p_{jW_k}^{k} - \dfrac{w_j}{w_j + w_{W_k}}\right)^2}{\dfrac{w_j}{w_j + w_{W_k}}} \right) + \\[4em] \sum_{j=1}^{n} \left(\dfrac{\left(r_{jB_k}^{k} - \dfrac{w_j}{w_j + w_{B_k}}\right)^2}{\dfrac{w_j}{w_j + w_{B_k}}} \right) + \sum_{j=1,j \neq B_k}^{n} \left(\dfrac{\left(r_{W_kj}^{k} - \dfrac{w_{W_k}}{w_{W_k} + w_j}\right)^2}{\dfrac{w_{W_k}}{w_{W_k} + w_j}} \right) \end{array} \right)$$

$$\text{s.t.} \begin{cases} \sum_{j=1}^{n} w_j = 1 \\ w_j \geq 0, \ j \in N \end{cases}$$

(M-7.16)

7. **LDM**

$$\min \ F(w) = \sum_{k=1}^{m} \left(\sum_{j=1}^{n} \left(\frac{r_{B_kj}^{k}}{r_{jB_k}^{k}} \frac{w_j}{w_{B_k}} + \frac{r_{jB_k}^{k}}{r_{B_kj}^{k}} \frac{w_{B_k}}{w_j} - 2 \right) \right.$$

$$\left. + \sum_{j=1,j \neq B_k}^{n} \left(\frac{r_{jW_k}^{k}}{r_{W_kj}^{k}} \frac{w_{W_k}}{w_j} + \frac{r_{W_kj}^{k}}{r_{jW_k}^{k}} \frac{w_j}{w_{W_k}} - 2 \right) \right)$$

(M-7.17)

$$\text{s.t.} \begin{cases} \sum_{j=1}^{n} w_j = 1 \\ w_j \geq 0, \ j \in N \end{cases}$$

8. **GPM**

$$\min \ J = \sum_{k=1}^{m} \left(\sum_{j=1}^{n} \left(d_{B_kj,k}^{+} + d_{Bj,k}^{-} \right) + \sum_{j=1,j \neq B_k}^{n} \left(d_{jW_k,k}^{+} + d_{jW_k,k}^{-} \right) \right)$$

$$\text{s.t.} \begin{cases} \left(r_{B_kj}^{k} w_j - r_{jB_k}^{k} w_B \right) - d_{B_kj,k}^{+} + d_{B_kj,k}^{-} = 0, \ k \in M, j \in N \\ \left(r_{jW_k}^{k} w_{W_k} - r_{W_kj}^{k} w_j \right) - d_{jW_k,k}^{+} + d_{jW_k,k}^{-} = 0, k \in M, j \in N, j \neq B_k \\ \sum_{j=1}^{n} w_j = 1 \\ w_j \geq 0, j \in N \\ d_{B_kj,k}^{+} \geq 0, \ d_{B_kj,k}^{-} \geq 0, \ k \in M, j \in N, j \neq B_k \\ d_{jW_k,k}^{+} \geq 0, \ d_{jW_k,k}^{-} \geq 0, \ k \in M, j \in N \end{cases}$$

(M-7.18)

Remark 7.3 The above models are extensions of (M-7.1)–(M-7.10). It should be noted that there is no model for eigenvector method with a group of DMs.

7.3 Monte Carlo Simulations and Discussions

In order to compare their performances of different methods, some Monte Carlo simulations are carried out. We randomly generate 1000 FBWM matrices for different dimensions ranging from 3 to 9. Then we apply different methods to derive the priority weights, and calculate the mean values of FCR, MD, and MAD for each method, which are shown in Tables 7.1, 7.2, and 7.3. These values are visualized in Figs. 7.1, 7.2, and 7.3, respectively.

According to Table 7.1 and Fig. 7.1, the mean values of FCR for all methods decrease with the increase of n. The higher the order of an FBWM matrix, the higher the consistency degrees. Generally, the GPM has the lowest consistency degree for all orders, followed by LAEM and LSM-II. LDM and LLSM have the same consistency degree, and they have the highest degree for all the methods. From Tables 7.2 and 7.3, and Figs. 7.2 and 7.3, it can be observed that the mean values of MD and MAD increase with the increase of n. From these figures, we can see that the orders of the different methods are almost same. The GPM and LAEM methods have the highest MA and MAD values, followed by LSM-II, EM, LDM, LSM-I, and CSM. For the MAD values, the FBWM has the best performance, which shows the effectiveness of the FBWM. From the mean values of FCR in Table 7.1, it shows that all of the values are smaller than 0.1, indicating that all the methods to deriving

Table 7.1 The mean value of FCR by different methods

	$n = 3$	$n = 4$	$n = 5$	$n = 6$	$n = 7$	$n = 8$	$n = 9$
FBWM	0.0245	0.0148	0.0119	0.0092	0.0074	0.0057	0.0054
LAEM	0.0709	0.0262	0.0217	0.0160	0.0126	0.0095	0.0086
LSM-I	0.0287	0.0149	0.0112	0.0085	0.0067	0.0053	0.0049
LSM-II	0.0282	0.0175	0.0142	0.0112	0.0090	0.0071	0.0066
LLSM	0.0221	0.0131	0.0103	0.0080	0.0064	0.0051	0.0047
CSM	0.0259	0.0144	0.0110	0.0085	0.0067	0.0053	0.0049
LDM	0.0221	0.0131	0.0103	0.0080	0.0064	0.0051	0.0047
GPM	0.0711	0.0419	0.0254	0.0213	0.0150	0.0125	0.0111
EM	0.0248	0.0149	0.0119	0.0093	0.0074	0.0059	0.0054

the weights are effective.

Table 7.2 The mean value of MD by different methods

	$n = 3$	$n = 4$	$n = 5$	$n = 6$	$n = 7$	$n = 8$	$n = 9$
FBWM	0.0480	0.0719	0.0974	0.1051	0.1153	0.1068	0.1221
LAEM	0.2212	0.2418	0.3265	0.3634	0.3674	0.3374	0.3539
LSM-I	0.0699	0.0873	0.1049	0.1131	0.1211	0.1134	0.1256
LSM-II	0.0500	0.1076	0.1639	0.1988	0.2184	0.2121	0.2493
LLSM	0.0230	0.0537	0.0748	0.0874	0.0949	0.0918	0.1037
CSM	0.0560	0.0775	0.0975	0.1075	0.1159	0.1104	0.1234
LDM	0.0230	0.0530	0.0741	0.0865	0.0941	0.0910	0.1029
GPM	0.2219	0.3522	0.4029	0.4826	0.4506	0.4521	0.4888
EM	0.0402	0.0846	0.1254	0.1498	0.1635	0.1578	0.1826

Table 7.3 The mean value of MAD by different methods

	$n = 3$	$n = 4$	$n = 5$	$n = 6$	$n = 7$	$n = 8$	$n = 9$
FBWM	0.0177	0.0259	0.0331	0.0369	0.0412	0.0408	0.0432
LAEM	0.0427	0.0613	0.0761	0.0825	0.0836	0.0855	0.0853
LSM-I	0.0214	0.0312	0.0410	0.0454	0.0475	0.0480	0.0498
LSM-II	0.0320	0.0469	0.0610	0.0687	0.0721	0.0739	0.0776
LLSM	0.0228	0.0333	0.0425	0.0463	0.0484	0.0490	0.0508
CSM	0.0190	0.0310	0.0397	0.0444	0.0465	0.0471	0.0491
LDM	0.0228	0.0333	0.0425	0.0463	0.0483	0.0489	0.0508
GPM	0.0608	0.0820	0.0889	0.0993	0.0985	0.1011	0.1025
EM	0.0270	0.0403	0.0524	0.0587	0.0617	0.0630	0.0659

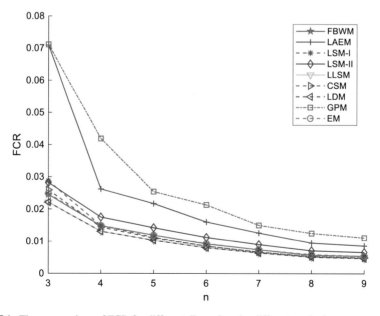

Fig. 7.1 The mean values of FCR for different dimensions by different methods

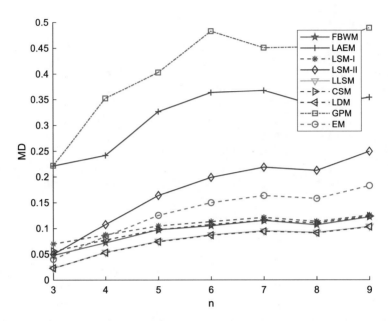

Fig. 7.2 The mean values of MD for different dimensions by different methods

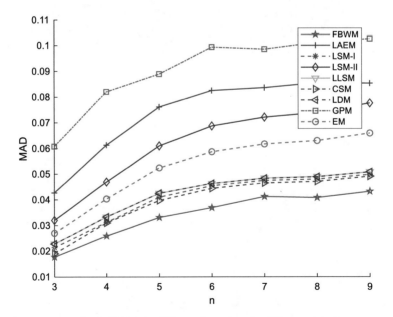

Fig. 7.3 The mean values of MAD for different dimensions by different methods

7.4   Illustrative Examples and Comparative Analyses

In this section, two examples are illustrated to show the application and verification of the different methods for priority of FBWM. Example 7.1 depicts the priority of criteria by different methods of an FBWM matrix in R&D performance evaluation. Example 7.2 applies different priority methods from a group of FBWM matrices for water pollution emergency management schemes in group decision-making.

Example 7.1 The R&D Performance Evaluation A firm needs to evaluate the R&D performance to take more effective strategies to improve the firm's R&D performance. Considering the vagueness and uncertainty of the DM when he/she carries out the evaluation, an FBWM matrix is provided.

There are four criteria, namely "quality of output (c_1)," "customer satisfaction (c_2)," "creativity (c_3)," and "efficiency (c_4)" selected for R&D performance evaluation issue. The "customer satisfaction (c_2)" and the "efficiency (c_4)" are, respectively, the best and the worst criteria on account of the opinion from the firm. The FBV and FWV are listed in Table 7.4.

To use the proposed methods to derive the weights, the following steps are involved:

Step 1. According to Table 7.4, the FBWM matrix R can be established:

$$R = \begin{pmatrix} 0.5 & 0.3 & - & 0.6 \\ 0.7 & 0.5 & 0.6 & 0.8 \\ - & 0.4 & 0.5 & 0.6 \\ 0.4 & 0.2 & 0.4 & 0.5 \end{pmatrix}$$

Step 2. By solving the models (M-7.2)–(M-7.10), the optimal priorities of four criteria can be obtained. To show the performances of these methods, the values of FCR, MD, and MAD are also listed in Table 7.5.

Step 3. From Table 7.5, the ranking of the four criteria is $c_2 \succ c_3 \succ c_1 \succ c_4$.

Table 7.4 FBV and FWV given by the DM

Best criterion	c_1	c_2	c_3	c_4
c_2	0.7	0.5	0.6	0.8
Worst criterion	c_4			
c_1	0.6			
c_2	0.8			
c_3	0.6			
c_4	0.5			

Table 7.5 The priorities of different methods and the values of FCR, MD, and MAD of FBWM

Methods	w_1	w_2	w_3	w_4	FCR	MD	MAD
FBWM	0.1955	0.4283	0.2408	0.1354	0.0111	0.0552	0.0401
LAEM	0.18	0.42	0.28	0.12	0.0202	0.1984	0.1
LSM-I	0.1942	0.4300	0.2408	0.1349	0.0110	0.0517	0.0410
LSM-II	0.1871	0.4250	0.2584	0.1295	0.0123	0.0818	0.0661
LLSM	0.1919	0.4381	0.2393	0.1307	0.0105	0.0398	0.0467
CSM	0.1934	0.4322	0.2405	0.1339	0.0107	0.0461	0.0425
LDM	0.1919	0.4380	0.2393	0.1308	0.0105	0.0397	0.0467
GPM	0.1827	0.4264	0.2843	0.1066	0.0335	0.3402	0.1273
EM	0.1886	0.4300	0.2505	0.1308	0.0111	0.0599	0.0569

From Table 7.5, the "customer satisfaction (c_2)" has the largest weight and the "efficiency (c_4)" has the smallest weight for all the methods. Moreover, the preference orders of four criteria by different methods are the same although there are slight differences among each of the criteria weights. It should be noted that the weights obtained by LLSM and LDM are identical, as well as FCR, MD, and MAD. According to the weights obtained by these methods, FCR values are calculated, and all are less than 0.1. Therefore, the results obtained by these methods all meet the consistency, but the degrees of consistencies are different. Among them, LLSM and LDM have the highest consistency degree, followed by CSM, LSM-I, and FBWM, while the consistency degrees of EM, LSM-II, GPM, and LAEM are worse than those five methods. Moreover, LLSM and LDM also have better performance on MD. The performance of FBWM is superior to all the other methods on MAD. LAEM and GPM have worse performances than the other methods for all the FCR, MD, and MAD indices. FBWM has the smallest MAD; this is not strange, because its goal is to minimize the MAD value. For the real application of the problem, the weights derived by FBWM, LDM, LLSM, and CSM could be adopted.

Example 7.2 Emergency Management Scheme Selection for Water Pollution In recent years, the problem of water pollution is becoming more and more serious in China. For the DMs of water resource management department, how to choose an efficient and feasible emergency management scheme for water pollution is a big challenge. Currently, there are four schemes to select. Because each scheme has its own advantages and disadvantages, the water resource management department needs to choose the fastest and most reliable scheme. For this reason, the evaluation team of the department invited three DMs to make group decisions and gave the evaluation information of pairwise comparisons of the four alternatives; they are listed in Tables 7.6, 7.7, and 7.8.

Table 7.6 FBV and FWV given by the first DM

Best criterion	a_1	a_2	a_3	a_4
a_4	0.8	0.9	0.7	0.5
Worst criterion	a_2			
a_1	0.6			
a_2	0.5			
a_3	0.7			
a_4	0.9			

Table 7.7 FBV and FWV given by the second DM

Best criterion	a_1	a_2	a_3	a_4
a_4	0.8	0.6	0.6	0.5
Worst criterion	a_1			
a_1	0.5			
a_2	0.7			
a_3	0.6			
a_4	0.8			

Table 7.8 FBV and FWV given by the third DM

Best criterion	a_1	a_2	a_3	a_4
a_3	0.9	0.7	0.5	0.6
Worst criterion	a_1			
a_1	0.5			
a_2	0.7			
a_3	0.9			
a_4	0.8			

Step 1. Based on Tables 7.6, 7.7, and 7.8, the following FBWM matrices can be constructed, respectively:

$$R_1 = \begin{pmatrix} 0.5 & 0.6 & - & 0.2 \\ 0.4 & 0.5 & 0.3 & 0.1 \\ - & 0.7 & 0.5 & 0.3 \\ 0.8 & 0.9 & 0.7 & 0.5 \end{pmatrix}, \quad R_2 = \begin{pmatrix} 0.5 & 0.3 & 0.4 & 0.2 \\ 0.7 & 0.5 & - & 0.4 \\ 0.6 & - & 0.5 & 0.4 \\ 0.8 & 0.6 & 0.6 & 0.5 \end{pmatrix},$$

$$R_3 = \begin{pmatrix} 0.5 & 0.3 & 0.1 & 0.2 \\ 0.7 & 0.5 & 0.3 & - \\ 0.9 & 0.7 & 0.5 & 0.6 \\ 0.8 & - & 0.4 & 0.5 \end{pmatrix}.$$

Step 2. The optimal weights of four schemes can be achieved by solving the models (M-7.11)–(M-7.18) in group decision-making presented in Table 7.9.

Step 3. From Table 7.9, we can find that the ranking of the four schemes is $a_4 \succ a_3 \succ a_2 \succ a_1$ except LAEM. The ranking of LAEM is slightly different from the other methods, which ranks the third scheme best, followed by the fourth, second, and first schemes.

Table 7.9 Priorities of different methods for FBWM

Methods	w_1	w_2	w_3	w_4
FBWM	0.1125	0.1375	0.3375	0.4125
LAEM	0.0783	0.1826	0.4261	0.3131
LSM-I	0.0933	0.1417	0.3380	0.4269
LSM-II	0.1085	0.1483	0.3238	0.4194
LLSM	0.0964	0.1373	0.3326	0.4337
CSM	0.1092	0.1531	0.3211	0.4166
LDM	0.0957	0.1346	0.3338	0.4359
GPM	0.1135	0.1297	0.3027	0.4541

7.4.1 Comparative Analyses

1. The computational complexity comparison for an FBWM matrix and a complete fuzzy reciprocal preference relation
   As we have pointed out in Sect. 7.1, the FBWM matrix is intrinsically an incomplete fuzzy reciprocal preference relation. Thus, first we compare the methods with the traditional methods using complete RPRs. In Example 7.1, only five comparisons are given by the DM, and six comparisons are necessary for the complete fuzzy reciprocal preference relation. More generally, the comparisons for an FBWM matrix are $2n - 5$ and $n(n - 1)/2$ (n is the order of the matrix) for the complete fuzzy reciprocal preference relation. Figure 7.4 portrays the number of comparisons for the FBWM matrix and complete fuzzy reciprocal preference relation. From Fig. 7.4, it shows that the number of comparisons for FBWM matrix is a linear function of n, while it is quadratic function of n for complete fuzzy reciprocal preference relation. That is, their computational complexity is $o(n)$ and $o(n^2)$, respectively. This means that the larger the value n, the bigger the difference of computational complexity between the FBWM matrix and complete fuzzy reciprocal preference relation.
2. The consistency comparison for different methods by an FBWM matrix and a complete fuzzy reciprocal preference relation
   In order to further compare the performances using the FBWM matrix and the traditional complete fuzzy reciprocal preference relation, we show the FCR values by different methods. As FCR is the consistency index of a fuzzy reciprocal preference relation, it could indicate the differences between the FBWM matrix and the complete fuzzy reciprocal preference relation when the weights are derived by different methods. To do this, Case 1 is used to illustrate the differences. In Example 7.1, the DM gives his best criterion as c_2 and the worst criterion as c_4. Thus, from R, we know that r_{13} and r_{31} are missing. In the following, we show the FCR values derived by different priority methods when $r_{13} = 0.1, 0.2, \ldots, 0.9$ ($r_{31} = 0.9, 0.8, \ldots, 0.1$), respectively. In Table 7.10, 0 denotes that r_{13} is missing, which is an FBWM matrix. When R is a complete fuzzy reciprocal preference relation, there is no FBWM. From Eq. (7.11), we know that FBWM is a special case of GLAE when $\lambda = \infty$. To compute the weights and FCR by GLAE, it should be that B and W are also from 1 to n in Eq. (7.11). Therefore, we still use FBWM to denote the GLAE in Table 7.10.

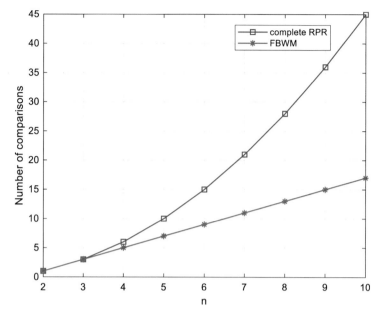

Fig. 7.4 The number of comparisons for an FBWM matrix and a complete fuzzy reciprocal preference relation

From Table 7.10, it is clear that the FCR values in the second column derived by the FBWM matrix (i.e., $r_{13} = 0$) are smaller than those by the complete-incomplete fuzzy reciprocal preference relation for all the methods, indicating that the FBWM matrix is more consistent than the corresponding complete-incomplete fuzzy reciprocal preference relation. This shows the advantage of the proposed methods. For all the methods, the FCR values decrease when r_{13} is from 0.1 to 0.5, but they increase when r_{13} is from 0.5 to 0.9. For each method, the FCR value is smallest when $r_{13} = 0$. Further, all the FCR values are smaller than 0.1 when $r_{13} = 0$, indicating that the FBWM matrix is consistent. There is little difference among them, which shows the effectiveness of the proposed methods to derive the weights from an FBWM matrix. We have the following features and advantages of the proposed methods:

1. An FBWM matrix is intrinsically an incomplete fuzzy reciprocal preference relation.
2. The proposed methods, including FBWM, LAEM, LSM-I, LSM-II, LLSM, CSM, LDM, GPM, and EM, are all effective to derive the weights from an FBWM matrix.
3. The FBWM matrix has fewer comparison than the corresponding complete fuzzy reciprocal preference relation, and thus has fewer computational complexity.
4. The FCR values by the different methods are all smaller than 0.1, indicating the usefulness of the proposed methods to derive the priorities from the FBWM matrix.

Table 7.10 The FCR values by different methods when $r_{13} = 0.1, 0.2, \ldots, 0.9$

	0	0.1	0.2	0.3	0.4	0.5	0.6	0.7	0.8	0.9
FBWM	0.0111	0.2064	0.0771	0.0311	0.0132	0.0142	0.0322	0.0692	0.1402	0.3068
LAEM	0.0202	0.3909	0.1102	0.0359	0.0174	0.0202	0.0359	0.0916	0.2309	0.6861
LSM-I	0.0110	0.2251	0.0763	0.0292	0.0125	0.0133	0.0296	0.0652	0.1369	0.3328
LSM-II	0.0123	0.2322	0.0778	0.0292	0.0133	0.0146	0.0308	0.0685	0.1515	0.3928
LLSM	0.0105	0.2038	0.0755	0.0290	0.0121	0.0128	0.0290	0.0650	0.1362	0.3074
CSM	0.0107	0.2403	0.0778	0.0293	0.0123	0.0131	0.0294	0.0655	0.1404	0.3606
LDM	0.0105	0.2033	0.0755	0.0290	0.0121	0.0128	0.0290	0.0650	0.1360	0.3057
GPM	0.0335	0.2275	0.0872	0.0332	0.0151	0.0160	0.0360	0.0882	0.1874	0.4138
EM	0.0111	0.2220	0.0764	0.0292	0.0125	0.0133	0.0297	0.0662	0.1420	0.3552

7.5 Summary

In 2015, Rezaei (2015) proposed a promising vector-based MCDM method called BWM. With the characteristics of fuzziness and intangibility, combined with the fuzzy theory, FBWM is then proposed by Xu et al. (2021). Traditionally, FBWM can be solved according to the solution idea of BWM. In FBWM, the preference comparison is identified by the FBV and FWV. Additionally, one or two incomplete fuzzy reciprocal preference relations can be constructed by FBV and FWV. In this view, this chapter proposes several methods for priority from FBWM matrices. Two examples are illustrated to show how the proposed method deals with the real decision-making problems. Monte Carlo simulation experiments are implemented to show the performances of the different methods. However, consistency is also an important problem of BWM (Liang et al., 2020). The consistency of FBWM is not discussed in this chapter; it will be an interesting work in the future.

References

Badri Ahmadi, H., Kusi-Sarpong, S., & Rezaei, J. (2017). Assessing the social sustainability of supply chains using Best Worst Method. *Resources, Conservation and Recycling, 126,* 99–106.

Gong, Z. W. (2008). Least-square method to priority of the fuzzy preference relations with incomplete information. *International Journal of Approximate Reasoning, 47*(2), 258–264.

Gupta, H., & Barua, M. K. (2016). Identifying enablers of technological innovation for Indian MSMEs using best–worst multi criteria decision making method. *Technological Forecasting and Social Change, 107,* 69–79.

Gupta, P., Anand, S., & Gupta, H. (2017). Developing a roadmap to overcome barriers to energy efficiency in buildings using best worst method. *Sustainable Cities and Society, 31,* 244–259.

Liang, F. Q., Brunelli, M., & Rezaei, J. (2020). Consistency issues in the best worst method: Measurements and thresholds. *Omega, 96,* 102175.

Liu, W. F., & He, X. (2012). Two nonlinear programming models for obtaining priority of incomplete complementary judgment matrix. *Computer Engineering and Applications, 48*(31), 49–52.

Rezaei, J. (2015). Best-worst multi-criteria decision-making method. *Omega, 53,* 49–57.

Rezaei, J. (2016). Best-worst multi-criteria decision-making method: Some properties and a linear model. *Omega, 64,* 126–130.

Salimi, N., & Rezaei, J. (2016). Measuring efficiency of university-industry Ph.D. projects using best worst method. *Scientometrics, 109*(3), 1911–1938.

Salimi, N., & Rezaei, J. (2018). Evaluating firms' R&D performance using best worst method. *Evaluation and Program Planning, 66,* 147–155.

Xu, Y. J., Chen, L., Li, K. W., & Wang, H. M. (2015a). A chi-square method for priority derivation in group decision making with incomplete reciprocal preference relations. *Information Sciences, 306,* 166–179.

Xu, Y. J., Chen, L., & Wang, H. M. (2015b). A least deviation method for priority derivation in group decision making with incomplete reciprocal preference relations. *International Journal of Approximate Reasoning, 66,* 91–102.

Xu, Y. J., Patnayakuni, R., & Wang, H. M. (2013). Logarithmic least squares method to priority for group decision making with incomplete fuzzy preference relations. *Applied Mathematical Modelling, 37*(4), 2139–2152.

Xu, Y. J., Zhu, X. T., Wen, X. W., & Herrera-Viedma, E. (2021). Fuzzy best-worst method and its application in initial water rights allocation. *Applied Soft Computing, 101,* 107007.

Xu, Z. S. (2004). Goal programming models for obtaining the priority vector of incomplete fuzzy preference relation. *International Journal of Approximate Reasoning, 36*(3), 261–270.

Chapter 8
Weighted Least Square Method

In this chapter, we propose a method called weighted least square method (WLSM) for priority of an incomplete fuzzy reciprocal preference relation (Xu & Da, 2008). It is similar with Gong (2008)'s least square method.

8.1 WLSM for Priority from an Incomplete Fuzzy Reciprocal Preference Relation

When the complete fuzzy reciprocal preference relation is multiplicatively consistent, then $r_{ij} = w_i/(w_i + w_j)$, $\forall i, j \in N$. As $r_{ij} + r_{ji} = 1$, we have

$$r_{ji}w_i = r_{ij}w_j, \quad i,j \in N \tag{8.1}$$

That is:

$$w_i = \frac{r_{ij}}{r_{ji}}w_j, \quad i,j \in N \tag{8.2}$$

Summing on both sides in Eq. (8.2), and $\sum_{i=1}^{n} w_i = 1$, then

$$w = \left(1/\sum_{i=1}^{n}(r_{i1}/r_{1i}), 1/\sum_{i=1}^{n}(r_{i2}/r_{2i}), \ldots, 1/\sum_{i=1}^{n}(r_{in}/r_{ni}) \right)^{T} \tag{8.3}$$

When the fuzzy reciprocal preference relation is incomplete, i.e., there are missing elements, we cannot use Eq. (8.3) to derive the priority weights. We need to estimate the missing values.

For the missing elements, we can use Eq. (1.37) to construct the matrix.

Then, the incomplete fuzzy reciprocal preference relation can be denoted as

$$\overline{c}_{ij} = \frac{w_i}{w_i + w_j} \tag{8.4}$$

That is:

$$\overline{c}_{ij} w_j = \overline{c}_{ji} w_i \tag{8.5}$$

Generally, Eq. (8.5) does not hold. We introduce the deviation ε_{ij}, that is,

$$\varepsilon_{ij} = \overline{c}_{ij} w_j - \overline{c}_{ji} w_i \tag{8.6}$$

Obviously, the smaller the value ε_{ij}, the better the weights. Thus, we can construct the following optimization model:

$$\min F(w) = \sum_{i=1}^{n} \sum_{j=1}^{n} \varepsilon_{ij}^2 = \sum_{i=1}^{n} \sum_{j=1}^{n} \left(\overline{c}_{ij} w_j - \overline{c}_{ji} w_i \right)^2$$
$$\text{s.t.} \begin{cases} \sum_{j=1}^{n} w_j = 1 \\ w_i \geq 0, i \in N \end{cases} \tag{M-8.1}$$

(M-8.1) can be denoted as

$$\min F(w) = w^T Q w$$
$$\text{s.t.} \begin{cases} e^T w = 1 \\ w \geq 0 \end{cases} \tag{M-8.2}$$

where $w = (w_1, w_2, \ldots, w_n)^T$, $e = (1, 1, \ldots, 1)^T$, $Q = (q_{ij})_{n \times n}$, and

$$q_{ii} = 2 \sum_{\substack{k=1 \\ k \neq i}}^{n} \overline{c}_{ki}^2, i \in N$$

$$q_{ij} = 2 \left(\overline{c}_{ij}^2 - c_{ij} \right), \ i, j \in N, i \neq j$$

To solve model (M-8.2), we can construct the Lagrange function:

$$L(w, \lambda) = w^T Q w + 2\lambda \left(e^T w - 1 \right)$$

Let $\frac{\partial L}{\partial w} = 0$ and $\frac{\partial L}{\partial \lambda} = 0$, and we have

$$Qw + \lambda e = 0 \tag{8.7}$$

$$e^T w = 1 \tag{8.8}$$

Solve Eqs. (8.7) and (8.8), and we have

$$w = \frac{Q^{-1}e}{e^T Q^{-1}e} \tag{8.9}$$

It is called WLSM for incomplete fuzzy reciprocal preference relation (ICWLSM). In Eq. (8.9), the matrix Q has the elements which are denoted by Eq. (8.4); thus, it is also a function for w_i in the right of Eq. (8.9). It cannot be solved directly. To solve the problem, we can use the symbol matrix in Matlab to solve. The matrix Q can be denoted by symbol matrix using "sym" command in Matlab, and we can also obtain the reverse of Q by Matlab, and then obtain the right part of Eq. (8.9), and with the left side of Eq. (8.9), we obtain a series of equations. Then, we can use Matlab or Lingo to solve the equations and obtain the weight vector w. Furthermore, we have the following results.

Remark 8.1 Gong (2008) proposed the LSM for incomplete fuzzy reciprocal preference relation, which is similar with the proposed method. The difference is that it is 0 when the value is missing in Eq. (8.5), while the missing value is instead by Eq. (8.4).

Theorem 8.1 *Let $C = (c_{ij})_{n \times n}$ be an incomplete fuzzy reciprocal preference relation; if C is not multiplicative consistent, then there exists Q^{-1}, and Q is positive definite matrix.*

Theorem 8.2 *Let w be the weight vector obtained by ICWLSM, and then $w \geq 0$.*

8.2   The Improvement of ICWLSM

From Theorem 8.1, we know that if C is multiplicatively consistent, then Q^{-1} does not exist. Further, if $n \geq 5$, then the obtained equation by Eq. (8.9) is very complicate. In the following, we propose an improvement method to solve the problem.

As (M-8.1) (or (M-8.2)) is a quadratic problem, we can solve it using the quadratic programming method. By Lemma 2.1 of Kuhn-Tucker condition, we obtain the following result:

Theorem 8.3 *The necessary condition of quadratic programming problem* (M-8.1) is

$$
\begin{cases}
\displaystyle\sum_{i=1}^{n} \bar{c}_{ij}^{2} w_j - \sum_{k=1}^{n} \bar{c}_{jk}\bar{c}_{kj} w_k - \lambda - \gamma_j = 0, j \in N \\[2ex]
\displaystyle\sum_{j=1}^{n} w_j = 1 \\[2ex]
\gamma_j w_j = 0, j \in N \\[1ex]
w_j \geq 0, \gamma_j \geq 0, j \in N
\end{cases}
\tag{M-8.3}
$$

As λ is a free variable, let $\lambda = \lambda' - \lambda''$, and $\lambda', \lambda'' \geq 0$, $\lambda'\lambda'' = 0$, and introduce a variable v, and then we can establish the following (M-8.4) linear programming model:

$$
\min z = v
$$
$$
\begin{cases}
\displaystyle\sum_{i=1}^{n} \bar{c}_{ij}^{2} w_j - \sum_{k=1}^{n} \bar{c}_{jk}\bar{c}_{kj} w_k - \lambda' - \lambda'' - \gamma_j = 0, j \in N \\[2ex]
\displaystyle\sum_{j=1}^{n} w_j + v = 1 \\[2ex]
\gamma_j w_j = 0, j \in N \\[1ex]
\lambda'\lambda'' = 0 \\[1ex]
w_j \geq 0, \gamma_j \geq 0, j \in N \\[1ex]
\lambda', \lambda'' \geq 0, v \geq 0
\end{cases}
\tag{M-8.4}
$$

8.3   Illustrative Examples

Example 8.1 Let C be an incomplete fuzzy reciprocal preference relation as follows:

$$
C = \begin{bmatrix} 0.5 & - & 0.6 \\ - & 0.5 & 0.6 \\ 0.4 & 0.4 & 0.5 \end{bmatrix}
$$

Its auxiliary matrix is

$$
\bar{C} = \begin{bmatrix} 0.5 & \dfrac{w_1}{w_1 + w_2} & 0.6 \\[2ex] \dfrac{w_2}{w_2 + w_1} & 0.5 & 0.6 \\[2ex] 0.4 & 0.4 & 0.5 \end{bmatrix}
$$

To solve the Example 8.1 by (M-8.4), we construct the following model:

$\min z = v$

$$\begin{cases} \left(0.5^2 + \dfrac{w_2^3}{(w_2+w_1)^2} + 0.4^2\right)w_1 - \left(0.5^2 w_1 + \dfrac{w_1 w_2}{(w_2+w_1)^2}w_2 + 0.24 w_3\right) - \lambda' - \lambda'' - \gamma_1 = 0 \\[2mm] \left(\dfrac{w_1^3}{(w_2+w_1)^2} + 0.5^2 + 0.4^2\right)w_2 - \left(\dfrac{w_1 w_2}{(w_2+w_1)^2}w_1 + 0.5^2 w_2 + 0.24 w_3\right) - \lambda' - \lambda'' - \gamma_2 = 0 \\[2mm] \left(0.6^2 + 0.6^2 + 0.5^2\right)w_3 - \left(0.24 w_1 + 0.24 w_2 + 0.5^2 w_3\right) - \lambda' - \lambda'' - \gamma_3 = 0 \\[1mm] w_1 + w_2 + w_3 + v = 1 \\ \gamma_1 w_1 = 0 \\ \gamma_2 w_2 = 0 \\ \gamma_3 w_3 = 0 \\ \lambda' \lambda'' = 0 \\ w_j \geq 0, \gamma_j \geq 0, j = 1,2,3 \\ \lambda', \lambda'', v \geq 0 \end{cases}$$

Solving the model, we obtain $w_1 = 0.375$, $w_2 = 0.375$, and $w_3 = 0.25$. Then

$$\overline{C} = \begin{bmatrix} 0.5 & 0.5 & 0.6 \\ 0.5 & 0.5 & 0.6 \\ 0.4 & 0.4 & 0.5 \end{bmatrix}$$

It is obvious that $\overline{C}$ is multiplicatively consistent.
If we use Gong (2008)'s method to solve, we obtain

$$Q = \begin{bmatrix} 0.16 & 0 & -0.24 \\ 0 & 0.16 & -0.24 \\ -0.24 & -0.24 & 0.72 \end{bmatrix}$$

However, Q^{-1} does not exist. Thus, Gong (2008)'s method can be used to solve the problem if C is multiplicatively inconsistent.

Example 8.2 Let C be an incomplete fuzzy reciprocal preference relation as follows:

$$C = \begin{bmatrix} 0.5 & x & 0.6 & 0.4 \\ 1-x & 0.5 & 0.3 & 0.7 \\ 0.4 & 0.7 & 0.5 & 0.6 \\ 0.6 & 0.3 & 0.4 & 0.5 \end{bmatrix}$$

Its auxiliary matrix is

$$\overline{C} = \begin{bmatrix} 0.5 & \dfrac{w_1}{w_1 + w_2} & 0.6 & 0.4 \\ \dfrac{w_2}{w_1 + w_2} & 0.5 & 0.3 & 0.7 \\ 0.4 & 0.7 & 0.5 & 0.6 \\ 0.6 & 0.3 & 0.4 & 0.5 \end{bmatrix}$$

To solve Example 8.2 by (M-8.4), we construct the following model:

$$\min z = v$$

$$\begin{cases} \left(0.5^2 + \left(\dfrac{w_2}{w_1 + w_2} \right)^2 + 0.4^2 + 0.6^2 \right) w_1 - \left(0.5^2 w_1 + \dfrac{w_1 w_2}{(w_2 + w_1)^2} w_2 + 0.24 w_3 + 0.24 w_4 \right) - \lambda' - \lambda'' - \gamma_1 = 0 \\ \left(\left(\dfrac{w_1}{w_1 + w_2} \right)^2 + 0.5^2 + 0.7^2 + 0.3^2 \right) w_2 - \left(\dfrac{w_1 w_2}{(w_2 + w_1)^2} w_1 + 0.5^2 w_2 + 0.21 w_3 + 0.21 w_4 \right) - \lambda' - \lambda'' - \gamma_2 = 0 \\ \left(0.6^2 + 0.3^2 + 0.5^2 + 0.4^2 \right) w_3 - \left(0.24 w_1 + 0.21 w_2 + 0.5^2 w_3 + 0.24 w_4 \right) - \lambda' - \lambda'' - \gamma_3 = 0 \\ \left(0.4^2 + 0.7^2 + 0.6^2 + 0.5^2 \right) w_4 - \left(0.24 w_1 + 0.21 w_2 + 0.24 w_3 + 0.5^2 w_4 \right) - \lambda' - \lambda'' - \gamma_4 = 0 \\ w_1 + w_2 + w_3 + w_4 + v = 1 \\ \gamma_1 w_1 = 0 \\ \gamma_2 w_2 = 0 \\ \gamma_3 w_3 = 0 \\ \gamma_4 w_4 = 0 \\ \lambda' \lambda'' = 0 \\ w_j \geq 0, \gamma_j \geq 0, j = 1,2,3,4 \\ \lambda', \lambda'', v \geq 0 \end{cases}$$

Solving the model, we obtain $w_1 = 0.275$, $w_2 = 0.2204$, $w_3 = 0.3003$, and $w_4 = 0.2042$. If we use Eq. (1.13) to check the consistency, we obtain $FCR = 0.1578 > 0.1$, which means that C is not of multiplicative consistency. If we return this matrix to the DM to re-evaluate, the DM gives the new incomplete fuzzy reciprocal preference relation as follows:

$$C = \begin{bmatrix} 0.5 & x & 0.6 & 0.8 \\ 1-x & 0.5 & 0.3 & 0.7 \\ 0.4 & 0.7 & 0.5 & 0.6 \\ 0.2 & 0.3 & 0.4 & 0.5 \end{bmatrix}$$

Its auxiliary matrix is

$$\overline{C} = \begin{bmatrix} 0.5 & \dfrac{w_1}{w_1+w_2} & 0.6 & 0.8 \\ \dfrac{w_2}{w_1+w_2} & 0.5 & 0.3 & 0.7 \\ 0.4 & 0.7 & 0.5 & 0.6 \\ 0.2 & 0.3 & 0.4 & 0.5 \end{bmatrix}$$

Similarly, we can construct the following model:

$$\min z = v$$

$$\begin{cases} \left(0.5^2 + \left(\frac{w_2}{w_1+w_2}\right)^2 + 0.4^2 + 0.2^2\right)w_1 - \left(0.5^2 w_1 + \frac{w_1 w_2}{(w_2+w_1)^2}w_2 + 0.24w_3 + 0.16w_4\right) - \lambda' - \lambda'' - \gamma_1 = 0 \\ \left(\left(\frac{w_1}{w_1+w_2}\right)^2 + 0.5^2 + 0.7^2 + 0.3^2\right)w_2 - \left(\frac{w_1 w_2}{(w_2+w_1)^2}w_1 + 0.5^2 w_2 + 0.21w_3 + 0.21w_4\right) - \lambda' - \lambda'' - \gamma_2 = 0 \\ \left(0.6^2 + 0.3^2 + 0.5^2 + 0.4^2\right)w_3 - \left(0.24w_1 + 0.21w_2 + 0.5^2 w_3 + 0.24w_4\right) - \lambda' - \lambda'' - \gamma_3 = 0 \\ \left(0.8^2 + 0.7^2 + 0.6^2 + 0.5^2\right)w_4 - \left(0.16w_1 + 0.21w_2 + 0.24w_3 + 0.5^2 w_4\right) - \lambda' - \lambda'' - \gamma_4 = 0 \\ w_1 + w_2 + w_3 + w_4 + v = 1 \\ \gamma_1 w_1 = 0 \\ \gamma_2 w_2 = 0 \\ \gamma_3 w_3 = 0 \\ \gamma_4 w_4 = 0 \\ \lambda' \lambda'' = 0 \\ w_j \geq 0, \gamma_j \geq 0, j = 1,2,3,4 \\ \lambda', \lambda'', v \geq 0 \end{cases}$$

Solving the model, we obtain $w_1 = 0.4503$, $w_2 = 0.1508$, $w_3 = 0.2814$, and $w_4 = 0.1174$. If we use Eq. (1.13) to check the consistency, we obtain FCR $= 0.0606 < 0.1$, which means that C is of multiplicative consistency.

If we use Gong (2008)'s method to solve for the original incomplete fuzzy reciprocal preference relation, we have

$$Q = \begin{bmatrix} 0.52 & 0 & -0.24 & -0.24 \\ 0 & 0.58 & -0.21 & -0.21 \\ -0.24 & -0.21 & 0.61 & -0.24 \\ -0.24 & -0.21 & -0.24 & 1.01 \end{bmatrix}$$

And by $w = Q^{-1}e/e^T Q^{-1}e$, we obtain $w_1 = 0.275$, $w_2 = 0.2204$, $w_3 = 0.3003$, and $w_4 = 0.2042$, which is same as our result.

For the improved incomplete fuzzy reciprocal preference relation, we have

$$Q = \begin{bmatrix} 0.2 & 0 & -0.24 & -0.16 \\ 0 & 0.58 & -0.21 & -0.21 \\ -0.24 & -0.21 & 0.61 & -0.24 \\ -0.16 & -0.21 & -0.24 & 1.49 \end{bmatrix}$$

By $w = Q^{-1}e/e^T Q^{-1}e$, we obtain $w_1 = 0.4503$, $w_2 = 0.1508$, $w_3 = 0.2814$, and $w_4 = 0.1174$, which is same as our result. This also shows the effectiveness of the proposed method.

8.4   Summary

In this chapter, we have proposed an ICWLSM. We propose several models to solve it.

References

Gong, Z. W. (2008). Least-square method to priority of the fuzzy preference relations with incomplete information. *International Journal of Approximate Reasoning, 47*(2), 258–264.

Xu, Y. J., & Da, Q. L. (2008). Weighted least-square method and its improvement for priority of incomplete complementary judgement matrix. *Systems Engineering and Electronics, 30*(7), 1273–1276.

Chapter 9
Priorities from Incomplete Hesitant Fuzzy Reciprocal Preference Relations

In the former chapters, we have introduced several priority methods for incomplete fuzzy reciprocal preference relations. In this chapter, we introduce another preference relation called hesitant fuzzy reciprocal preference relation and present how to derive the priority weights from incomplete hesitant fuzzy reciprocal preference relations.

9.1 Preliminaries

In this section, we give the definitions of hesitant fuzzy set (HFS), hesitant fuzzy element (HFE), hesitant fuzzy reciprocal preference relation, and incomplete hesitant fuzzy reciprocal preference relation.

9.1.1 HFS

Torra (2010) originally developed the definition of HFSs as follows:

Definition 9.1 (Torra & Narukawa, 2009; Torra, 2010) Let X be a reference set, and an HFS on X is defined in terms of a function $h_A(x)$ that returns a non-empty subset of $[0, 1]$ when it is applied to X, i.e.,

$$A = \{\langle x, h_A(x) \rangle | x \in X\} \tag{9.1}$$

where $h_A(x)$ is a set of some different values in $[0, 1]$, representing the possible membership degrees of the element $x \in X$ to A. $h_A(x)$ is called an HFE, a basic unit of HFS.

Y. Xu, *Deriving Priorities from Incomplete Fuzzy Reciprocal Preference Relations*, https://doi.org/10.1007/978-981-99-3169-9_9

9.1.2   Hesitant Fuzzy Preference Relation

On the basis of HFSs and fuzzy reciprocal preference relation, Xia and Xu (2013) introduced hesitant fuzzy reciprocal preference relations as follows:

Definition 9.2 Let $X = \{x_1, x_2, \ldots, x_n\}$ be a fixed set; then a hesitant fuzzy reciprocal preference relation H on X is represented by a matrix $H = (h_{ij})_{n \times n} \subset X \times X$, where $h_{ij} = \left\{ \gamma_{ij}^l | l = 1, \ldots, \#h_{ij} \right\}$ ($\#h_{ij}$ is the number of values in h_{ij}) is an HFE indicating all the possible values of preference degrees of the alternative x_i over x_j. For all $i, j \in N$, h_{ij} should satisfy the following conditions:

$$\begin{cases} \gamma_{ij}^{\sigma(l)} + \gamma_{ji}^{\sigma(l)} = 1 \\ h_{ii} = \{0.5\} \\ \#h_{ij} = \#h_{ji} \end{cases} \tag{9.2}$$

where $\gamma_{ij}^{\sigma(l)}$ is the lth smallest element in h_{ij}.

9.1.3   Incomplete Hesitant Fuzzy Reciprocal Preference Relation

As described in the introduction, incomplete fuzzy reciprocal preference relations do not merely permit the DMs to provide all of the possible values, but also allow them to give null values when comparing two alternatives. This is formally defined as follows:

Definition 9.3 (Xu et al., 2016) Let $X = \{x_1, x_2, \ldots, x_n\}$ be a fixed set; then an incomplete hesitant fuzzy reciprocal preference relation H on X is represented by a matrix $H = (h_{ij})_{n \times n} \subset X \times X$, for all known HFEs $h_{ij} = \left\{ \gamma_{ij}^l | l = 1, \ldots, \#h_{ij} \right\}$ ($\#h_{ij}$ is the number of values in h_{ij}) indicate all the possible values of preference degrees of the alternative x_i over x_j and should satisfy the following conditions:

$$\begin{cases} \gamma_{ij}^{\sigma(l)} + \gamma_{ji}^{\sigma(l)} = 1 \\ h_{ii} = \{0.5\} \\ \#h_{ij} = \#h_{ji} \end{cases} \tag{9.3}$$

where $\gamma_{ij}^{\sigma(l)}$ is the lth smallest value in h_{ij}.

Remark 9.1 Definitions 9.2 and 9.3 require that the values in h_{ij} of the upper triangular are arranged in ascending order, and $\gamma_{ij}^{\sigma(l)}$ is the lth smallest element in

h_{ij}, i.e., $\gamma_{ij}^{\sigma(l)} < \gamma_{ij}^{\sigma(l+1)}$ $(i < j)$. In Zhu and Xu (2013) and Zhu et al. (2014), $\gamma_{ij}^{\sigma(l)}$ is the lth largest value in h_{ij}; it is contrary to Definitions 9.2 and 9.3 and does not conform to their examples. However, Xu et al. (2017) defined the hesitant fuzzy reciprocal preference relation, in which there is no requirement for the values in h_{ij}, i.e., γ_{ij}^l is the lth value in h_{ij}. This definition is more reasonable, as the elements in a set are not needed to be arranged in ascending or descending order. Xu et al. (2018) also pointed out that it will create consistency problem if the elements are arranged in ascending or descending order in Definitions 9.2, and 9.3. Here, we do not differentiate them; both definitions can be used as there is no difference to derive the priorities from the incomplete hesitant fuzzy reciprocal preference relation in the following sections.

For the convenience of computations, we construct an indication matrix $\Delta = (\delta_{ij})_{n \times n}$ of the incomplete hesitant fuzzy reciprocal preference relation $H = (h_{ij})_{n \times n}$, where

$$\delta_{ij} = \begin{cases} 0, & h_{ij} = - \\ 1, & h_{ij} \neq - \end{cases} \tag{9.4}$$

and $h_{ij} = -$ indicates a missing HFE h_{ij}.

It should be noted that when $\delta_{ij} = 1$ for all $i, j \in N$, incomplete hesitant fuzzy reciprocal preference relation becomes hesitant fuzzy reciprocal preference relation, indicating that the latter is a special case of the former.

Based on the concepts of multiplicative consistency fuzzy reciprocal preference relation and additive consistency fuzzy reciprocal preference relation, we will introduce the concept of multiplicative consistency incomplete hesitant fuzzy reciprocal preference relation and additive consistency incomplete hesitant fuzzy reciprocal preference relation in the following:

Definition 9.4 Let $H = (h_{ij})_{n \times n}$ be an incomplete hesitant fuzzy reciprocal preference relation; if the missing HFE of H can be determined by the known HFE, then H is called an acceptable incomplete hesitant fuzzy reciprocal preference relation; otherwise, H is not an acceptable incomplete hesitant fuzzy reciprocal preference relation.

Theorem 9.1 *Let $H = (h_{ij})_{n \times n}$ be an incomplete hesitant fuzzy reciprocal preference relation; the necessary condition of acceptable incomplete hesitant fuzzy reciprocal preference relation H is that there is at least one known HFE in each row or column of H except for the diagonal HFE, i.e., it needs at least $(n-1)$ judgments.*

Definition 9.5 Let $H = (h_{ij})_{n \times n}$ be an incomplete hesitant fuzzy reciprocal preference relation; then H is called a multiplicative consistency incomplete hesitant fuzzy reciprocal preference relation, if some of its HFEs cannot be given by the DM, which we denote by the symbol $-$, and the others can be provided by the DM, which satisfy

$$\frac{w_i}{w_i + w_j} = \gamma_{ij}^{\sigma(1)} \text{ or} \ldots \text{or } \gamma_{ij}^{\sigma(\#h_{ij})}, \quad i,j \in N \tag{9.5}$$

Definition 9.6 Let $H = (h_{ij})_{n \times n}$ be an incomplete hesitant fuzzy reciprocal preference relation; then H is called an additive consistency incomplete hesitant fuzzy reciprocal preference relation, if some of its HFEs cannot be given by the DM, which we denote by symbol $-$, and the others can be provided by the DM, which satisfy

$$\gamma_{ij}^{\sigma(1)} \text{ or} \ldots \text{or } \gamma_{ij}^{\sigma(\#h_{ij})} = 0.5 + \frac{n-1}{2}(w_i - w_j), i,j \in N \tag{9.6}$$

9.2 The Models to Derive Priority Weights from Incomplete Hesitant Fuzzy Reciprocal Preference Relations

Let us suppose a set of alternatives $X = \{x_1, x_2, \ldots, x_n\}$, and a constructed incomplete hesitant fuzzy reciprocal preference relation $H = (h_{ij})_{n \times n}$, where $h_{ij} = \{\gamma_{ij}^l \mid l = 1, \ldots, \#h_{ij}\}$. Each element in h_{ij} is a possible preference degree for the comparison of the alternative x_i over x_j.

1. By Eq. (9.5), the multiplicative consistency preferences can be obtained by

$$\delta_{ij} \frac{w_i}{w_i + w_j} = \delta_{ij} \left(\gamma_{ij}^{\sigma(1)} \text{ or} \ldots \text{or } \gamma_{ij}^{\sigma(\#h_{ij})} \right), \quad i,j \in N \tag{9.7}$$

Let $S(\gamma_{ij}) = \gamma_{ij}^{\sigma(1)}$ or $\ldots$ or $\gamma_{ij}^{\sigma(\#hij)}$, and by Eq. (9.7), we have

$$\delta_{ij} \frac{w_i}{w_i + w_j} = \delta_{ij} S(\gamma_{ij})$$

$$\Leftrightarrow \delta_{ij} w_i = \delta_{ij}(w_i + w_j)(S(\gamma_{ij}))$$

$$\Leftrightarrow \delta_{ij}(1 - S(\gamma_{ij}))w_i = \delta_{ij} S(\gamma_{ij})w_j, \quad i,j \in N \tag{9.8}$$

Due to the fact that $1 - S(\gamma_{ij}) = 1 - \gamma_{ij}^{\sigma(1)}$ or $\ldots$ or $1 - \gamma_{ij}^{\sigma(\#hij)}$, we have $1 - S(\gamma_{ij}) = S(\gamma_{ji})$; thus, Eq. (9.8) can be rewritten as

$$\delta_{ij} S(\gamma_{ji}) w_i = \delta_{ij} S(\gamma_{ij}) w_j, \quad i,j \in N \tag{9.9}$$

Nevertheless, Eq. (9.9) does not always hold in the general case. There is deviation between $\delta_{ij} S(\gamma_{ji})w_i$ and $\delta_{ij} S(\gamma_{ij})w_j$, and the deviation degree is given by Eq.(9.10):

$$\varepsilon_{ij} = \delta_{ij} \mid S(\gamma_{ji})w_i - S(\gamma_{ij})w_j \mid \qquad (9.10)$$

Thus, we could construct the following multi-objective programming model:

$$
\begin{aligned}
&\min \quad \varepsilon_{ij} = \delta_{ij} \mid S(\gamma_{ji})w_i - S(\gamma_{ij})w_j \mid, i,j \in N \\
&\text{s.t.} \sum_{i=1}^{n} w_i = 1, w_i \geq 0, \quad i \in N
\end{aligned}
\qquad \text{(M-9.1)}
$$

As $|S(\gamma_{ji})w_i - S(\gamma_{ij})w_j| = |S(\gamma_{ij})w_j - S(\gamma_{ji})w_i|$, the above minimization problem could be solved by solving the following programming model:

$$
\min \quad F = \sum_{i=1}^{n-1} \sum_{j=i+1}^{n} s_{ij} d_{ij}^{+} + t_{ij} d_{ij}^{-}
$$

$$
\text{s.t.} \begin{cases}
\delta_{ij}\big(S(\gamma_{ji})w_i - S(\gamma_{ij})w_j\big) - d_{ij}^{+} + d_{ij}^{-} = 0, & i,j \in N, \quad j > i \\
\sum_{i=1}^{n} w_i = 1, \quad w_i \geq 0, \quad i \in N \\
d_{ij}^{+}, d_{ij}^{-} \geq 0, \quad i,j \in N, \quad j > i
\end{cases}
\qquad \text{(M-9.2)}
$$

where d_{ij}^{+} is the positive deviation from the target of the goal ε_{ij}, defined as

$$
d_{ij}^{+} = \delta_{ij}\big(S(\gamma_{ji})w_i - S(\gamma_{ij})w_j\big) \vee 0.
$$

d_{ij}^{-} is the negative deviation from the target of the goal ε_{ij}, defined as

$$
d_{ij}^{-} = \delta_{ij}\big(S(\gamma_{ij})w_j - S(\gamma_{ji})w_i\big) \vee 0.
$$

s_{ij} and t_{ij} are the weights corresponding to d_{ij}^{+} and d_{ij}^{-}, respectively.

In order to solve the above problem, model (M-9.2) can be transformed into the following mixed 0-1 goal programming model:

$$\min \quad F = \sum_{i=1}^{n-1} \sum_{j=i+1}^{n} s_{ij}d_{ij}^+ + t_{ij}d_{ij}^-$$

$$\text{s.t.} \begin{cases} \delta_{ij}\left[\left(\sum_{l=1}^{\#h_{ji}} z_{ji}^{\sigma(l)}\gamma_{ji}^{\sigma(l)}\right)w_i - \left(\sum_{l=1}^{\#h_{ji}} z_{ji}^{\sigma(l)}\gamma_{ij}^{\sigma(l)}\right)w_j\right] - d_{ij}^+ + d_{ij}^- = 0, \quad i,j \in N, \ j>i \\[4mm] \sum_{i=1}^{n} w_i = 1 \\[4mm] \sum_{l=1}^{\#h_{ji}} z_{ji}^{\sigma(l)} = 1, \ i,j \in N, \ j>i \\[4mm] z_{ji}^{\sigma(l)} = 0 \text{ or } 1, \quad i,j \in N, l=1,2,\ldots,\#h_{ji}, j>i \\[2mm] w_i \geq 0, i \in N \\[2mm] d_{ij}^+, \ d_{ij}^- \geq 0, \quad i,j \in N, \ j>i \end{cases}$$

$$\text{(M-9.3)}$$

Without loss of generality, when we consider that all the goal functions ε_{ij} $(i, j \in N)$ are fair, then we can set $s_{ij} = t_{ij} = 1$ $(i, j \in N)$. Consequently, model (M-9.3) can be rewritten as follows:

$$\min \quad F = \sum_{i=1}^{n-1} \sum_{j=i+1}^{n} \left(d_{ij}^+ + d_{ij}^-\right)$$

$$\text{s.t.} \begin{cases} \delta_{ij}\left[\left(\sum_{l=1}^{\#h_{ji}} z_{ji}^{\sigma(l)}\gamma_{ji}^{\sigma(l)}\right)w_i - \left(\sum_{l=1}^{\#h_{ji}} z_{ji}^{\sigma(l)}\gamma_{ij}^{\sigma(l)}\right)w_j\right] - d_{ij}^+ + d_{ij}^- = 0, \quad i,j \in N, \ j>i \\[4mm] \sum_{i=1}^{n} w_i = 1 \\[4mm] \sum_{l=1}^{\#h_{ji}} z_{ji}^{\sigma(l)} = 1, \ i,j \in N, \ j>i \\[4mm] z_{ji}^{\sigma(l)} = 0 \text{ or } 1, \quad i,j \in N, j>i, l=1,2,\ldots,\#h_{ji} \\[2mm] w_i \geq 0, i \in N \\[2mm] d_{ij}^+, \ d_{ij}^- \geq 0, \quad i,j \in N, \ j>i \end{cases}$$

$$\text{(M-9.4)}$$

2. By Eq. (9.6), the additive consistency preferences can be obtained by

$$\delta_{ij}\left(\gamma_{ij}^{\sigma(1)} \text{ or} \dots \text{or } \gamma_{ij}^{\sigma(\#h_{ij})}\right) = \delta_{ij}\left[0.5 + \frac{n-1}{2}\left(w_i - w_j\right)\right], i,j \in N \qquad (9.11)$$

Let $S(\gamma_{ij}) = \gamma_{ij}^{\sigma(1)}$ or ... or $\gamma_{ij}^{\sigma(\#hij)}$, and by Eq. (9.11), we have

$$\delta_{ij}S(\gamma_{ij}) = \delta_{ij}\left[0.5 + \frac{n-1}{2}\left(w_i - w_j\right)\right]$$

Let $\varepsilon_{ij} = \delta_{ij}|S(\gamma_{ij}) - [0.5 + \frac{n-1}{2}(w_i - w_j)|$; to obtain as many additive consistency preferences as possible, we construct the following multi-objective programming model:

$$\min \quad \varepsilon_{ij} = \delta_{ij}\left|S(\gamma_{ij}) - \left[0.5 + \frac{n-1}{2}\left(w_i - w_j\right)\right]\right|, i,j \in N$$
$$\text{s.t. } \sum_{i=1}^{n} w_i = 1, w_i \geq 0, \quad i \in N$$

$$(\text{M-9.5})$$

The solution to the above minimization problem is found by solving the following goal programming model:

$$\min \quad F = \sum_{i=1}^{n-1}\sum_{j=i+1}^{n} s_{ij}d_{ij}^{+} + t_{ij}d_{ij}^{-}$$
$$\text{s.t.}\begin{cases} \delta_{ij}\left[S(\gamma_{ij}) - \left(0.5 + \frac{n-1}{2}\left(w_i - w_j\right)\right)\right] - d_{ij}^{+} + d_{ij}^{-} = 0, \quad i,j \in N, \ j > i \\ \sum_{i=1}^{n} w_i = 1 \\ w_i \geq 0, \quad i \in N \\ d_{ij}^{+}, \ d_{ij}^{-} \geq 0, \quad i,j \in N, \ j > i \end{cases}$$

$$(\text{M-9.6})$$

where d_{ij}^{+} is the positive deviation from the target of the goal ε_{ij}, defined as

$$d_{ij}^{+} = \delta_{ij}\left[S(\gamma_{ij}) - \left(0.5 + \frac{n-1}{2}\left(w_i - w_j\right)\right)\right] \vee 0.$$

d_{ij}^{-} is the negative deviation from the target of the goal ε_{ij}, defined as

$$d_{ij}^{-} = \delta_{ij}\left[\left(0.5 + \frac{n-1}{2}\left(w_i - w_j\right)\right) - S(\gamma_{ij})\right] \vee 0.$$

s_{ij} and t_{ij} are the weights corresponding to d_{ij}^{+} and d_{ij}^{-}, respectively.

Similarly, model (M-9.6) can be transformed into the following 0-1 mixed goal programming:

$$\min \quad F = \sum_{i=1}^{n-1} \sum_{j=i+1}^{n} s_{ij} d_{ij}^+ + t_{ij} d_{ij}^-$$

$$\text{s.t.} \begin{cases} \delta_{ij} \left[\sum_{l=1}^{\#h_{ij}} z_{ij}^{\sigma(l)} \gamma_{ij}^{\sigma(l)} - \left(0.5 + \dfrac{n-1}{2} (w_i - w_j) \right) \right] - d_{ij}^+ + d_{ij}^- = 0, \quad i,j \in N, \ j > i \\[4mm] \displaystyle\sum_{i=1}^{n} w_i = 1 \\[4mm] \displaystyle\sum_{l=1}^{\#h_{ij}} z_{ij}^{\sigma(l)} = 1, \ i,j \in N, \ j > i \\[3mm] z_{ij}^{\sigma(l)} = 0 \text{ or } 1, \quad i,j \in N, \ l = 1, 2, \ldots, \#h_{ij}, j > i \\[2mm] w_i \geq 0, i \in N \\[2mm] d_{ij}^+, \ d_{ij}^- \geq 0, \quad i,j \in N, \ j > i \end{cases}$$

$$(\text{M-9.7})$$

Without loss of generality, when we consider that all the goal functions ε_{ij} $(i, j \in N)$ are fair, then we can set $s_{ij} = t_{ij} = 1$ $(i, j \in N)$. Consequently, model (M-7) can be rewritten as follows:

$$\min \quad F = \sum_{i=1}^{n-1} \sum_{j=i+1}^{n} \left(d_{ij}^+ + d_{ij}^- \right)$$

$$\text{s.t.} \begin{cases} \delta_{ij} \left[\sum_{l=1}^{\#h_{ij}} z_{ij}^{\sigma(l)} \gamma_{ij}^{\sigma(l)} - \left(0.5 + \dfrac{n-1}{2} (w_i - w_j) \right) \right] - d_{ij}^+ + d_{ij}^- = 0, \quad i,j \in N, \ j > i \\[4mm] \displaystyle\sum_{i=1}^{n} w_i = 1 \\[4mm] \displaystyle\sum_{l=1}^{\#h_{ij}} z_{ij}^{\sigma(l)} = 1, \ i,j \in N, \ j > i \\[3mm] z_{ij}^{\sigma(l)} = 0 \text{ or } 1, \quad i,j \in N, \ j > i, l = 1, 2, \ldots, \#h_{ij} \\[2mm] w_i \geq 0, i \in N \\[2mm] d_{ij}^+, \ d_{ij}^- \geq 0, \quad i,j \in N, \ j > i \end{cases}$$

$$(\text{M-9.8})$$

Once we have developed an algorithm for solving a computational problem and analyzed its worst-case time requirements as a function of the size of its input (in terms of the o-notation), we analyze the complexity of computation of different models. Time complexity of (M-9.4)–(M-9.8) is $o(n^4 \times l)$, which depends on the product of n^4 (n is the number of alternatives) and l ($l = \prod_{i=1}^{n-1} \prod_{j=i+1}^{n} \#h_{ij}$, $i, j \in N, j > i$). Meanwhile, the space complexity of (M-9.4)–(M-9.8) is $o(1)$.

By solving this model, we can also obtain the priority vector $w = (w_1, w_2, \ldots, w_n)^T$ of the incomplete hesitant fuzzy reciprocal preference relation $H = (h_{ij})_{n \times n}$. We will extend the above models to obtain the collective priority vector of two or more incomplete hesitant fuzzy reciprocal preference relations.

Suppose that there are m incomplete hesitant fuzzy reciprocal preference relations $H_k = (h_{ij,k})_{n \times n}$ ($k \in M$), and $v = (v_1, v_2, \ldots, v_n)^T$ is their collective priority vector, where $v_i \geq 0, i \in N, \sum_{i=1}^{n} v_i = 1$. Let $E = \{e_1, e_2, \ldots, e_m\}$ be a finite set of experts, where e_k denotes the kth expert. Let $\lambda = (\lambda_1, \lambda_2, \ldots, \lambda_m)^T$ be the weighting vector of experts, where $\sum_{k=1}^{m} \lambda_k = 1, \lambda_k \geq 0$ and λ_k means the importance degree of expert e_k. We also construct m indication matrices $\Delta_k = (\delta_{ij})_{n \times n}$ ($k \in M$) of the incomplete hesitant fuzzy reciprocal preference relations $H_k = (h_{ij,k})_{n \times n}$ ($k \in M$), where

$$
\delta_{ij,k} = \begin{cases} 0, & h_{ij,k} = - \\ 1, & h_{ij,k} \neq - \end{cases}
$$

For the multiplicative consistency hesitant fuzzy reciprocal preference relation, $v = (v_1, v_2, \ldots, v_n)^T$ can be obtained by solving the following model, which is an extension of the model (M-9.4):

$$
\min \quad F = \sum_{k=1}^{m} \sum_{i=1}^{n-1} \sum_{j=i+1}^{n} \lambda_k \left(d_{ij,k}^+ + d_{ij,k}^- \right)
$$

$$
\text{s.t.} \begin{cases} \delta_{ij,k} \left(S(\gamma_{ji,k}) v_i - S(\gamma_{ij,k}) v_j \right) - d_{ij,k}^+ + d_{ij,k}^- = 0, & i, j \in N, j > i \\ \sum_{i=1}^{n} v_i = 1 \\ v_i \geq 0, \quad i \in N \\ d_{ij,k}^+, d_{ij,k}^- \geq 0, \quad i, j \in N, j > i, \quad k \in M \end{cases} \quad \text{(M-9.9)}
$$

where $d_{ij,k}^+$ is the positive deviation, defined as

$$
d_{ij,k}^+ = \delta_{ij,k} \left(S(\gamma_{ji,k}) v_i - S(\gamma_{ij,k}) v_j \right) \vee 0.
$$

$d_{ij,k}^-$ is the negative deviation, defined as

$$d_{ij,k}^- = \delta_{ij,k}\left(S\left(\gamma_{ij,k}\right)v_j - S\left(\gamma_{ji,k}\right)v_i\right) \vee 0.$$

Model (M-9.9) can be transformed into the following 0-1 mixed goal programming:

$$\min \quad F = \sum_{k=1}^{m}\sum_{i=1}^{n-1}\sum_{j=i+1}^{n} \lambda_k\left(d_{ij,k}^+ + d_{ij,k}^-\right)$$

$$\text{s.t.} \begin{cases} \delta_{ij}^{(k)}\left[\left(\sum_{l=1}^{\#h_{ji,k}} z_{ji,k}^{\sigma(l)}\gamma_{ji,k}^{\sigma(l)}\right)v_i - \left(\sum_{l=1}^{\#h_{ji,k}} z_{ji,k}^{\sigma(l)}\gamma_{ij,k}^{\sigma(l)}\right)v_j\right] - d_{ij,k}^+ + d_{ij,k}^- = 0, \quad i,j \in N, j > i, k \in M \\[4mm] \sum_{i=1}^{n} v_i = 1 \\[4mm] \sum_{l=1}^{\#h_{ji,k}} z_{ji,k}^{\sigma(l)} = 1, \quad i,j \in N, j > i, k \in M \\[4mm] z_{ji,k}^{\sigma(l)} = 0 \text{ or } 1, \quad i,j \in N, j > i, k \in M, l = 1,2,\ldots,\#h_{ji,k} \\[2mm] v_i \geq 0, \quad i \in N \\[2mm] d_{ij,k}^+, \ d_{ij,k}^- \geq 0, \quad i,j \in N, \ j > i, \quad k \in M \end{cases}$$

$$\text{(M-9.10)}$$

For the additive consistency hesitant fuzzy reciprocal preference relation, $v = (v_1, v_2, \ldots, v_n)^T$ can be obtained by solving the following model, which is an extension of the model (M-9.8):

$$\min \quad F = \sum_{k=1}^{m}\sum_{i=1}^{n-1}\sum_{j=i+1}^{n} \lambda_k\left(d_{ij,k}^+ + d_{ij,k}^-\right)$$

$$\text{s.t.} \begin{cases} \delta_{ij,k}\left[S\left(\gamma_{ij,k}\right) - \left(0.5 + \dfrac{n-1}{2}\left(v_i - v_j\right)\right)\right] - d_{ij,k}^+ + d_{ij,k}^- = 0, \quad i,j \in N, \ j > i \\[4mm] \sum_{i=1}^{n} v_i = 1 \\[4mm] v_i \geq 0, i \in N \\[2mm] d_{ij,k}^+, \ d_{ij,k}^- \geq 0, \quad i,j \in N, \ j > i, \ k \in M \end{cases}$$

$$\text{(M-9.11)}$$

where $d_{ij,k}^+$ is the positive deviation, defined as

$$d_{ij,k}^+ = \delta_{ij,k}\left[S\left(\gamma_{ij,k}\right) - \left(0.5 + \frac{n-1}{2}\left(v_i - v_j\right)\right)\right] \vee 0.$$

$d_{ij,k}^-$ is the negative deviation ε_{ij}, defined as

$$d^-_{ij,k} = \delta_{ij,k} \left[\left(0.5 + \frac{n-1}{2}(v_i - v_j) \right) - S(\gamma_{ij,k}) \right] \vee 0$$

Model (M-9.11) can be transformed into the following 0-1 mixed goal programming:

$$\min \quad F = \sum_{k=1}^{m} \sum_{i=1}^{n-1} \sum_{j=i+1}^{n} \lambda_k \left(d^+_{ij,k} + d^-_{ij,k} \right)$$

$$\text{s.t.} \begin{cases} \delta_{ij,k} \left[\sum_{l=1}^{\#h_{ij,k}} z^{\sigma(l)}_{ij,k} \gamma^{\sigma(l)}_{ij,k} - \left(0.5 + \frac{(n-1)}{2}(v_i - v_j) \right) \right] - d^+_{ij,k} + d^-_{ij,k} = 0, \quad i,j \in N, j > i \\[2mm] \sum_{i=1}^{n} v_i = 1 \\[2mm] \sum_{l=1}^{\#h_{ij,k}} z^{\sigma(l)}_{ij,k} = 1, \quad i,j \in N, j > i, k \in M \\[2mm] v_i \geq 0, i \in N \\[2mm] z^{\sigma(l)}_{ij,k} = 0 \text{ or } 1, \quad i,j \in N, j > i, k \in M, l = 1, 2, \ldots, \#h_{ij,k} \\[2mm] d^+_{ij,k}, \ d^-_{ij,k} \geq 0, \quad i,j \in N, \ j > i, \ k \in M \end{cases}$$

$$(\text{M-9.12})$$

9.3   Illustrative Cases of Study

In this section, two numerical examples are provided to demonstrate the practicality and effectiveness of the developed models.

9.3.1   Case of Study with Four Decision Alternatives and an Incomplete Hesitant Fuzzy Reciprocal Preference Relation

Consider a single DM's decision problem with four alternatives x_i ($i = 1, 2, 3, 4$). The DM provides his/her preferences over the four decision alternatives, as an incomplete hesitant fuzzy reciprocal preference relation as follows:

$$H = \begin{bmatrix} \{0.5\} & - & \{0.6, 0.7\} & \{0.4\} \\ - & \{0.5\} & \{0.4\} & - \\ \{0.4, 0.3\} & \{0.6\} & \{0.5\} & \{0.3, 0.4\} \\ \{0.6\} & - & \{0.7, 0.6\} & \{0.5\} \end{bmatrix}.$$

Based on Theorem 9.1, we know that H is an acceptable incomplete hesitant fuzzy reciprocal preference relation, which means that the priority weights can be derived by the known HFEs.

1. According to the model (M-9.4), we can construct the following 0-1 goal programming model:

$$\min \quad F = \sum_{i=1}^{3} \sum_{j=2}^{4} \left(d_{ij}^{+} + d_{ij}^{-} \right)$$

$$\text{s. t.} \begin{cases} -d_{12}^{+} + d_{12}^{-} = 0 \\ \left(z_{31}^{\sigma(1)} \times 0.4 + z_{31}^{\sigma(2)} \times 0.3 \right) w_1 - \left(z_{31}^{\sigma(1)} \times 0.6 + z_{31}^{\sigma(2)} \times 0.7 \right) w_3 - d_{13}^{+} + d_{13}^{-} = 0 \\ 0.6 w_1 - 0.4 w_4 - d_{14}^{+} + d_{14}^{-} = 0 \\ 0.6 w_2 - 0.4 w_3 - d_{23}^{+} + d_{23}^{-} = 0 \\ \left(z_{43}^{\sigma(1)} \times 0.7 + z_{43}^{\sigma(2)} \times 0.6 \right) w_3 - \left(z_{43}^{\sigma(1)} \times 0.3 + z_{43}^{\sigma(2)} \times 0.4 \right) w_4 - d_{34}^{+} + d_{34}^{-} = 0 \\ w_1 + w_2 + w_3 + w_4 = 1 \\ z_{31}^{\sigma(1)} + z_{31}^{\sigma(2)} = 1 \\ z_{43}^{\sigma(1)} + z_{43}^{\sigma(2)} = 1 \\ z_{31}^{\sigma(1)}, z_{31}^{\sigma(2)}, z_{43}^{\sigma(1)}, z_{43}^{\sigma(2)} = 0 \text{ or } 1 \\ w_i \geq 0, i = 1, 2, 3, 4 \\ d_{ij}^{+}, d_{ij}^{-} \geq 0, \quad i, j = 1, 2, 3, 4, \ j > i \end{cases}$$

By solving the above optimization problem, we have
$F = 0.004$, $w_1 = 0.28$, $w_2 = 0.12$, $w_3 = 0.18$, $w_4 = 0.42$, $d_{12}^{+} = d_{12}^{-} = 0$, $d_{13}^{+} = 0.004$, $d_{13}^{-} = 0$, $d_{23}^{+} = d_{23}^{-} = 0$, $d_{14}^{+} = d_{14}^{-} = 0$, $d_{24}^{+} = d_{24}^{-} = 0$, and $d_{34}^{+} = d_{34}^{-} = 0$.

Therefore, the ranking of these four alternatives is $x_4 \succ x_1 \succ x_3 \succ x_2$.

2. According to the model (M-9.8), we can build this optimization problem as follows:

$$\min \quad F = \sum_{i=1}^{3} \sum_{j=2}^{4} \left(d_{ij}^+ + d_{ij}^- \right)$$

$$\text{s.t.} \begin{cases} -d_{12}^+ + d_{12}^- = 0 \\ z_{13}^{\sigma(1)} \times 0.6 + z_{13}^{\sigma(2)} \times 0.7 - (0.5 + 1.5(w_1 - w_3)) - d_{13}^+ + d_{13}^- = 0 \\ 0.4 - (0.5 + 1.5(w_1 - w_4)) - d_{14}^+ + d_{14}^- = 0 \\ 0.4 - (0.5 + 1.5(w_2 - w_3)) - d_{23}^+ + d_{23}^- = 0 \\ -d_{24}^+ + d_{24}^- = 0 \\ z_{34}^{\sigma(1)} \times 0.3 + z_{34}^{\sigma(2)} \times 0.4 - (0.5 + 1.5(w_3 - w_4)) - d_{34}^+ + d_{34}^- = 0 \\ w_1 + w_2 + w_3 + w_4 = 1 \\ z_{13}^{\sigma(1)} + z_{13}^{\sigma(2)} = 1 \\ z_{34}^{\sigma(1)} + z_{34}^{\sigma(2)} = 1 \\ z_{13}^{\sigma(1)}, z_{13}^{\sigma(2)}, z_{34}^{\sigma(1)}, z_{34}^{\sigma(2)} = 0 \text{ or } 1 \\ w_i \geq 0, i = 1, 2, 3, 4 \\ d_{ij}^+, d_{ij}^- \geq 0, \quad i, j = 1, 2, 3, 4, \ j > i \end{cases}$$

By solving the above optimization problem, we have
$F = 0$, $w_1 = 0.2833$, $w_2 = 0.1500$, $w_3 = 0.2167$, $w_4 = 0.35$, $d_{12}^+ = d_{12}^- = 0$,
$d_{13}^+ = d_{13}^- = 0$, $d_{23}^+ = d_{23}^- = 0$, $d_{14}^+ = d_{14}^- = 0$, $d_{24}^+ = d_{24}^- = 0$, and $d_{34}^+ = d_{34}^- = 0$.

So, the ranking of these four alternatives is $x_4 \succ x_1 \succ x_3 \succ x_2$, which is same as that obtained by the model (M-9.4).

To further compare the performances of these two models in fitting incomplete hesitant fuzzy reciprocal preference relations, the following evaluation criteria are introduced:

Maximum deviation (MD) for incomplete hesitant fuzzy reciprocal preference relation:

$$\text{MD} = \max_{i,j,k} \left\{ \delta_{ij,k} \left(\frac{\gamma'_{ij,k}}{\gamma'_{ji,k}} \frac{w_j}{w_i} + \frac{\gamma'_{ji,k}}{\gamma'_{ij,k}} \frac{w_i}{w_j} - 2 \right) \middle| i, j \in N, k \in M \right\} \tag{9.12}$$

where $\gamma'_{ij,k}$ is the value of $S(\gamma_{ij,k})$ when the F gets the minimal value.

Maximum absolute deviation (MAD) for incomplete hesitant fuzzy reciprocal preference relation:

Table 9.1 Performance comparisons for Example 9.1

Methods	w^*	Ranking	MD	MAD
Model (M-9.4)	$(0.2800, 0.1200, 0.1800, 0.4200)T$	$x_4 \succ x_1 \succ x_3 \succ x_2$	0.0013	0.0087
Model (M-9.8)	$(0.2833, 0.1500, 0.2167, 0.3500)T$	$x_4 \succ x_1 \succ x_3 \succ x_2$	0.1369	0.0824

$$\mathrm{MAD} = \max_{i,j,k} \left\{ \delta_{ij,k} \left| \gamma'_{ij,k} - \frac{w_i}{w_i + w_j} \right| \middle| i,j \in N, k \in M \right\} \qquad (9.13)$$

where $d_{ij,k} = \gamma'_{ij,k} - w_i/(w_i + w_j)$ is the fitting error for $\gamma'_{ij,k}$. If the priority vector $w = (w_1, w_2, \ldots, w_n)^T$ is able to precisely fit the incomplete hesitant fuzzy reciprocal preference relation H_k, then $|d_{ij,k}| \equiv 0$; otherwise, $|d_{ij,k}| > 0$.

From Table 9.1, it is observed that the model (M-9.4) achieves an identical ranking as model (M-9.8). Model (M-9.4) performs better than model (M-9.8) in terms of two performance evaluation criteria, MD and MAD, which partly shows the advantage of the model (M-9.4).

9.3.2　GDM Problem with Three Alternatives and Three Experts

In the following, we further illustrate the practicality of incomplete hesitant fuzzy reciprocal preference relations in group decision-making by utilizing a practical example (adapted from (Parreiras et al., 2010)).

The enterprise's board of directors, which includes three members e_k ($k = 1, 2, 3$), have to plan the development of large projects (strategy initiatives) for the following 5 years. Suppose that there are three possible projects x_i ($i = 1, 2, 3$) to be evaluated. It is necessary to compare these projects in order to select that which is the most important as well as order them from the viewpoint of their importance, taking into account four criteria suggested by the balanced scorecard methodology: (1) financial perspective; (2) customer satisfaction; (3) internal business process perspective; and (4) learning and growth perspective. First, the specialists are asked to give their opinion relative to each project. Because of the uncertainty of the attributes, it is difficult for the DMs to use just one value to provide their preferences. To facilitate the elicitation of their preferences, HFS is just an effective tool to deal with such situations. Furthermore, some experts may be lacking in knowledge and have limited expertise related to the problem domain, and thus, these members give their incomplete hesitant fuzzy reciprocal preference relations as follows:

$$H_1 = \begin{bmatrix} \{0.5\} & \{0.6\} & - \\ \{0.4\} & \{0.5\} & \{0.2,0.3\} \\ - & \{0.8,0.7\} & \{0.5\} \end{bmatrix}, H_2 = \begin{bmatrix} \{0.5\} & - & \{0.3,0.4\} \\ - & \{0.5\} & \{0.3\} \\ \{0.7,0.6\} & \{0.7\} & \{0.5\} \end{bmatrix},$$

$$H_3 = \begin{bmatrix} \{0.5\} & \{0.3,0.4\} & \{0.4\} \\ \{0.7,0.6\} & \{0.5\} & - \\ \{0.6\} & - & \{0.5\} \end{bmatrix}.$$

From Theorem 9.1, we know that H_k ($k = 1, 2, 3$) are all acceptable incomplete hesitant fuzzy reciprocal preference relations. That is, the priority vector can be obtained through the known HFEs. Without loss of generality, we set $\lambda_1 = \lambda_2 = \lambda_3 = 1/3$.

1. According to model (M-9.10), we can build this optimization problem as follows:

$$\min \quad F = \sum_{k=1}^{3} \sum_{i=1}^{2} \sum_{j=i+1}^{3} \lambda_k \left(d_{ij,k}^{+} + d_{ij,k}^{-} \right)$$

$$\text{s.t.} \begin{cases} 0.4v_1 - 0.6v_2 - d_{12,1}^{+} + d_{12,1}^{-} = 0 \\ - d_{13,1}^{+} + d_{13,1}^{-} = 0 \\ \left(z_{32,1}^{\sigma(1)} \times 0.8 + z_{32,1}^{\sigma(2)} \times 0.7 \right) v_2 - \left(z_{32,1}^{\sigma(1)} \times 0.2 + z_{32,1}^{\sigma(2)} \times 0.3 \right) v_3 - d_{23,1}^{+} + d_{23,1}^{-} = 0 \\ - d_{12,2}^{+} + d_{12,2}^{-} = 0 \\ \left(z_{31,2}^{\sigma(1)} \times 0.7 + z_{31,2}^{\sigma(2)} \times 0.6 \right) v_1 - \left(z_{31,2}^{\sigma(1)} \times 0.3 + z_{31,2}^{\sigma(2)} \times 0.4 \right) v_3 - d_{13,2}^{+} + d_{13,2}^{-} = 0 \\ 0.7v_2 - 0.3v_3 - d_{23,2}^{+} + d_{23,2}^{-} = 0 \\ \left(z_{21,3}^{\sigma(1)} \times 0.7 + z_{21,3}^{\sigma(2)} \times 0.6 \right) v_1 - \left(z_{21,3}^{\sigma(1)} \times 0.3 + z_{21,3}^{\sigma(2)} \times 0.4 \right) v_2 - d_{12,3}^{+} + d_{12,3}^{-} = 0 \\ 0.6v_1 - 0.4v_3 - d_{13,3}^{+} + d_{13,3}^{-} = 0 \\ - d_{23,3}^{+} + d_{23,3}^{-} = 0 \\ v_1 + v_2 + v_3 = 1 \\ z_{32,1}^{\sigma(1)} + z_{32,1}^{\sigma(2)} = 1 \\ z_{31,2}^{\sigma(1)} + z_{31,2}^{\sigma(2)} = 1 \\ z_{21,3}^{\sigma(1)} + z_{21,3}^{\sigma(2)} = 1 \\ z_{32,1}^{\sigma(1)}, z_{32,1}^{\sigma(2)}, z_{31,2}^{\sigma(1)}, z_{31,2}^{\sigma(2)}, z_{21,3}^{\sigma(1)}, z_{21,3}^{\sigma(2)} = 0 \text{ or } 1 \\ v_i \geq 0, i = 1, 2, 3 \\ d_{ij,k}^{+}, d_{ij,k}^{-} \geq 0, \quad i,j = 1, 2, 3, \ j > i, \ k = 1, 2, 3 \end{cases}$$

By solving the above optimization problem, we have

$F = 0.0379$, $v_1 = 0.3182$, $v_2 = 0.2045$, $v_3 = 0.4773$, $d^+_{12,1} = 0.45 \times 10^{-2}$, $d^-_{12,1} = 0$, $d^+_{13,1} = d^-_{13,1} = 0$, $d^+_{23,1} = d^-_{23,1} = 0$, $d^+_{12,2} = d^-_{12,2} = 0$, $d^+_{13,2} = d^-_{13,2} = 0$, $d^+_{23,2} = d^-_{23,2} = 0$, $d^+_{12,3} = 0.1091$, $d^-_{12,3} = 0$, $d^+_{13,3} = d^-_{13,3} = 0$, and $d^+_{23,3} = d^-_{23,3} = 0$.

Therefore, the ranking of these three alternatives is $x_3 \succ x_1 \succ x_2$.

2. According to the model (M-9.12), we can build this optimization problem as follows:

$$\min \quad F = \sum_{k=1}^{3} \sum_{i=1}^{3} \sum_{j=2}^{3} \lambda_k \left(d^+_{ij,k} + d^-_{ij,k} \right)$$

$$\text{s.t.} \begin{cases} 0.6 - (0.5 + v_1 - v_2) - d^+_{12,1} + d^-_{12,1} = 0 \\[4pt] - d^+_{13,1} + d^-_{13,1} = 0 \\[4pt] \left[z^{\sigma(1)}_{23,1} \times 0.2 + z^{\sigma(2)}_{23,1} \times 0.3 - (0.5 + v_2 - v_3) \right] - d^+_{23,1} + d^-_{23,1} = 0 \\[4pt] - d^+_{12,2} + d^-_{12,2} = 0 \\[4pt] \left[z^{\sigma(1)}_{13,2} \times 0.3 + z^{\sigma(2)}_{13,2} \times 0.4 - (0.5 + v_1 - v_3) \right] - d^+_{13,2} + d^-_{13,2} = 0 \\[4pt] 0.3 - (0.5 + v_2 - v_3) - d^+_{23,2} + d^-_{23,2} = 0 \\[4pt] \left[z^{\sigma(1)}_{12,3} \times 0.3 + z^{\sigma(2)}_{12,3} \times 0.4 - (0.5 + v_1 - v_2) \right] - d^+_{12,3} + d^-_{12,3} = 0 \\[4pt] 0.4 - (0.5 + v_1 - v_3) - d^+_{13,3} + d^-_{13,3} = 0 \\[4pt] - d^+_{23,3} + d^-_{23,3} = 0 \\[4pt] v_1 + v_2 + v_3 = 1 \\[4pt] z^{\sigma(1)}_{23,1} + z^{\sigma(2)}_{23,1} = 1 \\[4pt] z^{\sigma(1)}_{13,2} + z^{\sigma(2)}_{13,2} = 1 \\[4pt] z^{\sigma(1)}_{12,3} + z^{\sigma(2)}_{12,3} = 1 \\[4pt] z^{\sigma(1)}_{23,1}, z^{\sigma(2)}_{23,1}, z^{\sigma(1)}_{13,2}, z^{\sigma(2)}_{13,2}, z^{\sigma(1)}_{12,3}, z^{\sigma(2)}_{12,3} = 0 \text{ or } 1 \\[4pt] v_i \geq 0, i = 1, 2, 3 \\[4pt] d^+_{ij,k}, d^-_{ij,k} \geq 0, \quad i,j = 1, 2, 3, \ j > i, \ k = 1, 2, 3 \end{cases}$$

By solving the above optimization problem, we have

$F = 0.0667$, $v_1 = 0.3333$, $v_2 = 0.2333$, $v_3 = 0.4333$, $d^+_{12,1} = d^-_{12,1} = 0$, $d^+_{13,1} = d^-_{13,1} = 0$, $d^+_{23,1} = d^-_{23,1} = 0$, $d^+_{12,2} = d^-_{12,2} = 0$, $d^+_{13,2} = d^-_{13,2} = 0$, $d^+_{23,2} = d^-_{23,2} = 0$, $d^+_{12,3} = 0.2$, $d^-_{12,3} = 0$, $d^+_{13,3} = d^-_{13,3} = 0$, and $d^+_{23,3} = d^-_{23,3} = 0$.

So, the ranking of these three alternatives is $x_3 \succ x_1 \succ x_2$, which is same as that obtained by the model (M-9.10).

Table 9.2 Performance comparisons for Example 9.2

Methods	w^*	Ranking	MD	MAD
Model (M-9.10)	$(0.3182, 0.2045, 0.4773)^T$	$x_3 \succ x_1 \succ x_2$	0.0013	0.0088
Model (M-9.12)	$(0.3333, 0.2333, 0.4333)^T$	$x_3 \succ x_1 \succ x_2$	0.0523	0.0500

The results of comparisons are shown in Table 9.2, from which we can see that model (M-9.10) achieves the same ranking $x_3 \succ x_1 \succ x_2$ as model (M-9.12). Moreover, model (M-9.10) has smaller MD and MAD than model (M-9.12).

Remark 9.2 It should be noted that many methods have been proposed to derive the weighting vector for fuzzy reciprocal preference relations and to solve group decision-making problems. However, these methods fail when addressing situations in which the input arguments take the form of hesitant fuzzy reciprocal preference relations. In the following, we discuss some advantages and differences as compared with the existing different kinds of methods for GDM problems.

1. In the above case study, Parreiras et al. (2010) proposed a flexible consensus scheme for GDM problems under linguistic assessments. However, in their approach, they first transformed the linguistic variables into triangular fuzzy numbers, which led to information losing. Second, they used the consensus scheme to rank the alternatives, which is very complicated, while our method can rank the alternatives directly.

2. For the incomplete fuzzy reciprocal preference relations, for example, Xu (2004) and Xu et al. (2011), their methods did not consider the hesitant situation, which limits their application. However, if there is only one value in each pairwise value in the hesitant fuzzy reciprocal preference relations, the methods proposed in this chapter will be reduced to the traditional incomplete fuzzy reciprocal preference relations.

3. Zhu et al. (2014) presented the ranking methods with hesitant fuzzy reciprocal preference relations in GDM environments. These methods only consider the multiplicative consistency of hesitant fuzzy reciprocal preference relations. Generally, the cardinal consistency of fuzzy reciprocal preference relations includes multiplicative consistency and additive consistency. In this chapter, we consider these different types of consistencies for hesitant fuzzy reciprocal preference relations. Furthermore, if $\delta_{ij} = 1$ for all $i, j \in N$ in all the models (M-9.1)–(M-9.12), then the proposed methods can be used to derive the rankings for the complete hesitant fuzzy reciprocal preference relations, which means that the proposed methods can deal with both the complete and incomplete hesitant fuzzy reciprocal preference relations, while Zhu et al. (2014)'s method is only suitable to deal with the complete ones. In other words, Zhu et al. (2014)'s method would be considered as a special case of the proposed method.

9.4 Summary

We have investigated group decision-making problems, where preference information offered by DMs is hesitant and incomplete. For the sake of a better description of this situation, we have proposed a new concept of incomplete hesitant fuzzy reciprocal preference relations, which are an effective tool to collect and present preferences provided by DMs in decision-making. Incomplete hesitant fuzzy reciprocal preference relations do not merely permit the DMs to provide all of the possible values but also allow them to give null values when comparing two alternatives. In this chapter, we also introduced the concept of multiplicative consistency incomplete hesitant fuzzy reciprocal preference relation and additive consistency incomplete hesitant fuzzy reciprocal preference relation. Moreover, to obtain the priority vector of an incomplete hesitant fuzzy reciprocal preference relation, we have proposed two programming models based on multiplicative consistency and additive consistency, respectively. These two goal programming models are also extended to obtain the collective priority vector of several incomplete hesitant fuzzy reciprocal preference relations. Finally, the practicality and effectiveness of the developed models have been verified using two illustrative examples.

References

Parreiras, R. O., Ekel, P. Y., Martini, J. S. C., & Palhares, R. M. (2010). A flexible consensus scheme for multicriteria group decision making under linguistic assessments. *Information Sciences, 180*, 1075–1089.

Torra, V. (2010). Hesitant fuzzy sets. *International Journal of Intelligence Systems, 25*(6), 529–539.

Torra, V., & Narukawa, Y. (2009). On hesitant fuzzy sets and decision. In: Fuzzy Systems, 2009. FUZZ-IEEE 2009. IEEE International Conference on Fuzzy Systems. IEEE. pp. 1378–1382.

Xia, M. M., & Xu, Z. S. (2013). Managing hesitant information in GDM problems under fuzzy and multiplicative preference relations. *International Journal of Uncertainty, Fuzziness and Knowledge-Based Systems, 21*(6), 865–897.

Xu, Y. J., Cabrerizo, F. J., & Herrera-Viedma, E. (2017). A consensus model for hesitant fuzzy preference relations and its application in water allocation management. *Applied Soft Computing, 58*, 265–284.

Xu, Y. J., Chen, L., Rodríguez, R. M., Herrera, F., & Wang, H. M. (2016). Deriving the priority weights from incomplete hesitant fuzzy preference relations in group decision making. *Knowledge-Based Systems, 99*, 71–78.

Xu, Y. J., Da, Q. L., & Wang, H. M. (2011). A note on group decision-making procedure based on incomplete reciprocal relations. *Soft Computing, 15*(7), 1289–1300.

Xu, Y. J., Li, C. Y., & Wen, X. W. (2018). Missing values estimation and consensus building for incomplete hesitant fuzzy preference relations with multiplicative consistency. *International Journal of Computational Intelligence Systems, 11*, 101–119.

Xu, Z. S. (2004). Goal programming models for obtaining the priority vector of incomplete fuzzy preference relation. *International Journal of Approximate Reasoning, 36*(3), 261–270.

Zhu, B., & Xu, Z. S. (2013). Regression methods for hesitant fuzzy preference relations. *Technological and Economic Development of Economy, 19*(sup 1), s214–s227.

Zhu, B., Xu, Z. S., & Xu, J. P. (2014). Deriving a ranking from hesitant fuzzy preference relations under group decision making. *IEEE Transactions on Cybernetics, 44*(4), 1328–1337.

Correction to: Deriving Priorities from Incomplete Fuzzy Reciprocal Preference Relations

Correction to:
Yejun Xu, *Deriving Priorities from Incomplete Fuzzy*
Reciprocal Preference Relations,
https://doi.org/10.1007/978-981-99-3169-9

The original version of this book was inadvertently published with typographical errors. The following corrections have been made in the book after publication.

1. Chapter 3 (p. 62), above Step 1, $\overline{P}_v = nv$ has been corrected as $\overline{P}v = nv$.
2. Chapter 4 (p. 77), Eq.(4.16) has been corrected as

$$W_{n-1} = \left[\ln w_1, \ln w_2, \ldots, \ln w_{n-1}\right]^T.$$

3. Chapter 5 (p. 96), in Table 5.1 column heading, $|\eta 2|$, $|\eta 3|$, and $|\eta 4|$ have been corrected as $|\eta_2|$, $|\eta_3|$, and $|\eta_4|$, respectively, and $w2$, $w3$, and $w4$ as w_2, w_3, and w_4, respectively.
4. Chapter 5 (p. 97), in Table 5.2 column "Ranking", $x1$, $x2$, $x3$, and $x4$ have been corrected as x_1, x_2, x_3, and x_4, respectively.
5. Chapter 5 (p. 98), in Table 5.3 column heading, $|\eta 2|$, $|\eta 3|$, and $|\eta 4|$ have been corrected as $|\eta_2|$, $|\eta_3|$, and $|\eta_4|$, respectively.
6. Chapter 5 (p. 98), in Table 5.3 column "Ranking", $x1$, $x2$, $x3$, and $x4$ have been corrected as x_1, x_2, x_3, and x_4, respectively.
7. Chapter 5 (p. 100), in Table 5.4 column "Ranking", $x1$, $x2$, $x3$, and $x4$ have been corrected as x_1, x_2, x_3, and x_4, respectively.
8. Chapter 5 (p. 101), in Table 5.5 column "Ranking", $x1$, $x2$, $x3$, and $x4$ have been corrected as x_1, x_2, x_3, and x_4, respectively.

The updated version of the book can be found at
https://doi.org/10.1007/978-981-99-3169-9

9. Chapter 5 (p. 103), in Table 5.6 column "Ranking", $x1$, $x2$, $x3$, and $x4$ have been corrected as x_1, x_2, x_3, and x_4, respectively.
10. Chapter 5 (p. 104), in Table 5.7 column "Ranking", $x1$, $x2$, $x3$, and $x4$ have been corrected as x_1, x_2, x_3, and x_4, respectively.
11. Chapter 5 (p. 105), in Table 5.8 column "Ranking", $x1$, $x2$, $x3$, and $x4$ have been corrected as x_1, x_2, x_3, and x_4, respectively.
12. Chapter 6 (p. 115), below Example 6.1, "c3" has been moved to the next line and placed before the respective matrix, (i.e.) corrected as

$$C_3 = \begin{bmatrix} 0.5 & 0.3 & 0.4 & 0.6 \\ 0.7 & 0.5 & - & 0.5 \\ 0.6 & - & 0.5 & 0.7 \\ 0.4 & 0.5 & 0.3 & 0.5 \end{bmatrix}.$$

13. Chapter 6 (p. 117), in Table 6.3 column heading, $|\eta 2|$, $|\eta 3|$, and $|\eta 4|$ have been corrected as $|\eta_2|$, $|\eta_3|$, and $|\eta_4|$, respectively.
14. Chapter 6 (p. 119), in Table 6.4 column heading, $|\eta i(w(L))|$ has been corrected as $|\eta_i(w(L))|$.
15. Chapter 7 (p. 125), below Eq. (7.2), $0.5 \leq rjW \leq 1$ corrected as $0.5 \leq r_{jW} \leq 1$.
16. Chapter 7 (p. 143), in Step 1, "R_3" has been moved to the next line and placed before the respective matrix.
17. Chapter 9 (p. 165; Line 5), the blank space between # and h_{ij} has been deleted in the equation $l = \prod_{i=1}^{n-1} \prod_{j=i+1}^{n} \# h_{ij}$.

Printed in the United States
by Baker & Taylor Publisher Services